# DETOURS
## TO THE
# GOOD
# STUFF

## A RAY OF
## GOLDEN SUNLIGHT

# Vickie McGillis

outskirtspress

DENVER, COLORADO

## DEDICATION

This book is dedicated to my beloved grandparents and all the wonderful grandparents out there who love their grandchildren unconditionally, inspiring them to be true to themselves so that they may become solid citizens and successful parents and grandparents themselves one day. As you will discover in the following stories, it truly does take a village to raise a child…and I believe grandparents are sovereign.

My cherished grandparents have left an indelible imprint on my heart. Although many years have passed since they left this earth, I will miss them until the moment I utter my last breath. Thank you both for your strength, courage, wisdom, guidance and, most of all, your moral example. Until we meet again, may you rest in peace…

Vickie K. McGillis

# Contents

# Prologue

In the spring of 1970, as Katie Munson celebrated her twenty-fifth birthday, the single mother of four young children looked back on her life. Feeling grateful and relieved that her estranged and violent ex-husband, Darren Munson, had remarried and moved on, Katie was finally able to leave her sordid past behind. At long last, the young mother and her family had risen from the depths of despair, eager to rebuild their shattered lives.

But starting over is never easy. After having relocated to a small rural town in southeastern Minnesota, the young divorcee felt isolated, frightened and alone. Katie's first priority was finding a decent job so that she could support her four little children. Once she had established herself financially, Katie set her sights on restoring some form of social life for herself...and she never lost hope of finding that special someone with whom she could fall in love, settle down, and enjoy a happy, healthy relationship.

In this second installment of the Munson family saga, you will become more familiar with Katie's four children--Keith, Judith Ivy, Darcy and Samantha--as their unique personalities materialize through their individual trials, tribulations and triumphs. In the springtime of their lives, with the love and support of their mother, grandparents and childhood friends, the extraordinary Munson children gradually evolve into fun-loving, compassionate and kindhearted kids, despite the blemish of their father's terrifying memory and legacy of abuse.

Set against the backdrop of small-town Minnesota life in the carefree 1970s, this exhilarating drama is overflowing with nostalgia, history, music, suspense and shocking events. Whether you're young or young at heart, there's something for everyone in this thrilling joyride back in time as Katie Munson and her children navigate the river of life, both together as a family and independently from one another, in hopes of discovering the ultimate treasure...in search of "the good stuff."

*This book is based on a true story and inspired by actual events. All character names have been changed to protect privacy*

# Part II
# A Ray of Golden Sunlight

## *Chapter 1*
# Leader of the Pack

It was a gorgeous, warm spring Saturday afternoon in May of 1970. Katie Munson had put in a long, hard work week and was ready to go out and have some well-deserved fun. A select group of her girlfriends from the vocational school were taking her out on the town in Lumberton that evening to celebrate her twenty-fifth birthday.

While Katie was in the bedroom applying her makeup, her four children were running rampant through the house like wild animals. They were obviously still buzzing from sugar overload, since they had exchanged their entire weekly allowances for penny candy, bubble gum and licorice whips, which they had purchased earlier that morning at the Stone Valley grocery and candy store down on Main Street.

On that particular evening, however, Katie had somehow managed to harness enough restraint to ignore all the fighting, horseplay and sibling rivalry goings-on just a few feet away in the living room. She simply cranked the clock radio on her dresser top a little louder, unwrapped another piece of Bazooka bubble gum that she had previously swiped from Keith's "secret" candy stash, and proceeded to roll multiple strands of her long, shiny blonde hair into pink plastic curlers.

Katie was in an especially good mood that evening because she knew that in just a little over an hour, the babysitter was due to arrive, and then she would be released from the binding responsibilities of motherhood to partake in an evening of adult conversation and reckless abandon, if only for a short while.

She sang along gleefully to one of her favorite tunes, "Ain't No Mountain High Enough" by Diana Ross, blowing pink bubbles intermittently during the brief gaps in lyrics, while she thrashed her bedroom closet in search of the perfect outfit to wear for her fun night out with the girls.

Eventually, Katie settled on a black-and-white checkered, button-down sweater, her black leather miniskirt and matching go-go boots, with accessories to include her large white hoop earrings, complemented by her white pearl necklace and a black patent-leather clutch handbag to complete the youthful ensemble.

As she checked her look in the mirror, Katie felt grateful to her sister, Roberta, for the many hand-me-down clothes she had passed down to her over the years, for Katie would never have been able to afford such "fun" clothes on her salary; and since Roberta was well into her thirties by then (at the age of 36), Katie's sister felt that she had long ago exceeded the era of adorning herself with such adolescent costumes.

"Wow, twenty-five already!" Katie proclaimed to her mirrored reflection, shaking her head in utter disbelief. She was astonished at how quickly the years had passed since she had become pregnant with Keith, seven whole years ago.

Katie looked back on those seven years with a certain degree of ambivalence as she recalled some of the memorable events that had led to this incredibly joyous moment. At the same time, she was very proud of herself for all she had endured and accomplished during that time. Katie's life had undergone a remarkable transformation, indeed, particularly during the last 2-1/2 years.

When Katie's divorce from Darren Munson had been finalized at the end of 1967, Katie waived her right to financial assistance from Darren, as child support would entitle the man to regular visitation sessions with his children.

There was no doubt in Katie's mind that she had made the right decision in that regard. She had no intention of letting Darren anywhere near her children ever again. Thus, Katie made sure to keep the restraining order against Darren current and valid, until she was convinced that her ex-husband was no longer a threat to her or her family.

Interestingly, ever since her "awakening" in January of 1968 (when despair had nearly claimed her life), Katie's destiny led her in a new direction, and along her path to self-discovery, she found the courage and strength to accept her challenges and take back control of her life.

Unfortunately, as a result of her debilitating depression, and less-than-stellar attendance record, Katie had since been fired from her previous job at the Lumberton clothing factory. However, once she had reclaimed her confidence and had gotten back on her feet, Katie felt certain that she could find another job—an even better one.

She decided her first recourse would be to pay a visit to the local employment office, to find out what types of jobs were currently available within the community. On a rather mild winter's morning in February of 1968, Katie dropped the kids off across the street at Linda Reed's house and drove to the nearby city of Lumberton.

Feeling confident, poised and well-dressed in a white blouse and black dress slacks, Katie entered the Lumberton County Employment Office, where she was quickly approached by a middle-aged woman wearing a light-blue polyester pantsuit, with her dishwater-blonde hair tossed up and into an untidy bun secured by bobby pins.

"Can I help you, miss?" the woman beseeched. "Ah, yes," Katie answered, clearing her throat. "I'm here to look for a job."

The tall slender woman kindly replied, "Well, then…it looks like you've come to the right place. Please have a seat, and I'll be with you in a minute."

"Thank you," Katie replied, taking a seat in one of the orange plastic chairs aligned neatly against the wall of the bustling office filled with rows of filing cabinets.

While she waited, Katie studied the office secretaries seated behind cluttered desks, their typewriters buzzing with the sound of efficiency, and it suddenly occurred to her: "That's what I want to do for a career," she realized. "I want to be a secretary!"

The receptionist soon returned to the front desk and shuffled through some papers. She then motioned to her client that she was ready to assist her. Katie eagerly walked over to the receptionist's desk, which she subsequently found to be very disorganized and overly cluttered.

"Good morning...I'm Georgina," the slightly unkempt woman announced. "And you are..." she inquired.

"Katie Munson," her client answered. The receptionist then handed Katie a sheet of paper and stated, "Here's a list of current jobs that we have available."

"Oh, thank you, ma'am," Katie politely returned. "Is this your first visit to our office, Miss Munson?" Georgina inquired. "Yes, it is," Katie replied.

Georgina handed Katie another piece of paper and added, "Okay, then...first, you'll need to fill out this employment application, so we can get you added to our files. Then, take a look at the list of openings I gave you," she instructed. "When you've completed all the paperwork, just let me know, and I'll call one of our employment counselors to meet with you."

"Thank you," Katie returned. She then walked over to the centralized area, where she joined the other applicants who were also filling out employment applications.

Katie had hoped to find a clerical position, much like the medical file clerk job she had enjoyed working years ago at the Mayo Clinic, but most of the existing listings were seeking part-time help for the summer months and/or minimum wage type positions. One listing, however, had piqued Katie's interest; unfortunately, it also specified a secretarial degree and/or at least two years of prior secretarial experience.

When Katie had completed her application, she handed it back to Georgina, who asked her to once again take a seat while she summoned an employment counselor on the telephone. Katie waited impatiently for the interviewer, fidgeting in her chair, shifting her weight from side to side, all the while chewing on her thumb nails.

About 15 minutes later, a red-headed, freckle-faced woman appeared from behind a closed door. Georgina readily handed the counselor Katie's application.

"Good morning, Katie Munson," the stocky red-head greeted. "My name is Norma Jean. Please step into my office," she politely gestured.

Norma Jean offered Katie a chair and then seated

herself behind her desk. The interviewer briefly perused the nervous young woman's employment application and then commenced with the interviewing process. "I see here that you have <u>four </u>children," the woman remarked, with emphasis on the number four.

"Yes, I do," Katie answered curtly. "You're also divorced," Norma Jean commented. "That is correct," Katie conceded, wondering where the interview was leading. The interviewer inquired further. "Is it safe to assume, Mrs. Munson, that you're receiving fixed monthly child support payments from your ex-husband?"

Katie cleared her throat and answered, "No, ma'am...uh, actually, I don't receive any compensation from the children's father whatsoever."

Norma Jean appeared puzzled by Katie's situation, and then she boldly presumed, "Oh, then you must be getting support from our federal welfare system."

Katie became overly tense and started to fidget in her chair. She didn't much care for the sarcasm in the counselor's line of questioning. It was beginning to feel more like an interrogation than an employment counseling session. "No, ma'am!" Katie refuted.

"Then, if you don't mind my asking," Norma Jean pressed, tapping her pencil incessantly on her desktop, "how are you currently supporting your four children?"

"Well, Ms...ah, Norma Jean," Katie stammered, "that's why I'm here. I just recently became unemployed, as you can see from my application," she explained. "I'm hoping to secure a long-term, respectable job so that I can become self-sufficient and never have to rely on anyone else but myself to support my kids."

Norma Jean smiled and leaned back in her chair. She laid her pencil down on top of Katie's employment application and asserted, "Well, that's very commendable of you, Mrs. Munson. I wish more people shared your sense of responsibility…seems like everyone's looking for a handout these days."

"I know what you mean," Katie concurred. "But, please, call me Katie."

Following that pivotal point in the conversation, it wasn't long before Katie and Norma Jean felt more comfortable with each other, and the employment interview quickly headed in a more productive direction.

"My father is a very wise man," Katie informed the counselor, seizing control of the interview for just a moment, with an added element of her charm and grace. Her intention was to share an example of Buster Wiederman's extensive insight with Norma Jean, so that she could better understand why Katie felt so strongly about supporting herself and her family.

"He taught us to be self-reliant," Katie proudly ascertained. "I remember him telling us kids on more than one occasion, 'If you <u>give</u> a man a fish, he'll eat for a day. If you <u>teach</u> a man to fish, he'll eat for a lifetime!'"

Norma Jean concurred with Katie's father's sensibility and replied, "Your father sounds like a very smart fellow, indeed."

While Katie had expressed specific interest in the secretarial opening, she readily admitted to her obvious lack of qualifications. At the same time, however, she apprised Norma Jean of her prior work experience and the various office skills she had acquired while working at the Mayo Clinic as a medical file clerk, in hopes that her clerical background might help counterbalance her apparent limitations.

"Are you aspiring to expand your clerical experience into the secretarial field?" Norma Jean queried. "Oh, yes!" Katie exclaimed. "I loved my file clerk job at the Mayo Clinic, but I had to quit working there when I had my second baby…and after watching all the secretaries out in there in the lobby," she gushed, "I just knew that I wanted a respectable, high-classed job like that."

"I assume that you have a high-school diploma…is that correct, Katie?" The red-headed woman inquired. "Yes, ma'am! I graduated in 1963," Katie asserted.

Norma Jean bolted upright from her office chair and walked over to the filing cabinet. She quickly retrieved a stapled paper packet from an over-filled manila file folder and happily offered the documents to Katie. "I think I have the perfect solution for you, Katie Munson," she shared, with a charitable smile on her freckled face.

While Katie examined the foreign information, Norma Jean proceeded to briefly describe for Katie a government-funded program in which they would grant Katie the tuition funds, thus allowing her to study the course of her choice at the vocational technical institute in Lumberton.

"If you'll notice on page two, Katie," Norma Jean pointed out, "the technical institute has a general secretarial course, as well as many other fine trades you might wish to consider."

"Wow, that would be great!" Katie exclaimed. "But, how can I possibly go back to school when I need to work full time in order to support my family?"

"Now, don't get discouraged, Katie," Norma Jean retorted. "The government program can help with that as well," she expounded. "In addition to paying for your schooling, the program will also provide you with a monthly stipend, to assist you with your household budget...you know, to cover your utility bills, groceries, even daycare expenses while you attend school full time."

"Gee, that sounds almost too good to be true!" Katie yelped, in surprise.

"Well, we all believe in helping those who want to help themselves--even the government," Norma Jean remarked. "Besides, this way you'll be able to contribute to society, rather than becoming yet another burden on the welfare system."

Imbued with excitement, Katie couldn't wait

to sign up for the next general secretarial course at the vocational technical institute. Unfortunately, she would have to wait until September to start the next class, and there was still plenty of snow yet to melt before springtime. Although she was ecstatic, Katie still felt a bit frustrated.

"Well, I definitely want to get signed up for technical school," Katie asserted, with a heavy sigh, "but I still have to find a job to carry us through the next six and a half months." The disappointment in her tone was markedly evident.

The employment counselor spent a few more minutes helping Katie scan the current job listings. There was a temporary job available at another Lumberton factory that specialized in making spices and natural health remedies. Katie wasn't all that concerned with the type of work, since it was just temporary, as long as the position was full time and it paid at least the minimum wage.

At her urging, Norma Jean set up the interview for Katie. In the meantime, she initiated the paperwork to enroll Katie in the secretarial course starting in the fall. She also assisted Katie with the legal documentation and necessary paperwork to get her registered for the government subsidy program.

When Katie had returned home from her very productive job search, the first thing she did was telephone her parents and tell them all about the government program and how excited she was to have the opportunity to attend the general secretarial program at the technical school beginning in September.

Buster and Sally Wiederman were equally as happy for their daughter. They were thrilled that Katie's life was finally heading in the right direction. Thus, to show their support of her long-range career goals, Katie's parents benevolently offered to help care for the children during the summer months, in addition to providing financial assistance to help make ends meet before starting school in the fall.

A couple of days later, Katie received a telephone call from the spice manufacturing plant's office supervisor, who offered Katie the temporary position. She gladly accepted without hesitation.

During her employment there, from March through August of 1968, Katie performed various duties in the packaging department, but she also volunteered to assist with clerical duties in the office whenever she could.

As the warm summer breezes turned cool and crisp, changing the leaves of green to hues of lemon-yellow, carrot-orange, ruby-red and maple-plum, fall was fast approaching, and the Lumberton Vocational Technical Institute was beckoning.

At long last, the day after Labor Day, Katie eagerly attended her very first session of the secretarial course at the vocational school. She was very enthusiastic about her studies, and she truly enjoyed each and every one of her classes from the very beginning.

Katie knew that she would remain forever grateful to her employment counselor, Norma Jean, for she had meticulously coordinated everything in such a way that Katie's tuition and books were covered by the federal subsidy, and Katie had immediately begun to receive the monthly stipend checks to help counterbalance her household budget and daycare expenses for the coming academic year.

While excelling in all of her business, typing and shorthand classes, in addition to making new friends and enjoying the social interaction with her fellow students, the nine-month secretarial course just flew by. Katie was excited to graduate alongside her classmates in June of 1969, and she was most eager to catapult herself into the workforce and discover the fantastic job opportunities that awaited her.

Being the mother of four small children, and the only divorcee in the tiny town of Stone Valley (population 395), Katie Munson hadn't had much time or opportunity to make friends. Fortunately, that changed significantly, as Katie had made dozens of friends during her rewarding collegiate experience at the vocational school.

As the graduation ceremony commenced, Katie cheered with heartfelt pride as, one by one, her fellow graduates marched up to the podium to collect their diplomas...and then, it was Katie's turn to be summoned to the platform for recognition of her academic achievement.

She quickly arose from her seat when she heard her name being called on the loudspeaker, echoing throughout the enormous gymnasium. As Katie proudly promenaded past her friends in the bleachers, gliding toward the stage, she happily reflected on her memorable scholastic experience.

Katie felt wonderful, as if she were a teenager again. She fondly recalled how, for the past nine months, she didn't see herself as a mother, a divorcee, or even a 24-year-old woman, for that matter...until she was suddenly reminded of all that when she heard the cheers and familiar infantile cries wailing from the second row of bleachers in the high school gymnasium, where the graduation ceremony was being held.

Buster and Sally had made sure to bring Katie's children to the momentous event so they, too, could bear witness to this spectacular milestone in their mother's life. As soon as Katie was handed her secretarial degree, her cheering section stood up proudly and applauded loudly, shouting, "Way to go, Katie!"

Mr. Wiederman managed to snap a Polaroid picture of his daughter before she descended the podium. Then, in a flash, Katie had disappeared from view, lost in the sea of graduating students, faculty and family members as the next graduate was summoned to the stage.

During those precious moments, as Katie clutched her trade-school diploma in her hand, Mrs. Wiederman had never been more proud of her baby girl. Sally's eyes welled with tears, as she acknowledged that her daughter had just achieved the most monumental of all goals she had ever set for herself. At last, their youngest daughter was on the road to fulfilling her dreams and making the most of her future.

Buster and Sally insisted on keeping the kids overnight so that Katie could go out and celebrate with her girlfriends. Katie readily accepted their generous offer because she realized that it would probably be a very long time before an opportunity such as this would arise again, once she started working a full-time job.

Katie and her fellow graduates started the evening out with a few cocktails at a hot spot that catered to young adults from Lumberton area colleges. After that, they enjoyed fine dining at a well-established seafood restaurant, topping off the night at a popular dance club, where they intended to rock to the Beatles and "twist" off the exorbitant calories from the rich chocolate desserts they had consumed earlier.

The secretarial school graduates had a marvelous time! Katie knew that night would be an evening to remember, so she pasted the memory into her mental scrapbook, where it would never be forgotten. It suddenly occurred to her, however, that, come Monday morning, her life was about to be modified once again, as Katie had already set the wheels in motion to scour the Lumberton vicinity in search of her dream job.

Her search for clerical work didn't take long. After making a return visit to the Lumberton employment office, Katie revisited with her former employment counselor; and with Norma Jean's assistance once again, Katie had secured a very lucrative secretarial job at the Lumberton Community College.

Working in the Education Office, as the secretary to one of the college's numerous administrators, Katie enjoyed a wide array of duties including typing, short-hand and answering the telephones, while also acting as receptionist for students, faculty and visitors, along with filing and miscellaneous record-keeping tasks.

In addition to her monthly salary, which Katie felt was more than satisfactory for a fresh secretarial school graduate, she couldn't have been more grateful for the generous amount of school holidays, in addition to two weeks of paid vacation time allotted each year, granting Katie even more quality time to spend with her children.

In August of that summer, a close-knit group of Katie's girlfriends had invited her to join them on a road trip to Upstate New York, to attend the "1969 Woodstock Festival and Concert." Betty Lou, Tiffany and Susie had been planning this special all-girl pilgrimage across states lines for months.

While her younger girlfriends (all between the ages of 18 and 20) had been holding on to the hope that their fun-loving, free-spirited buddy would join them on their exciting excursion to Woodstock, 24-year-old Katie Munson regretfully declined.

That didn't stop them from pleading with Katie,

however. The gal-pals tried to lure her even further by disclosing that they would be driving to New York in style, motoring down the highway in Betty Lou's brand-new blue Chrysler convertible, which was bestowed upon her in June by her wealthy parents as a graduation present.

No matter how much she had yearned to embark upon such a liberating journey, Katie knew in her heart that she had far too much responsibility now to accompany her girlfriends to New York State for a week's worth of undisciplined abandon.

That was a decision Katie would eventually come to regret for the rest of her life, having missed out on what her girlfriends referred to as "the ultimate, most hip and far-out experience of a lifetime," but Katie enjoyed hearing all about their electrifying road trip and the intimate (sometimes incriminating) details that would often be recalled during many a casual conversation.

Although her weekly schedule was extremely hectic, Katie endeavored to keep in contact with her close friends (Betty Lou, Tiffany and Susie) from the vocational school. The relationships she had formed with those three young women and their cherished get-togethers constituted her only reprieve from the precarious hazards of her daily life.

Unfortunately, after the exhausted female trio had returned from their post-graduation summer tour to the Woodstock Festival, their paths started heading in different directions. Inevitably, the fun-loving four-some began to part ways.

However, before letting their friendship fizzle out altogether (like so many post-graduates do), the four friends made a collective pact to get together and celebrate special birthdays, as well as any other im-portant milestones or life-altering events that might impact their lives.

Thus, in honor of that special friendship covenant, Katie received a highly anticipated telephone call from Betty Lou the following spring, in May of 1970. The pleasant voice on the other end of the line glee-fully reminded Katie that her 25th birthday was fast ap-proaching and that she had better be ready by 7 p.m. sharp next Saturday for her night out with the girls, in accordance with their agreement last fall.

Late that Saturday afternoon, Katie got all decked out in her pre-selected miniskirt and sweater outfit. As she slid her sleek black go-go boots over her smooth calves, she heard a familiar tune begin to serenade her through the speaker of her clock radio. She swiftly sprang up from her bed to amplify the volume and immediately started singing along to the Partridge Family's hit song, "I Think I Love You."

Katie then twirled around in front of the vanity mirror affixed to her chest of drawers. She examined her appearance from left to right, and then she opened up her compact mirror and turned around, catching a glimpse of her backside.

Finding herself surprisingly pleased with her festive choice of attire for this special occasion, Katie began to unroll at least a dozen hair curlers from her uncomfortably taught scalp. When the last remaining pink plastic curler had been removed, Katie tossed her blonde mane upside down and gave her hair a good shake, letting the curly locks cascade over her slender shoulders.

She fumbled hastily for the near-empty can of hairspray, which lay amid an untidy clutter of beauty aids, cosmetics and hair curlers that shrouded the dresser's surface. Katie proceeded to mist her entire mane, at which point she became engulfed in a thin fog of aerosol fumes, which eventually caused her to cough and sputter (much like the old "blue bomber," her 1958 Chevy Impala).

Katie was most relieved to have achieved instantaneous satisfaction with the aesthetic outcome of her golden locks on her first hairdo attempt, as it was already half past six, and she knew from experience that her vocational school chums were usually quite punctual.

"Would you kids PLEASE quiet down out there!" Katie hollered from her bedroom. She polished off the last gulp from her pink diet soda can and shouted, "The babysitter will be here any minute, so you'd better be on your best behavior!"

Obviously, Katie didn't want the new babysitter to hear the quarreling and chaos that was currently echoing throughout the house. Tonight was "Lulu's" first time sitting for Katie's children, and she didn't want her little hellions to scare Lulu off before she even got started on the job.

Although Katie's four children were typically fairly well-behaved, their close ages (6-1/2, 5, 4, 3) prompted constant bickering, sibling rivalry and, of course, the ultimate conquest to be in charge over one another; and at the going rate of 50 cents per hour compensation for babysitting services, the list of Stone Valley prospects willing to return for more of the Munson kids' punishment was ever-dwindling.

Fortunately, for Katie, it was 6:30 p.m. and time for one of her children's favorite television shows to air. "Hey, kids…*Hee Haw* is starting," Katie announced loudly, feeling confident that the popular variety show would keep them occupied, entertained, and relatively quiet for the next half-hour.

Keith, Judith Ivy, Darcy and Samantha immediately dropped what they were doing and raced to the television set, where they pushed and shoved one another in order to claim the ideal viewing spot from the area rug on the living room floor.

A short time later, Katie heard a knock at the door. While she had expected one of her kids to answer it, the children were so engrossed with Roy Clark, Buck Owens, and the whole "Kornfield Kounty" gang that their eyes were glued to the picture tube, where the feeble foursome remained completely oblivious to their guest's arrival.

"Gee, don't bother getting up, kids…by all means, let <u>me</u> get the door," Katie sarcastically remarked in passing. Her scowl at the children went completely unnoticed. "Well, at least they're quiet now," she mumbled, as her noisy high-heeled boots clickety-clacked across the hardwood kitchen floor.

"Mrs. Munson?" greeted a petite, teenaged lass. She was dressed in an orange, green and yellow poncho, with a flowing beige skirt down to her ankles and matching sandals. Her hair was parted in the back, with two long, cornsilk-colored pigtails resting on her shoulders, accented by large peace-sign earrings dangling from her earlobes.

"Yes, I'm Katie Munson," the children's mother replied. "You must be Lulu," Katie presumed. "Please, come in."

Although Katie had never met Lulu before, she had come highly recommended by Katie's neighbor and daycare provider (Linda Reed) as a dependable seventeen-year-old and an experienced babysitter.

Contrarily, Katie couldn't help but assume, based solely on her outward appearance, that Lulu must have been one of those girls who hung out with Stone Valley's "hippie" crowd.

From what Katie had heard around town, those hippie types were usually pot-heads and/or trouble-makers. Nevertheless, regardless of her initial impression, Katie decided to set aside her prejudice and trust her neighbor's favorable reference.

During a commercial break halfway through the *Hee Haw* presentation, Katie introduced the new babysitter to her children, from oldest to youngest. She then proceeded with Lulu's brief orientation of the Munson household. Before she was able to finish reciting Lulu's duties and instructions, however, the women were interrupted by the sound of a car honking outside in front of the old white house.

Katie parted the kitchen curtains and peered out the window. "Oh, my gosh! The girls are here already!" she frantically announced, adding, "I gotta run!" Katie then grabbed her black patent-leather clutch handbag from her bed, blew her children a kiss goodbye, and headed for the door.

Before she let the screen door slam shut, Katie informed the babysitter, "I left some written instructions for tonight on the kitchen table. If you need any assistance or have any problems or an emergency, just contact Linda Reed across the street," she shouted. "Her number's written on the paper. I should be home by one o'clock...or two at the very latest," Katie promised.

"Okay, Mrs. Munson...have a good time!" Lulu yelled back, as Katie hopped into the rear seat of Betty Lou's pretty '69 Chrysler convertible.

Lulu watched with curiosity as Mrs. Munson was whisked away by a carload of loud-mouthed, giddy ladies. The moment that heavy side door was closed, the blue convertible screeched its tires, after which the vehicle sped off into the warm, cloud-covered spring evening.

"Huh…sounds like the party already started," Lulu mumbled, shaking her head. She then addressed the Munson brood, now that their television program was over. "So, kids…what do you guys wanna do?"

"I know," four-year-old Darcy volunteered. "Let's play hide-n-seek."

"Sure, that sounds like fun," Lulu responded. "You kids go run and hide, and then I'll come find you."

"No, not in the house," Keith protested. "We like to play Starlight Moonlight outside…in the graveyard," he informed their newest Saturday-night guardian.

"The graveyard!" Lulu shrieked. "But, it's gonna be dark out soon," she acknowledged, in an effort to persuade the kids to stick around the house.

"So what!" Keith stated defiantly. "We do it all the time."

"No, I don't think that's such a good idea," Lulu argued. "How 'bout we pop up a huge bowl of pop-corn and watch a scary movie instead."

"Nah, we wanna go outside and play, right guys?" Keith maintained, rallying his sisters to side with him. "Yeah, let's play Starlight Moonlight," Judith Ivy sec-onded. "Can Laverne and Jeannie play too?" she be-seeched their new sitter.

"Who are Laverne and Jeannie?" Lulu asked. "Oh, they're our best friends," Judith Ivy affirmed. "They live across the street, over by the park."

Laverne and Jeannie Crawford were the youngest of nine children—five boys and four girls. The Crawford family lived kitty-corner from the Munsons and adjacent to the Stone Valley Park, where Katie's daughters frequently played.

It was at the park where they had met Laverne and Jeannie, and they ultimately became the best of friends. Although there were five boys in the Crawford family, they were years older than Keith Munson, so aside from being their babysitter on occasion, the teenaged Crawford boys didn't have much to do with the six-year-old.

"Come on, you guys!" Keith hollered, taking command of the game, as usual. "I get to be the ghost," he blurted. Before Lulu could even pose an argument, the four little children had darted out the front door, bounded down the porch steps, and scattered off, in opposite directions.

Judith Ivy and Darcy were already making their way across the street to call on the Crawford girls, while Keith was halfway through the cemetery, in search of the optimal hiding place in which the "ghost" would lie in wait. Lulu and three-year-old Samantha were left behind to wait for the girls on the front porch.

When Judy, Darcy, Laverne and Jeannie returned, Lulu and Samantha joined them. The female party of six clasped hands, clinging close to one another as the pack bravely forged ahead, into the eerie graveyard. Together, the girls began to chant loudly so that their "ghost" would hear them and initiate the game. "Starlight, moonlight, hope to see a ghost tonight..."

Nightfall was fast upon them. Luckily, the radiance of the full moon peered intermittently through the breaks in cloud cover just long enough to light their way through the deepening darkness. At the same time, however, those bouts of visual clarity also illuminated the countless granite and quartz monuments, casting enormous shadows beyond the tombstones, which closely resembled gargoyles and other grotesque demonic creatures of the night.

Lulu felt the panic begin to envelop her body, and soon goose bumps had formed on her arms and legs. "I don't think I like this game," the unnerved 17-year-old admitted, which added an extra element of fear to the notoriously spooky game.

The girls all huddled together, and as their terror intensified, they advanced with trepidation, clinging ever tighter to one another. From any given direction, the frightened females expected their "ghost" to suddenly appear, jumping out from behind a gravestone or tomb, and start chasing them, rendering the first victim caught to be the designated ghost in the next round of the game.

Lulu had never ventured through a graveyard in the daylight, and she certainly didn't much care for it in the dark of night. Her imagination began to run away with her thoughts, as she started to envision apparitions and unsightly monsters lurking behind each and every tree, shrub or headstone. Her heart pounded steadily and her pulse quickened with every step. She could only imagine how terrified the young girls she was supposed to be protecting must have felt.

"I'm scared!" little Samantha finally cried out. "Come here, sweetheart," the babysitter enticed, with open arms. The three-year-old instantly jumped into her bosom with an embrace so tight that it made Lulu gasp for air. "Stick close with me girls," Lulu instructed the youngsters, with a shaking whisper.

Laverne had grown frustrated as well. "Is your brother even out there, Jude?" she tauntingly remarked. "He should be after us by now!"

The women chanted one more time to summon the ghost, but still he did not materialize. The girls had run out of patience. "That's it, Keith!" Lulu screamed. "We're going back to the house...game's over!"

Bewildered and weary, the gang of girls gave up on the game and started traipsing back to the house, deciding to devise an alternate agenda for the evening's entertainment. Then, as the little women deliberated with great intensity, a dark figure suddenly appeared directly in front of their path, having descended from an overhead tree limb. Lulu and the five young girls screamed in blood-curdling horror.

In fear for their lives, the tightly woven band of babes broke loose and scattered with the winds, running as fast as they could towards the old white Munson house. Lulu sprinted with three-year-old

Samantha in tow, leaving the rest of the girls to fend for themselves.

Once inside the house, Lulu turned off the light, and then the six young ladies huddled closely together in the far corner of the kitchen, where they could keep an eye on the front door. They crouched down on their knees, paralyzed with fright, trying to remain silent as they struggled to breathe.

The screen door slammed hard a second time, ushering an ominous, elongated shadow in through the doorway from out of the moonlit darkness.

"I really got you guys!" Keith bellowed, with bursts of intense, somewhat sinister laughter. He seemed to derive a sense of perverse gratification from terrorizing his little sisters, not to mention the neighbor girls, as well as their latest babysitter.

"You are really sick, Keith!" Judith Ivy screamed, once Keith had turned on the kitchen light to reveal his identity.

"Keith Munson, do you have any idea what you've done?" Lulu wailed. "You scared us nearly half to death! Your sister Samantha wet her pants because she was so scared!" Lulu then exercised her authoritative right and commanded, "I think you had better go on up to your room, mister, and think about what you've done...go on!"

Once Keith had been banished to his bedroom, the babysitter got Samantha cleaned up and changed into her pajamas. Lulu then addressed the pint-sized sorority and inquired, "So, what do you girls wanna do now?"

"Let's play some records," Judith Ivy eagerly proposed, adding, "Our mom has lots of really good records we can dance to!"

The five-year-old darted over to the gold-plated slotted record stand that housed her mother's precious collection of LP record albums, to include such iconic artists as Connie Francis, Bobby Vinton, Hank Williams, Patsy Cline, Loretta Lynn, Tammy Wynette, Ricky Nelson, Johnny Cash, The Beach Boys, and Katie's favorite artist, the legendary Elvis Presley.

Judith Ivy first selected the Connie Francis album. While the popular female vocalist sang her poignant breakup ballad, "Who's Sorry Now," Judy couldn't help but notice the sudden change in the babysitter's facial expression. "What's the matter, Lulu?" the petite brown-eyed girl asked, with genuine wide-eyed concern.

"Oh, I'm just bummed out because my boyfriend and I broke up last week," Lulu sniveled. "And I just...I really miss him, that's all," she despairingly disclosed, to the only companions she had for the evening. Lulu then wiped a solitary tear from the corner of her eye, smudging her thick black mascara in the process. "Why don't you guys play something a little more upbeat?" she urged, in an effort to dispel her sullen mood.

After slipping the large black vinyl disc back into its thin paper sheath, Judith Ivy gently placed her mother's "Leader of the Pack" LP record on the turn-table. When the Shangri-Las started singing their first track, Lulu's olive-green eyes opened wide with inter-est. "Hey, that's my favorite album!" she perked up, declaring, "Your mom has good taste...crank it up!"

The six girls then hosted their own little dance party right there in the living room. Lulu taught the eager pupils a few dance steps she had learned in high school, in addition to some new moves she had picked up recently while watching the hit television show, *American Bandstand*. Kicking the rugs off to the side, the girls then proceeded to twist, shimmy, shake, swim, pony and twirl one another across the hardwood floor.

Judith Ivy and Laverne danced together as a cou-ple, alongside Darcy and Jeannie. Samantha tried to mimic her sisters by bopping around the room and pretending to sing along to the lyrics of the former number-one hit, "The Leader of the Pack." Each of them tried to override the others, singing louder and louder with the Shangri-Las.

All the girls seemed to be having a wonderful time, including the babysitter. However, when Lulu heard the sound of the motorcycle engine revving in the background on the well-known recording, her carefree, energetic spirit took a melancholy turn. She marched over to the turntable and disengaged the sty-lus, thus souring the girls' dance party with a screech and an abrupt silence.

"Hey, what did you do that for?" Laverne Crawford queried, obviously annoyed, with her hands on her hips. "We were having fun!"

"I'm sorry," Lulu replied. "That's just a hard song for me to listen to right now."

"How come?" Judith Ivy implored her babysitter.

"It has to do with my boyfriend…well, my ex-boy-friend now, I guess," Lulu lamented, hanging her head in sorrow. "But, you guys don't wanna hear that story."

"Sure we do," four-year-old Darcy chimed in. "We like stories."

As the rest of the group echoed Darcy's sentiment, Lulu felt unexpectedly comforted. Though she was surprised at the somewhat odd interest the young girls were expressing with regard to her love affairs, Lulu found them to be mature beyond their prepubescent years; and since she really had no one else to confide in that night, she thought, "What the heck?"

She gathered the Munson girls and the Crawford girls around the living room sofa and proceeded to tell them all about how she had met her boyfriend at the homecoming football game last fall. Lulu had actually been forced to attend that football game by her parents, in an effort to demonstrate their familial support of her younger brother, who played the trombone in Lumberton High School's marching band.

Lulu and some of her "hippie" wannabe girlfriends were walking laps around the perimeter of the football field when she first noticed him. His name was Paul…

and when he pulled up to the concession stand on his gleaming Triumph Bonneville motorcycle, revving it up loudly as if to herald his arrival, every female eye within earshot was fixated on the mysterious dark-haired dreamboat draped in black leather.

From the moment Paul and Lulu had struck up a conversation over two bottles of refreshing cola, a spark had ignited between them, lighting a fire that kept them warm in each other's arms for months to follow...that was, however, until eighteen-year-old Paul had begun to develop doubts about being committed to a serious relationship.

Just last weekend, according to Lulu, Paul had coldly informed Lulu that he needed more time to figure out what he wanted to do and that she needed to give him some space. Lulu read more into Paul's words than he had intended, presuming the worst—that their relationship was over.

The babysitter tried to rationalize for the young girls just how devastated their breakup had left her. Paul was the only long-term boyfriend Lulu had ever had. She subsequently admitted that she was in love with the boy, at which point she broke down and wept. "So now, whenever I hear that song, or any song about a guy on a motorcycle," Lulu sobbed, "I think about Paul...and how much I miss him!"

Offering the only insightful advice the 5-1/2-year-old could reckon, Laverne innocently blurted, "Maybe you should just call Paul and tell him you miss him."

That was the last thing Lulu had in mind. It suddenly dawned on her that she was bearing her soul to a bunch of tiny tots. "Well, maybe you girls should just go on upstairs and get changed into your PJs," Lulu retorted, as she wiped the black streaks of tears from her flushed red cheeks with her hand-crocheted, multicolored poncho.

"Can Laverne and Jeannie stay overnight tonight, Lulu?" Darcy petitioned.

"Oh, I don't know," Lulu wavered. "I'm not sure how your mom would feel about having two overnight guests," she reluctantly returned. "Besides...why didn't you kids ask your mother when she was home not too long ago?"

"Because...we just thought it up now," Darcy explained. "Don't worry, Lulu, our mom won't mind," she convincingly added. "She always says 'yes'."

"Well, if it's okay with your friends' mom, Mrs. Crawford...and you're <u>positive</u> that your mother won't mind, then...I guess it's okay with me," Lulu acceded. With a hint of reservation in her voice, however, she warned, "But you better not be pulling one of your little stunts, like your naughty brother Keith did in the cemetery!"

Laverne raced to the telephone in the kitchen and called her mom, requesting permission for the two of them to stay overnight at the Munson house. Mrs. Crawford readily granted the request, as she was in the midst of a nasty brotherly squabble at home, so she was just happy to have her two youngest daughters out of the house.

"Yay!" Laverne shouted. "We get to stay!" The five happy little girls jumped and cheered with joy. Judith Ivy then led the female pack upstairs to change into their pajamas and, at the same time, search for some sleep wear to fit the significantly taller Crawford girls.

At last, Lulu had finally found some time to herself. She took a deep breath and sighed, thankful for the relaxing moment. She couldn't stop thinking about Laverne's quick-witted advice, however. "Maybe I should just call him," she pondered. "What's the harm in saying hello?" Lulu reasoned. "I'd be happy just to hear his voice."

While the noisy girls were engaged in what sounded like a pillow fight upstairs, and Keith had locked himself in his room during his exile, the babysitter took refuge in the kitchen, reveling in the placid moment.

Lulu picked up the telephone receiver and very nervously dialed Paul's number. Although she had no idea how Paul might react to her calling him so soon after his request for more space just one week earlier, she summoned the courage and decided to follow through. Surprised to find Paul at home on a Saturday night, the palms of her hands began to perspire, in anticipation of an undoubtedly passionate discussion.

At one point during their meaningful telephone conversation, one of the Munson girls came sliding down the wooden staircase inside of a brown paper grocery sack. Lulu paid no attention as the youngster ran back up the stairs and offered the paper bag to the next girl in line to slide down the steps, and so on, and so on.

A short time later, after deciding that he had been recluse in his bedroom long enough, Keith eventually joined his siblings, and he was the next ruffian to come tumbling down those stairs in the brown paper sack.

As a result of the children's hysterical laughter and ear-piercing screams, Lulu was forced to cut her phone call short. She angrily confronted the boisterous little rascals and bellowed, "What on earth are you guys doing?"

"We're stair sledding," Darcy enlightened the babysitter. "We do it all the time."

"Yeah, it's really fun," Judith Ivy added, with a giggle. "Wanna try it, Lulu?"

"No thanks, guys. I think I'll pass," their guardian scoffed. Lulu shook her head in astonishment as she walked into the living room, mumbling, "Goofy kids." She then placed another record album on the turntable while the children continued their exhilarating, albeit bizarre, horseplay.

The moment they heard American heartthrob Ricky Nelson singing "Teenage Idol," however, the giggling stair-sledders immediately stopped what they were doing, and the dance party in the living room suddenly recommenced.

Keith didn't much care for dancing, so he became quickly bored with watching his sisters and their two little friends flailing about like spastic rag dolls. Feeling neglected and ignored, Keith decided to entertain himself. "I'm gonna go make some popcorn," he informed the babysitter, as he stormed off into the kitchen.

"Wait! Let me help you," Lulu interrupted the willful young lad, "before you go and make a complete mess of the place!"

Once they had caught a whiff of the savory buttered popcorn Keith and Lulu were preparing, the girls instinctively followed their sense of smell, which led them to the kitchen. "Judy, you go and get the soda pop," Lulu delegated. "And, Darcy, you can fetch the glasses while I get the ice cubes."

Laverne removed the caps from the bottles of Dr. Pepper, since she was much bigger and stronger than Judy. Darcy then dropped a few ice cubes into each of the seven glasses, and her older sister poured the sodas. While Keith seasoned their late-night snack with salt, Lulu retrieved seven small bowls from the kitchen cupboards, at which point the babysitting gang gathered around the kitchen table and dug in.

Lulu and the children were laughing and having a grand old time as they enjoyed their ice-cold sodas and greasy buttered popcorn, although they did have to sort out a handful of burnt black kernels, which Keith collected in a separate bowl, so he could feed them and the "old maids" to the squirrels and birds in the morning.

Then, while Keith was attempting to shoot popcorn kernels into the girls' mouths from across the kitchen table, the faint whirr of a motorcycle engine arose from somewhere off in the distance. The rumbling clamor grew increasingly audible as it drew nearer, and soon the powerful roar was unmistakable, as the thunderclap of a parade of steel horses descended upon the tranquil streets of Stone Valley.

Keith pushed his chair back and scurried to the kitchen door to take a peek outside. He flung the door wide open, and then the rest of the troops rushed to his side. Lulu picked up little Samantha in her arms as the inquisitive bunch crowded around the screen door to investigate the mysterious commotion.

Lulu instantly recognized the leader of this leather-clad pack. She could hardly believe her eyes, for it was her beloved Paul! He and a half-dozen of his biker buddies were parking their motorcycles along the curb in front of the Munson residence.

One by one, the biker gang shut down their engines, restoring tranquility once again to the peaceful little town of Stone Valley. The gentlemen, however, remained stoically perched upon their majestic scooters.

The babysitter quickly set Samantha down on the kitchen floor, and then she and Keith hustled outside to greet Paul and his comrades. Curiosity had gotten the better of the girls, so they trailed closely behind, bounding out into the dark of night wearing nothing by their nightgowns and pajamas.

"Wow!" Keith exclaimed. "Look at all the motorcycles!"

"Paul, what are you doing here?" the dumfounded Lulu asked. She glanced around at the handful of comrades who accompanied him, recognizing but a few of his friends, who utilized the unscheduled pit stop to smoke a cigarette.

"Well, after you called me earlier tonight," Paul divulged, "I got to thinking...maybe I was wrong about the things I said to you last weekend."

Unfortunately, Keith had interrupted their potential moment of reconciliation by blurting, "Can I have a ride on your cool motorcycle, mister?"

"Keith, we were talking!" Lulu chastised the six-year-old. "Don't you know that it's rude to interrupt people?"

Once the embarrassed youngster had apologized, Lulu agreed to let Paul give Keith a short ride on his bike, just around the park and back. In the meantime, while the two of them were circling the block, the remainder of the biker gang and the babysitting gang became better acquainted.

During that most unusual meeting of leathers and pajamas, beneath the moon of a bewitching May sky, Judith Ivy and Laverne disappeared for a spell, as they had gone back inside the house to change the record album. Laverne cranked the volume to the maximum level, as the five-year-olds wanted to be able to hear the music from the yard.

She and Judy then raced back outside as fast as they could, so as not to miss a single beat of the Beach Boys record. "Dance, Dance, Dance" was the most anticipated tune of the evening. Accordingly, when the upbeat song began to play, the Munson and Crawford girls instantaneously started twisting and gyrating, putting into practice the dance steps their babysitter had taught them earlier that evening.

When Paul and little Keith subsequently returned from their brief jaunt on Paul's silver-blue Triumph Bonneville, the leather-clad lad couldn't believe the goings-on he was witnessing in the front yard of the Munson residence.

"I don't believe it!" Paul uttered in awe, for out there on the lawn were six of his closest friends, the most macho assortment of guys he knew, twirling and bopping with a bunch of pint-sized teenyboppers wearing nightgowns and pajamas, dancing to the music of the Beach Boys!

"Come on, let's go!" Keith urged his new biker buddy, Paul, and then he firmly grasped his weathered hand and yanked him over towards the yard party.

Even though he didn't care to dance, Keith had a sudden change of heart. He figured that, if the big guys didn't feel silly and foolish for dancing, then it was okay for him to do it too. Trying his best to mimic the cool moves of his male elders, Keith inconspicuously blended in with the rest of the crowd.

"So, why did you come here tonight, Paul?" Lulu asked her star-crossed lover, now that they finally had a moment to talk semi-privately.

"I don't know…I guess I just wanted to see you," Paul confessed. "I know it's only been a week, but I've missed you something awful…and, well…me and the guys were on a road trip not far from here, so I decided to make a pit stop."

"But, I thought you wanted some space…to figure out what you wanted to do with your life," Lulu reiterated, still unable to comprehend the agonizing problem he was having with their relationship.

"Believe me, Lulu, it's not you!" Paul assured her. "It's my parents," he started to explain. "They've been pressuring me and telling me things like…how I shouldn't be spending all my time with just one girl… and that I should play the field and not get too serious because we're so young, and…"

"Really?" Lulu beseeched, through misty green eyes. "It was all your parents' doing? I thought it was all over for us," she whimpered with a sigh, now that a glimmer of hope had emerged from the darkness. "Last weekend you sounded like you were breaking up with me for good," she sniveled.

"I know, and I'm sorry about that," Paul apologized. "I love you, Lulu," he professed, "and I want us to be together…regardless of what my parents think or say."

"You really mean that?" Lulu implored, while nervously wrapping strands of hair from her blonde pigtail around her index finger.

"With all my heart," Paul avowed. "I know you're the only girl for me, so...will you go steady with me?" He carefully pried his 1969 class ring from his finger and presented it to his beloved, who readily accepted both the ring and his proposal.

"Yes, Paul, I would love to go steady with you!" Lulu affirmed. In an instant, those looming feelings of uncertainty and despair that had been hanging over her head were blown away with the wind, leaving her feeling exhilarated and joyful.

Paul wiped a salty tear from Lulu's fair-skinned face, and then he softly kissed her glossy lips, in validation of his profound intentions.

The happily reunited couple rejoiced with a lengthy embrace, after which they, too, joined in the dance party, alongside the rest of the biker/babysitting bunch. All of the kids, both big and small, male and female, the tough and the not-so-tough, were having a marvelous time...until their fun suddenly came to a screeching halt.

Around midnight, a blue 1969 Chrysler convertible pulled up unexpectedly and abruptly terminated their good time. "What the hell is going on here?" a very irate, petite blonde woman wearing black go-go boots bellowed, as she exited the large vehicle.

"Oh, uh...hello, Mrs. Munson," the babysitter

sheepishly returned, feeling as if she were about to be harshly reprimanded in front of her boyfriend and all of his pals. "What are you doing home so early?" Lulu inquired.

"I got a terrible headache, so I decided to come home and sleep it off," Mrs. Munson apprised her children's caretaker. "And it's a good thing I did," Katie angrily stated, "because when I get home, I find a black-leather biker gang partying with my little girls outside in the yard in the middle of the night! What kind of a babysitter would allow such inappropriate behavior?" she screamed.

Katie was unmistakably furious. Apparently, her twenty-fifth birthday night out with the girls hadn't turned out quite the way she had planned, so she was already in a rotten mood long before her girlfriends drove her back home to Stone Valley.

"Mom, we were having so much fun!" Judith Ivy exclaimed. She then made an attempt to defend her new favorite babysitter. "Please don't be mad at Lulu, Mom," she pleaded. "We really like her!"

"Well, that's too bad!" Katie retorted. "I'm sorry, but that irresponsible hippie is never babysitting for you kids ever again!"

Mrs. Munson hastily fumbled for the coin purse tucked deep inside her clutch handbag. She counted out $2.50 and then handed Lulu her compensation for the five hours that she had spent watching over her children.

"Here's your pay for the evening," Katie gruffly told the seventeen-year-old girl as she placed the cash in her hands. "Now, tell your friends to get on home, and don't ever come back! You're no longer welcome here…is that clear?" she snapped.

"But, Mrs. Munson…" Lulu pleaded, struggling to offer some sort of an explanation, but Katie wouldn't grant her the opportunity.

"Please, just go! Get out of here…every last one of you!" Mrs. Munson bellowed, placing the palm of her left hand against her forehead. During that startling confrontation, Katie's headache pain had escalated with unbearable intensity.

Upon Lulu's immediate termination, the biker/babysitting bunch quickly disbanded, as their dance party was officially over.

Katie's children watched with sadness as their new favorite babysitter swiftly climbed onto the back of Paul's motorcycle. The remaining crew of bikers mounted their steel horses in succession, firing up their noisy engines, which further aggravated Mrs. Munson's pounding head.

As Lulu and her friends in leather jackets departed, they waved a collective farewell to their newest young comrade, Keith Munson, and to all their dainty dance partners who, for a fraction of an evening, had unknowingly reminded them that it was okay to feel childlike and uninhibited, even downright silly, every once in a while.

That was the last the Munson children ever saw of the delightfully entertaining Lulu or her "leader and his pack" as they rode out of Stone Valley, into the ebony May sky, and out of their lives forever.

The next morning, during an unusually quiet Sunday breakfast, Katie Munson handed out punishments like she was dishing out extra helpings of blueberry pancakes. In addition to assigning piles of nonstandard household chores, all four children found themselves grounded from watching television for an entire week.

The Munson kids accepted their harsh sentences honorably and without objection, for Keith, Judith Ivy, Darcy and Samantha (and even Laverne and Jeannie Crawford) had already established that their experience with Lulu and the biker gang last night was, by far, the most exciting and thrilling event of their juvenile lives...and as far as they were concerned, the reward far outweighed the penance!

## Chapter 2
# All Right Now

When Labor Day weekend arrived later that year, in September of 1970, Katie Munson and the kids were excited to spend the extended weekend in Huntington with her parents. Buster and Sally Wiederman had invited Katie and her brood to join them on Saturday for a day of fishing at Buster's boathouse, which floated amid a humble boathouse club in a small harbor on the backwaters of the mighty Mississippi River, just a few miles north of Lumberton.

Keith Munson was already dreading the start of first grade, knowing that he would have to sit in school for the whole day, unlike his sister, Judith Ivy, who would be starting kindergarten and only had to attend school for half the day. Thus, Keith was eager to get some more fishing time in before becoming imprisoned within the schoolhouse walls every Monday through Friday, week after boring week.

On Sunday, the plan was for Katie and the kids to help Buster and Sally after church services, preparing their homestead for the annual Labor Day picnic on Monday, for which the entire Wiederman clan would come together to enjoy a full day of potluck picnic food and softball games in the spacious pasture land behind their barn, sheds and garage.

Katie looked forward to seeing her three older brothers and her sister, Roberta, along with all the nieces and nephews. She couldn't wait to catch up on all that had been going on in their lives since their last big family get-together on Memorial Day.

As usual, Grandpa Buster had spent most of Saturday afternoon helping Darcy and Samantha wrangle worms onto their tiny fish hooks and/or removing little bitty sunfish, one right after the other, from the lines of their miniature homemade bamboo fishing rods. Buster didn't seem to mind at all. In fact, his heart danced when he saw his little granddaughters' faces light up with each successful catch.

Keith and Judith Ivy, unlike their little sisters, were already experienced fishermen, having discovered their passion for fishing at about the age of two. Buster had been taking Keith fishing with him since he had learned to walk, and as soon as Judy was steadily ambulatory, she insisted on tagging along with her big brother and Grandpa Buster on their fishing expeditions.

"When am I gonna catch a big fish, Grandpa?" four-year-old Darcy whined, after her grandfather released the seventh tiny sunfish she had reeled in that afternoon into the warm, shallow Mississippi waters.

"Don't worry, Gravel Gertie," Buster assured his impatient granddaughter. "You'll catch a keeper eventually. Have patience, my dear, for that's a big part of fishing," he assured the young lass. Darcy responded with a heavy sigh, and then she dug around the fresh, moist black dirt inside the large coffee can, in search of another earthworm to bait her hook.

After branding his grandson Keith with the nickname "Oscar" (fashioned after his good buddy from the Marine Corps), Grandpa Buster continued that tradition with each of Katie's girls as well. Mr. Wiederman had invented some interesting nicknames for the Munson kids, as well as several other grandchildren, each of which reflected Buster's unique comical nature.

When Judith Ivy was born, Grandpa Buster had likened her appearance to that of a wrinkled old man; and because she was such an ornery little cuss (cried and whined a lot), he wittily started calling her "Snuffy," in emulation of that old hillbilly-moonshiner, "Snuffy Smith," who was Buster's favorite troublemaker from the popular *Barney Google and Snuffy Smith* comic strip series, which ran through the Great Depression era.

Mr. Wiederman was also a big fan and regular reader of the *Dick Tracy* comic strip series, ever since its inception in 1931 (the year he married his beloved Sally).

He especially got a kick out of the mysterious "Gravel Gertie," a recurring character in *Dick Tracy* who lived in a gravel pit outside of the city. Although she was quite homely on the outside, "Gravel Gertie" had a beautiful singing voice, was a skilled mandolin player, and became the inspiration for the namesake Buster would eventually allocate to Katie's third-born child, Darcy Lynn.

Samantha Jo Munson was "born with smiling eyes," Grandpa Buster always said. From the moment he beheld the newborn's twinkling eyes in the nursery, he instinctively began to sing, "When Irish eyes are smiling, sure it's like a morning spring..." From that day forward, Samantha became forever known by her grandfather as "Irish."

As the sun's late-afternoon heat grew more intense, so did the complaints stemming from the two youngest fisher-women, Darcy and Samantha. While the pint-sized beginners questioned why their sunfish were not worthy to take home for supper, Buster was relieved to hear the sound of splashing water coming from the other end of the boathouse, where Keith and Judith Ivy were angling for keepers in the deeper waters.

"I got one, Grandpa, I got one!" Keith hollered loudly, so as to solicit Buster's attention. "And it's a big one too!" he announced with excitement, while skillfully reeling the undisclosed monstrous fish toward the boathouse.

Buster quickly rose to his feet, thankful for the disruption. He clumsily maneuvered around the open tackle box, fishing poles, and the five-quart ice cream pail full of night crawlers (which he and Keith had plucked from the freshly soaked topsoil after last night's rain), in order to investigate the commotion.

"Hey, you've got a big one there, Oscar!" Buster hailed, once the six-year-old had successfully landed the husky smallmouth bass inside the boathouse.

"Yeah…way to go, Keith!" his jealous, but supportive, sister applauded. Judith Ivy and Keith had long been harmonious fishing partners; and just as her big brother had taught, the five-year-old lass remembered to pull up her fishing line and clear out of Keith's way, once her brother had become entangled in the dance of landing the big one.

"Let's see how much my big bass weighs, Grandpa!" the thrilled young boy replied, clinging desperately to his heavy fishing rod with both hands as the slimy fish flip-flopped frantically on the filthy aluminum boathouse floor.

Buster fumbled hastily for the weighting scale inside his rusty red tackle box. Once located, he quickly untangled it from some loose fishing line and eagerly presented it to his grandson, graciously letting the lad enjoy the pleasure of weighing his first large-scale fish.

Kneeling down beside his grandson, Buster carefully removed the barbed hook from the great fish's mouth. Keith then slipped the hook of the scale apparatus through the gill, lifting the heavy scale with both hands. He held the scale up at eye level, so that he and Grandpa Buster could examine the measurement together.

"Wow, you've just caught yourself a four-pound lunker, Oscar!" Buster boasted, as he mussed up the sun-bleached locks on Keith's shaggy blonde head, in gentlemanly appreciation. "That'll make for some mighty good eatin'," Buster asserted, licking his lips. "Especially with your grandma's famous pan-fry coating."

While Grandpa Buster and his mess of tiny tots continued to fish for their supper, the children's mother and grandmother lounged on lawn chairs set atop the wooden dock, on the shallow side of the boathouse, yet in close view of the wee ones.

Unlike the rest of the group, Grandma Sally and Katie had chosen to unwind that Saturday afternoon, catching up on each other's lives while basking in the warmth of the abundant late-summer Minnesota sunshine.

As usual, Sally was wearing her faded blue-denim visor. The 58-year-old grandmother freckled easily and wanted to inhibit the appearance of any new age spots. Katie, on the other hand, welcomed the sun's rays, as the 25-year-old mother of four rarely found time to soak up the sun and/or just sit back, relax and do absolutely nothing.

"Hey, you guys, come over here and see my big fish!" Keith bellowed to his clan. "Hurry up, before we put it down in the fish basket!"

Katie grudgingly made her way to her beaming son, while Sally helped Darcy and Samantha meander through the labyrinth of fishing paraphernalia that littered the boathouse floor. "Gee, that is a nice fish, Keith!" his mother applauded.

While the gang carried on about Keith's big catch of the day, Buster lobbed the hefty bass into the live fishing basket, lowering their supper into the murky waters through the ice fishing hole, cut out of the center of the boathouse floor.

"All we need now is another keeper or two like that one, and we can have ourselves a great big fish fry tonight," Buster proudly hailed.

Imbued with enthusiasm, the children quickly scattered back to their original fishing posts, each one aspiring to catch the next great whopper. "Okay, troops," their 60-year-old grandfather commanded, with a clap of his hands, "Let's go catch some more fish!"

The Labor Day weekend's Saturday afternoon fishing expedition had proven to be a successful one, indeed. Grandma Sally fried a substantial mess of fresh fish for supper that evening, including several Bluegill sunfish, Keith's four-pound bass, a couple of crappies, and a 3-1/2-pound northern pike that Buster had caught, once the "beginners" had decided to give up on fishing and go hunting for agates on the gravel road just beyond the boathouse dock.

After supper, Buster thanked Sally for the delicious

meal, kissed her on the cheek, and excused himself from the kitchen table. He then retreated to the living room, where he intended to smoke his evening tobacco pipe and catch the Minnesota Twins game on television.

While the TV set warmed up, Buster claimed his cozy rocking chair, and then he carefully ignited the brown tobacco leaves. The spicy aroma wafted through the house like an incense, eventually masking the lingering stench of greasy pan-fried fish.

Keith was the first to join his grandfather in the living room, after being forced by his grandmother to take a long-overdue bath; and since Katie was busy tidying up the bathroom and drawing a new bath for her daughters, Sally was left behind to clear the table and wash the supper dishes.

During a sponsor break in the baseball game, Keith trotted back into the kitchen to see how things were coming along with the cleanup, as he had an ulterior motive. "Can I go down to the basement and get the ice cream now?" he asked his grandmother, as she drained the water from the kitchen sink.

"Sure, go ahead, Keith," Grandma Sally answered, after having scalded the dishes with a pan of boiling water. She then wiped the beads of sweat from her forehead with her apron and sighed, "I think we'll just let the dishes dry in the rack tonight."

Keith darted downstairs to the deep freezer and retrieved a five-quart pail of New York vanilla ice cream, which had long ago become a staple in the Wiederman household, particularly during the steamy summer months. Whenever Katie and the kids spent the night, the family always graced their evening meal with a tantalizing ice cream dessert and desired toppings.

"Are you girls almost done in there?" Sally shouted through the closed bathroom door, where Katie was busy towel-drying the last of her daughters' wet heads after their shared bath. "Yeah, go ahead and dish up, Mom," Katie hollered back. "We just have to get into our pajamas, and then we'll be ready."

Keith stomped his way up the wooden basement steps, and then he heaved the nearly full, frosty ice cream pail onto the kitchen table cloth. Using a large, sturdy metal spoon, Sally began to scoop two mounds of vanilla ice cream into each of the seven plastic bowls, making sure to give Buster an extra helping.

"Don't forget the walnuts, Oscar!" Buster yelled out from his rocker, in an effort to remind the lad not to forget his most favorite ice cream topping of all. "I won't, Grandpa," his grandson reassured him.

Keith and his grandfather had spent hours the weekend prior shucking buckets full of bountiful yellowish-green walnuts, which they had harvested together from Buster's enormous walnut tree that provided shade for the majority of his huge front lawn.

Although Buster wore rugged leather hand gloves for better grip and skin protection, Keith's fingernails were still discolored with the residual dark stains from that exhausting hot and sticky afternoon of shelling and peeling walnut husks with his bare hands.

On Sunday morning, Sally got up early and started getting the kitchen table ready for a quick breakfast before the family headed off to church. With time being somewhat limited on Sunday mornings, she would immediately start the coffee in the percolator, and while that was brewing, retrieve the Sunday morning newspaper from the front porch steps, placing it neatly at Buster's customary place setting at the breakfast table.

Standing on her tiptoes, the petite grandmother yawned heavily as she wrangled an unopened box of breakfast cereal from the top cupboard shelf. Sally opened the box and placed it on the kitchen table next to the sugar bowl. She then plugged in the toaster and set out a loaf of white bread and some butter, alongside a jar of creamy peanut butter, as well as her homemade strawberry and raspberry preserves.

After dividing up the breakfast dishes, Sally rechecked her kitchen setup, making sure that everything was in order and all of her family's individual preferences were represented. When her husband caught a whiff of the freshly brewed coffee wafting into their bedroom, he quietly crept out of bed, so as not to awaken the slumbering children upstairs. Buster then joined his beloved wife in the kitchen.

"Mmm, something smells awfully good, Sweetheart,"

Buster acknowledged, with a groggy voice. He leaned in and kissed his wife's cool cheek as he brushed past the stove. Sally poured him a fresh cup of black coffee, and then she joined her husband at the table for a rejuvenating cup of hot coffee with cream, alongside two slices of lightly buttered toast.

Buster had already begun to peruse the *Lumberton Daily News*, at which point Sally decided to call down Katie and the Munson gang from their upstairs bedrooms. Convinced that they were all capable of helping themselves to breakfast that morning, Sally returned to her bedroom and proceeded to dress in her Sunday best.

Searching her bedroom closet for an ensemble befitting the summer-like, humid September morning, Sally decided to wear her favorite white cotton dress, speckled with violet flowers, and embroidered lace on the neckline, sleeves and hemline. It was light and airy, which precisely matched her mood that morning.

Sally then plucked the fluffy pink powder puff (which her daughter, Roberta, had given her last Christmas) from its plastic casing and dipped it in the lavender-scented, talcum body powder. After lightly dusting her upper torso, she slipped her Sunday dress over her knee-length, twice-mended, yellowing silk slip and worn nylon stockings.

Brushing through her tangled locks of wavy, slightly-graying brown hair, Sally was disappointingly reminded that her neglected mane was overdue for a good hair-washing. Unfortunately, she had felt that the children's baths were of higher priority last evening, so Sally decided that her shampoo would simply have to wait.

Sally then opened her top dresser drawer filled with hair trinkets and picked up a small gift box from amid the clutter of multicolored hair pins, combs, ribbons, and other hair accessories she had collected throughout the years.

She gingerly opened the dingy white gift box, still decorated with a faded light yellow ribbon. Inside the treasured box, lying on a bed of soft white cotton, were two brilliantly preserved, pristine, yellow gold hair combs. Running her dainty fingertips across the delicate craftsmanship along the edges of those lovely combs, Sally became momentarily lost in the reminiscence of their meaning.

"I can't believe almost forty years have passed since Buster gave me these combs for my twentieth birthday," she murmured, with a heavy, disbelieving sigh. Mrs. Wiederman then gazed up at her reflection in the mirror. "Where have all those years gone?" she pondered, while secretly mourning the rapidly progressing loss of her youth.

The bedroom was brightly illuminated by the clear, early morning light that was now grudgingly shining through Sally's homemade white lace curtains. She glanced over at the youthful wedding photo of her and Buster on top of the dresser. Reluctantly, she leaned forward, in order to take a closer look at her face in the vanity mirror.

Realizing that she was about to celebrate another birthday soon, Sally examined the crow's feet that accentuated her aging blue eyes, resenting how those tiny creases crept in without warning when she wasn't looking. She then probed the speckled pattern of age spots that continued to expand on the surface of her wrinkled and weathered gardener's hands.

Feeling somewhat bitter and disgusted, Sally Wiederman paused for a brief moment. Then she stood up straight and took a deep, cleansing breath. While slowly exhaling, she decided to let go of her indignation and just accept the fact that she was 58 years of age (almost 59) and embrace the wisdom that coincided with her years.

Following that brief brush with self-pity, Sally proceeded to style her unkempt hair using the beautiful golden combs, piling it up neatly beneath one of her elegant church hats. With each sweep of those treasured hair pieces, Sally was reminded of the thoughtfulness and generosity demonstrated by her very young and handsome beau just before they were married, back in November of 1931.

Before long, the disappointment she had so harshly entertained with regard to her aging reflection and fading youth was overshadowed by the everlasting memory of the young love she and Buster had once shared, complemented by the mature kind of love they now cherished.

It was almost 9:30 a.m. Sally was just about ready for church, so she laid out Buster's blue-gray suit for him, as her husband would be getting dressed shortly.

Judith Ivy was the first to finish her breakfast and excuse herself from the table. She trotted off toward the bathroom, but made a pit stop along the way. The toddler had an important question for her grandmother, so she knocked on the closed bedroom door.

"Come on in," Sally called out. "I'm done getting dressed."

"Grandma, will you help me get ready for church today?" the five-year-old beseeched, in her typically pleasant and cheerful morning demeanor. Sally was instantaneously charmed by the tiny tot's large fawn-like brown eyes looking up at her so affectionately.

"Of course I will, dear," Sally answered, as she knelt down in front of the little lass. "But it will cost you a great big bear hug first," she whispered. Judith Ivy instantly leaped into her arms.

At that moment, as she hugged her loving grand-daughter tightly, breathing in the fresh scent of baby shampoo that lingered on her clean, soft, light brown hair, it suddenly became very clear to Sally Wiederman that her life was unfolding as it should… and she wouldn't change a thing!

The Huntington Presbyterian Church was a modest and very close-knit congregation. Mrs. Wiederman periodically played the organ for their small assembly, substituting for the regular organist whenever she was unable to fulfill her duties, which happened to be the case for that particular Sunday morning.

Sally was delighted when her grandchildren could accompany her and Buster to church. She enjoyed sharing them with friends and neighbors, and the reverend was always happy to see their refreshing young faces looking back at him from the pulpit.

Once the church pews were filled and everybody was seated, Sally began to play a newly mastered hymn that had always been very dear to her heart. With the reverend's prompting, the congregation stood up, with their hymnals in hand, and then Sally began to play the endearing tune, "In the Garden."

Katie and the children joined in the chorus, singing, "And He walks with me, and He talks with me, and He tells me I am His own; and the joy we share as we tarry there, none other has ever known."

Whenever the Munsons attended Sunday morning service in Huntington, they were so well received that they would end up spending at least another half-hour or so afterwards just socializing and catching up with the townspeople. Katie always enjoyed returning to her hometown church, as she felt very comfortable there. No matter how many weeks or months (or longer) had transpired between visits, she was always greeted warmly and made to feel welcome and accepted.

The next day, the extended Wiederman clan trickled in for the annual Labor Day picnic. The weather couldn't have been more accommodating. While Katie's children were busy frolicking with their cousins of similar ages, the adults and older kids selected two teams and engaged in a friendly game of softball.

Grandma Sally tried to play hard, like her children and grandchildren, but the best she could do was bunt the ball and hope to get on first base before the pitcher could get her "out." Oftentimes, the pitcher (usually one of Roberta's sons) would feign incompetence just to let his grandmother get safely on base, which brought the entire family to their feet, cheering Sally on. It was a glorious day of family and fun!

The Munsons had such a good time that Keith didn't want to go home. Katie had to really fight with her son that night in order to get him into the car and leave his grandparents' house. Keith whined all the way to Stone Valley, while making it abundantly clear that he dreaded the thought of starting first grade in the morning.

"I wanna be with Grandpa," he incessantly cried. "I wanna be with Grandpa!"

Keith eventually started huffing and sputtering, coughing in between bellows throughout his infantile tantrum. Katie couldn't help but worry about the next time they visited her folks for an entire weekend and how difficult it would be on her son when it came time to leave again.

It had been more than 2-1/2 years since Katie's ex-husband had barged into their home during that terrible blizzard, intruding upon Keith's fourth birthday party with his menacing ways, ultimately terrorizing and beating his defenseless mother with a frying pan. But, as quickly as Darren Munson had stormed back into their lives on that harrowing Saturday afternoon, so had he also departed, for the children's father had all but been forgotten with the passage of time.

Katie and her folks had been apprised some time ago that Darren Munson had remarried and started a new family with another woman from a neighboring county, much to Katie's relief. "Good riddance!" was the universal consensus among the Wiederman clan, for they were all happy to learn that Katie's violent ex-husband had moved on with his life and was finally leaving their Katie alone.

For those fleeting moments when Darren did cross his son's mind, however, and Keith actually did inquire about his father, Katie provided the unpleasant, bitter truth about his father with one simple statement: "Your daddy is married to someone else and has a new family now."

Since Darren's incarceration and subsequent withdrawal from their lives, Katie realized that her own father had been fulfilling dual roles in her son's life—that of his grandfather as well as his father—for Buster was the only male role model for Keith.

Katie was ecstatic that the two had become so

closely bonded, yet it was becoming more and more difficult for her to tear Keith away from his grandpa when it came time to go home.

Sadly, and most annoyingly, Keith's relentless ranting continued. The 15-minute trek from Huntington to Stone Valley that night seemed like an hour-long commute to Katie, who kept checking the time on the dashboard clock, trying her hardest to ignore her son's childish behavior and concentrate on her driving.

In an effort to drown out Keith's ear-splitting outbursts, Katie turned on the radio, cranking up the volume loudly, in the hopes that she might spark a sing-a-long with her daughters and help take the boy's mind off of his troubles.

"Come on, girls, sing along with me," their mother urged, and then Katie started belting out the chorus to the new hit song, "All Right Now," by the band called Free. Unfortunately, her feeble attempt at soothing her inconsolable son had been in vain.

"I don't wanna go to school tomorrow!" Keith wailed in his mother's ear, standing up behind her in the back seat of the 1958 royal-blue Chevy Impala, Katie's "blue bomber."

Keith's mother had become fed up with his whining. "I know that, Keith!" she snapped, having lost her patience. "But you <u>have</u> to go to school tomorrow, and there's nothing you can do about it, so just sit down and be quiet!"

The following morning, Katie got herself prepared

for her secretarial job at the Lumberton Community College while, at the same time, getting her three girls ready to go to daycare at Linda Reed's house across the street. Katie had entrusted Keith with dressing himself for school that morning, and she was surprisingly pleased with the end result.

Before leaving for work, Katie pulled her two eldest children aside, to explain their itinerary for the day. She had a brief talk with Judith Ivy, reminding her that she was to leave her daycare mother's house ten minutes before noon, right after lunch, and then walk to school (just down the street, on the far side of the cemetery) for her very first day of kindergarten class.

"Now, listen to me, kids," Katie instructed. "When the bell rings at the end of the school day, I want you, Keith, to make sure to go and get your sister from her kindergarten classroom and walk her home from school." The first-grader nodded his head in affirmation. "Keith, do you have the house key that I gave you in your front pocket?" she quizzed.

"Yeah, Mom...right here," Keith answered, showing his mother the house key, but only after plucking two pea-sized lint balls from the front pockets of his brown trousers and placing them on top of Judith Ivy's head.

"Now, that wasn't very nice, Keith," his mother scolded. She grasped her son's arms with both hands, looked him square in the eyes, and issued her mandate: "This is Judith Ivy's first day of school, so I want you to be nice to your sister and look after her, do you hear me?"

"Why do I have to walk her home?" Keith argued. "Nobody ever walked me home from school when I was in kindergarten."

"Because I said so, that's why!" Katie retaliated. "Now, listen up!" she continued. "When you kids get home from school, I want you to lock the door behind yourselves and stay inside the house until I get home from work, around 5:30…and nobody is allowed to go outside until after I get home, understood?"

"Oh, man," Keith moaned, with discontent. "Do we really have to stay in the house, even if it's nice outside?"

"Yes, you do!" his mother reiterated. "And I'll be calling from work, after you get home from school, to make sure that both of you are home, safe and sound, and that you're taking good care of each other," Katie warned the seditious six-year-old.

For the past year and a half (since Katie secured her lucrative secretarial job at the Lumberton Community College), Mrs. Munson had spent a significant amount of her paychecks on daycare expenses, so she was very relieved that Keith was now attending school full time.

Since Keith would be turning seven in just a few short months, Katie felt confident that he was mature enough to watch himself, as well as Judith Ivy, for a few hours each day after school. Besides, Linda

Reed was right across the street, caring for Darcy and Samantha, so if the school children had any type of emergency or problem, their daycare mother would be more than happy to oblige.

The next few months went fairly smoothly. Keith had proven to be a very responsible young man in taking care of himself and his little sister after school on weekday afternoons. Although he and Judith Ivy continued to bicker and quarrel, like most kids, the time they spent alone together each day actually brought them closer.

Sometimes, Keith and Judith Ivy would rally together and pick up the clutter around the house, to surprise their mother and help ease her burdens. Katie was truly thankful for those transient episodes. Most often, however, the diminutive duo passed the idle hours by watching television, which kept them occupied and entertained until their mother got home from work.

When December came, the wicked winter season hit southeastern Minnesota hard. In light of the blizzard-like conditions and heavy amounts of snowfall predicted through the holidays, it had been advised (by the evening news team the night before Christmas) that all travel on Christmas Eve and Christmas Day be postponed, unless absolutely necessary.

The Munson family had always spent Christmas Eve back home in Huntington with Katie's parents and the entire Wiederman clan. Knowing how terribly disappointed the children would be, having to miss seeing their grandparents and cousins at Christmastime, Katie decided to wait until tomorrow to break the disheartening news, thus avoiding the inevitable riot tonight.

When she awoke the next morning, on Christmas Eve, Katie peeked out her bedroom window. "Darn!" she cussed. There was nothing to see outside but a white winter haze, as the light falling snow was being whirled about by cyclonic, howling winds. "The weatherman was right after all," she shuddered at the ghastly sight. Katie shivered as she closed her bedroom curtains, and then she headed into the kitchen to make a fresh percolator full of hot coffee.

Katie was at the kitchen stove stirring a large pot of warm oatmeal when the kids darted downstairs for breakfast. Almost instantly, the children could tell that something was amiss, as their mother was not her usual chipper self on such a special morning as Christmas Eve.

After turning the burner way down low, Katie gathered her excited, albeit curious, brood around the kitchen table. "I'm awfully sorry, kids," she started to explain. "It looks like we won't be able to drive to Huntington tonight for Christmas Eve," Katie lamented. "The weather has taken a turn, and it's supposed to be really, really bad…and they don't want anybody traveling on the county roads, except in the case of an emergency."

"What?" The children asked in unison, astounded by the dreadful news. Almost instantly, the tears began to fall. Once little Darcy had begun to sob, her sisters followed suit. Before long, profound sorrow had overcome the Munson children just as quickly as the measles had stricken them in the summer of 1969.

Keith, most especially, was utterly devastated by the horrible announcement. He had his heart set on being with Grandma and Grandpa for Christmas. The now seven-year-old lad had never missed a Christmas Eve with his grandparents, aunts, uncles and cousins for as long as he could remember…and he didn't intend to miss Christmas this year either.

"No way!" Katie's son disputed. "I'm still going to Grandpa's house, whether you go or not!" he informed his mother. Keith quickly stomped out of the room, in an effort to conceal the tears that were building in his sad blue eyes from his heavy, mournful heart.

"You mean, we have to stay home on…on Christmas Eve?" Judith Ivy questioned, obviously siding with her brother on this particular issue. "But that's not fair!" she wailed, wiping her runny nose on the sleeve of her blue flannel pajama top.

"I'm sorry, kids, but there's nothing we can do about it," Katie assured the bewildered bunch. "Hey, now…don't be sad. We can have our very own Christmas Eve right here at home, just the five of us…and it can be just as wonderful, you'll see," their mother promised, even though her bright blue eyes had suddenly turned red and misty as well.

At that moment, Katie felt a tiny tug on her pajama bottoms. Her youngest daughter, Samantha, beckoned, with tears overflowing from her innocent, big blue eyes. The very concerned three-year-old looked up at her mother and implored, "But how will Santa Claus find us if the weather is bad?"

Katie knelt down beside her troubled daughter and comforted her as best she could. "Don't worry, Honey," she said, reassuringly. "Rudolph has that big, bright red nose to guide Santa's sleigh through the wind and snow. He'll be able to find us."

"Oh yeah," Samantha recalled. "I almost forgot about that," she suddenly perked up. "Boy, Santa Claus sure is lucky to have Rudolph for a pet," the tiny tot remarked. "Hey, Mommy…when we leave cookies out for Santa tonight, can we leave a treat for Rudolph too?" Samantha suggested. "'Cause…without Rudolph, there wouldn't be any Christmas this year!"

"That's a wonderful idea, Sweetheart," her mother acclaimed. "I know…we'll pop a giant bowl of popcorn tonight, and then put some aside, just for Rudolph. How does that sound?" Katie proposed, in hopes of appeasing her thoughtful baby girl.

"Okay, Mommy," her three-year-old daughter consented, adding, "We just gotta make sure Keith doesn't eat it all!"

When Katie called her parents to inform them that they wouldn't be able to make it to Huntington that night, she was rather relieved to learn that her parents had already decided to cancel the 1970 Wiederman Christmas Eve celebration altogether, on account of the inclement weather and the dismal forecast for the remainder of the holiday weekend. "I was just about to call you and the rest of the kids," Sally reported.

Despite the devastating news that there would be no Christmas Eve at Grandma's house this year, Katie's girls wasted no time in getting on with their weekend fun. Therefore, while their mother was hiding out in her bedroom, wrapping the children's Christmas presents (which they usually opened on Christmas Day morning), her daughters were happily entertaining themselves in the living room, playing their mom's new Beatles album on the record player.

Mrs. Munson was amazed, albeit joyful, to hear her three little girls singing and dancing around the living room. Katie even caught herself singing along to one of her favorites while she wrapped the children's gifts, chanting, "She loves you, yeah, yeah, yeah…"

Although she hadn't heard a peep from her son in quite some time, Katie presumed that he had locked himself in his bedroom and was brooding like a baby. Unlike his sisters, Keith Munson wasn't nearly as forgiving, and he was miserably unhappy about the Christmas situation.

Apparently, Keith had meant what he said about

going to his grandparents' house, with or without his mother and sisters, if only he could find a way. Later that afternoon, while his mother was preoccupied in her bedroom, and his sisters were carrying on in the living room, Keith quietly slipped on his winter coat, boots and mittens, and then he sneaked out the kitchen door, completely undetected, under the cloud of loud music.

He quickly plucked his bicycle from the pile of tricycles, dump trucks and outdoor toys cluttering the front porch…and then he was gone!

Keith Munson was determined to get to Huntington before dark, so he knew he had to hustle. He hopped on the banana seat of his orange Schwinn and pedaled his bicycle as hard as he could, however, the frigid temperatures made it difficult for the boy to breathe, especially when he over-exerted himself.

About a half-hour into his 15-mile trek, the heavier snow began to fall, as predicted. At first, Keith was able to trudge through it, but then the flakes became thicker, after which they really started to accumulate. Eventually, the roads became too slippery for the tires to grip the asphalt. At that point, Keith realized that he was going to have to ditch the bicycle and finish his Christmas Eve journey on foot.

Meanwhile, back home in Stone Valley, once all the presents had been wrapped, Katie carried them into the living room and placed them beneath the boughs of the modest artificial Christmas tree, which the Munsons had adorned with tinsel and strings of popcorn, topped with homemade ornaments crafted from construction paper and Popsicle sticks, in addition to hand-painted holiday wooden cutouts.

Consumed with excitement, the girls gathered around the foot of the tree to get a glimpse of their brightly wrapped gifts, which would give them all something fanciful to dream about tonight. Katie's children weren't allowed to touch any of the packages until it came time to open them on Christmas morning, and so they obediently kept their hands to themselves.

"Which one's mine?" questioned four-year-old Darcy. "That one right there," Katie replied, pointing to the gift box on the left, wrapped in shiny red paper covered with pictures of white snowmen wearing blue scarves.

"There's mine!" Judith Ivy proclaimed, now that the kindergartener was able to read her name on the package. "And it's a big one too," she gushed.

"Can you guess which one is yours, Samantha?" Katie asked her three-year-old. "That one?" the toddler presumed, pointing to the smallest package under the tree. "Nope," her mother countered. "It's that one over there," she noted, referring to the largest package beneath the tree. "Wow!" Samantha exclaimed, her big blue eyes growing larger than Katie had ever seen. "Mine's the biggest one of all!"

"Yes, it is, Sweetheart," Katie assured the happy

little lass, with a hug and kiss. She then glanced around the living room and asked, "Where's your brother?"

"I don't know," Judith Ivy responded, with a shrug of her shoulders. "He's probably up in his room pouting like a big-old baby."

Mrs. Munson stood at the foot of the stairs and hollered up to her son. "Hey, Keith, come on down here! I just put the presents under the tree, so you can come and check out your Christmas present now." Strangely, there was no response.

When Keith didn't come downstairs after a few minutes, Katie asked Judith Ivy to run up to his room and see if she could coax him down…but when Judy got to his room, the door was wide open and her brother was nowhere in sight. His befuddled little sister bounded down the stairs and yelled, "Mom, Keith's not up here!"

"What? Are you sure?" Katie beseeched. "Yeah, his bedroom door is wide open," Judith Ivy reported. Keith had always kept his bedroom door closed when he was in his room, for he valued his privacy, especially with three nosey little sisters sharing the upstairs floor with him.

At that point, Katie began to worry. She glanced out the kitchen window and realized that the winter storm they had predicted earlier was fiercely upon them. Shortly thereafter, she noticed something else that hurled her mind into a frenzy. Keith's boots and winter coat were missing from the kitchen coat rack!

Katie quickly interrogated her daughters: "Did any of you girls see your brother leave the house today?"

"No, Mommy," all three sisters answered, while shaking their heads from side to side. "Well, did he say he was planning on going anywhere, or maybe he went over to a friend's house?" their mother panicked. Sadly, Katie received the same response. Her girls knew nothing of Keith's whereabouts.

Mrs. Munson then checked outside. She stood on the front porch, calling her son's name as loudly as she could, through the wind and the driving snow. A dead calm had fallen upon Stone Valley that blustery afternoon. The townspeople had evidently bunkered down in preparation for the cruel winter storm that awaited them, as there was not a single soul in sight.

The only sound that Katie could hear was the echo of her own voice calling out to her missing son. Still, there was no reply from seven-year-old Keith. On her way back into the house, Katie noticed something out of the corner of her eye. There was an odd disarray in the far corner of the porch, where the kids' outdoor toys had been stacked for the winter. Upon further investigation, Katie soon discovered that Keith's bicycle was gone as well.

She immediately got on the telephone and started calling their neighbors, as well as Keith's friends, apologizing in advance to everyone along the way for interrupting their holiday. Ultimately, Katie was disheartened to learn that nobody had seen nor heard from Keith in days, actually, since the last day of school before the winter break.

"Where could he be?" Mrs. Munson bewailed... and then she gasped, when a startling chill passed through her body. Katie felt the tiny hairs on the nape of her neck stand at attention, as she suddenly remembered Keith's last words replaying in her mind: "No way! I'm still going to Grandpa's house, whether you go or not!"

"Oh, my God!" Katie shrieked. "Could he possibly have taken off on his bike to his grandparents' house?" she pondered, horrified. If that were the case, Keith could be miles away by now, she feared. He could be lost in the blizzard or, heaven forbid, freezing to death!

Katie shuddered with agonizing fright. She decided to turn to her father for help. Buster would know what to do. Katie picked up the receiver and, with trembling hands, dialed her parents. "Come on, Dad, pick up...hurry up," she grumbled, pacing back and forth anxiously as she watched the snow piling up outside through the kitchen window.

After the fifth ring, Buster finally answered the phone. "Dad?" Katie gurgled. Her voice was barely audible, as a lump had formed in the back of her throat. Mr. Wiederman instantly recognized the panic in his youngest daughter's voice, however, as he had heard it many times before. "What's the matter, Katie?" he responded.

"It's Keith," Katie whimpered. "He got very upset when I told him that we can't come to your house tonight…and now he's gone, and we can't find him anywhere! I've already called all the neighbors and his friends," she wailed, "but no one has seen or heard from him today!"

"Dear Lord!" Buster reacted, bellowing, "Where on Earth could he have gone?"

At that point, Katie could hold back the tears no longer. Through labored breaths, she admitted, "I think he snuck out of the house while I was wrapping the kids' Christmas presents…and then I noticed his bike was missing from the front porch," she sniveled, "so he's probably on his way to your place."

"How long has he been gone?" Buster roared. "I don't know," Katie sobbed. "Maybe an hour or so… maybe even longer," she supposed.

Buster and Sally were absolutely mortified by the news. The thought of their seven-year-old grandson wandering around in that blinding blizzard utterly terrified them…and it would be dark soon. It was critical that they take immediate action.

"Listen, Katie," Buster instructed his distraught daughter, "I'm gonna jump in my Scout and start driving. I'll backtrack toward Stone Valley and look for Oscar. If I don't find him soon, we'll have to notify the sheriff so he can call out a search party. Just sit tight for now," he ordered, "and wait until you hear from me, whether I show up at your place, or I call you on the phone...so keep your telephone line open!"

"Okay, Dad...and thanks," Katie whimpered, in between sobs. "Please find my baby boy, Dad... please!" she pleaded. "And you be careful too!"

By the time Katie summoned her father, Keith had ridden his bike for several miles. He had already pedaled his way through the small town of Ashton, which was about one-third of the distance from Stone Valley to Huntington.

Unfortunately, now that the determined young lad had cleared the hills of the Mississippi River Valley (where the small community of Stone Valley is nestled), Keith was no longer surrounded by the majestic glacier-carved bluffs, which furnished some shelter from the piercing winds. Finding himself at the top of the ridge, the little boy was now at the mercy of the tempest, unable to see more than two feet in front of his face through the virtual whiteout.

The gales governing those ridge tops proved to be the fiercest of all of Keith's adversaries, past or present, producing gusts that fashioned small cyclones of snow all around the young boy. Keith was beginning to regret his decision, as it was becoming increasingly difficult to see the road and virtually impossible to steer the small Schwinn bicycle.

He had no choice but to relinquish his bike to the elements and abandon his most valued possession along the shoulder of the highway. Although Keith was very fond of that bicycle, he loved his grandparents far more, and he wanted more than anything to be with Grandpa Buster and Grandma Sally at Christmastime.

Since Keith had already come this far, he was determined to complete his journey. There was no turning back now. Therefore, the seven-year-old set out on foot, trudging through the snow as he continued to hike south along the highway that would lead him to Huntington, Minnesota.

His feet were getting awfully cold, and with the snow blowing in his face and eyes, it was incredibly challenging for Keith to see where he was going. He knew the general direction to Huntington, as he had made the trip so many times before in his mom's car, but he was losing his bearings in the intensifying blizzard.

At that point, Keith was feeling very disappointed in himself, for in his haste to leave the house, the lad had forgotten to grab his compass from his top dresser drawer. Keith always took his compass along when he went on scavenger hunts in the woods and/or scouting for new territories to explore.

"What a dope," Keith chastised himself, as he forged his way through the tormenting winds and driving snow. His eyes watered continuously, and his cheeks were so unbelievably cold that he couldn't even feel the tears rolling down his face, which instantly frosted over and turned into salty icicles.

The bewildered seven-year-old was growing tired,

weak and hungry. Keith's stomach was growling like he had never experienced in his entire life. It suddenly occurred to the youngster that he hadn't planned this trip very well at all...and now it was starting to get dark. "Oh, no," he whimpered. "I'm really in trouble now," he conceded, feeling defeated by the elements.

As the panic set in, Keith decided to take a break. He sat down at the edge of the road, which was no longer detectable through the blowing snow. The trail he had left behind was already buried, mere seconds after he had blazed it.

Looking around in every direction, shaking in despair, Keith could no longer determine his location. Succumbing to his anguish, there was only one thing left to do. The lost little boy resolved to sit down and pray. After all, it was Christmas Eve, a time for miracles.

"Dear God," he prayed, his hands shaking violently. "It's me, Keith Munson. I'm sorry for sneaking out of the house. I know it was a bad thing to do, but I just wanted to be with my grandpa for Christmas. You see, God...I don't have a daddy anymore," he began to sob. "All I have at home is girls, my mom and three little sisters...and sometimes I just wanna be with my grandpa. So, can you...can you please help me find him?" Keith begged, through his chattering teeth. "Thank you, God."

Sitting along the side of the road, bent over, hugging his knees, Keith lay his tired, weary head on his lap as he wept, which caused him to become overwhelmingly sleepy.

The downtrodden lad would have given almost anything to crawl into his warm bed at that particular moment and take a nice long nap. Sadly, his unrelenting shivering was a painful reminder that he was lost outside somewhere in the freezing cold, all alone, and now it was getting dark...and he couldn't even see where he was going!

Keith had never felt so lonely and desperate. Surrendering to his feelings of dread, hopelessness and regret, he started to bawl, setting his emotions free, like he had never done before in all his seven years. That was one day Keith Munson knew that he would not soon forget.

During that profoundly bleak moment, as he wiped the icy tears from his strained eyes with his snow-covered mittens, Keith thought he detected a flicker of light coming from up ahead in the distance. He peered up and, through horribly blurred vision, saw what appeared to be the glow from a pair of headlights beaming towards him.

At last, a glimmer of hope had warmed its way through Keith's frigid and vanquished soul. He picked himself up off the ground, dusted the white powder from his hood, coat sleeves and pants, and then he forged ahead toward the illumination, in the hopes of flagging down the driver of the automobile for assistance.

As he neared the only vehicle he had encountered during his treacherous odyssey, Keith's pulse quickened with anticipation...and then his heart overflowed with inspiration and awe, for he suddenly realized that God had, indeed, heard his prayer by the side of the road, and He had granted his request.

The driver slowly rolled down the side window. Keith immediately recognized the man behind the wheel. It was his beloved grandfather. "Oscar!" Buster shouted to his grandson. "What in God's name are you doing out here?"

When the green and white 1963 International Harvester Scout slowed to a complete stop, Keith ran around to the passenger side and immediately jumped inside. "I was coming to your house," the nearly frozen lad replied.

"What were you thinking?" Buster bellowed. "Do you know how upset your mother is? Why, she's worried half to death!" his grandfather scolded. "You know you're not supposed to leave the house without your mother's permission!"

"I know," Keith conceded, while trying to warm his frozen fingers by the heating element in the cab of the Scout. "I was mad that we couldn't drive to your house for Christmas Eve, so I...I decided to come by myself," he explained, his teeth still chattering. "I started out on my bike, but when it got too slippery, I had to leave my bike in the ditch."

"Well, I'm just glad I found you," his grandpa

sighed, through misty eyes. He hugged his grandson tightly and just held him in his arms. "It's all right now, son," Buster assured the shivering lad as he rocked him in his arms. "You're all right now."

A few minutes later, once his grandson had stopped shivering, and his frozen cheeks had begun to burn (a sure sign that Keith was thawing out), Buster stated, "Let's see if we can't find your bicycle on the way home and get you back to your mother."

Luckily, they were able to retrieve Keith's orange Schwinn before it had been completely obscured by white powder. Buster opened the tailgate of the Scout and tucked the bicycle safely inside. By the time he had returned to the driver seat, however, his grandson had an alternative plan in mind. "Take me to your house, Grandpa," Keith pleaded. "I don't wanna go back home!"

"No, Oscar," his grandfather objected. "I'm sorry, but I'm sure your mother wants you home with her and your sisters for Christmas."

"I don't care!" Keith refuted. "I wanna stay with you and Grandma! Please take me home to your house," he begged. "Mom will understand...really, she will," Keith assured.

"Oh, all right, Oscar," Buster surrendered, for he presumed the boy had been through enough that day. "If it means that much to you," he granted, "then we'll turn around and go home to Grandma."

"Oh, boy! Thanks, Grandpa!" the happy child

exclaimed. "And you can tell Mom that I promise to be good."

"As soon as we get home, I'll call your mother while your grandma gets you warmed up and into some dry clothes," Buster commented. "Are you hungry, Oscar?" he asked his knuckle-headed grandson.

"Hungry," Keith replied, "I'm starving! I'm so hungry, I could eat a cow...and I ain't kidding," the excited youngster clarified. "Hooves and all!"

"Well, we're having ham for supper, so you'll have to settle for pork," Buster chuckled, as the two men began to laugh and horse around as usual. "I'll make sure to have Grandma save the pig's snout just for you, Oscar," he teased.

Buster Wiederman was never more pleased or thankful to see his grandson laughing and smiling, after nearly freezing to death.

"Are we gonna go to church tonight, Grandpa?" Keith unexpectedly inquired. "Well, of course, Oscar," Buster answered. "We always go to church on Christmas Eve."

"Good," Keith responded, "'cause I wanna thank God tonight when I talk to him in church."

"Oh, yeah?" his grandfather remarked, wondering what had brought on Keith's sudden interest in church, as the boy had always disliked going to church.

"Yeah," Keith asserted. "When I got lost in the snow and couldn't find my way to your house, I prayed and asked God to help me find you...but instead,

God helped <u>you</u> find <u>me</u>," he explained. "Either way, I know He was watching over me. God saved my life today, so I just wanted to thank Him for that."

"Well, I think that's a mighty fine gesture, Oscar," his grandfather commended. "A mighty fine gesture… and I'm very proud of you, son."

Although Keith hadn't noticed, at that precise moment, a solitary tear fell from behind the black frames of his brawny grandfather's eyeglasses, for Buster had suddenly understood that he had some praise and thanks to give to the Good Lord that Christmas Eve as well.

When the two men arrived back home in Huntington, Grandma Sally instantly wrapped her warm, welcoming arms around her grandson, loving and reprimanding Keith at the same time. "Don't you <u>ever</u> do anything as senseless and disrespectful like that ever again, young man!" she snapped. "You had us all scared half to death!"

While Grandma Sally tended to the remorseful young lad, Grandpa Buster called Stone Valley and reassured his daughter that Keith was safe, warm, and in good hands. Katie was ecstatic to have received the joyous news, and after speaking with her son, was finally able to understand why it had meant so much to Keith that he spend Christmas with his grandparents.

Additionally, after much begging, pledging, and bargaining on Keith's part, his mother ultimately granted him permission to stay with his grandparents for the remainder of the elementary school's winter break. Keith, in turn, promised to never take off like that again.

As 1970 reached its end, Katie and her daughters spent New Year's Eve at home, watching Guy Lombardo and his big-band orchestra on television, eating popcorn while they all snuggled together on the couch beneath a thick quilt Grandma Sally had made for the Munson family years ago.

Although the four women had missed Keith's company that night, they looked forward to joining him the next day at Grandma and Grandpa's house.

Initially, when Katie and her three daughters, along with the rest of the extended Wiederman clan, gathered in Huntington for their annual New Year's Day celebration, they felt like they had missed out on Christmas that year, since they couldn't spend the holidays with their parents. But, as the day unfolded, they found themselves laughing, feasting on oyster stew, and singing Christmas carols alongside Grandma Sally, who accompanied them on the organ.

Katie glanced around the small living room jam-packed with siblings, nieces and nephews. Her girls were lively and happy, playing with their cousins and singing at the top of their lungs (whether they knew the words or not), and then she noticed Keith. Her son was glued to his grandfather's side, which is where he had wanted to be all along.

She quickly realized that they hadn't missed out

on Christmas that year, for it was all around them that day, in the sparkling eyes of the children and the rejoicing voices of the young and the young-at-heart.

On that very first day of 1971, Katie Munson's heart was warmed by the unshakable bonds of family, together with the purifying feeling that comes with the promise of a brand-new year ahead and the unlimited aspirations that coincide with the prospect of a new beginning.

## Chapter 3
# If Not for You

The new year brought with it many changes for Katie and the Munson family. The first resolution the 25-year-old divorcee decided to carry out in 1971 was to reestablish some form of a social life. Since her divorce from Darren three years ago, Katie had found herself becoming increasingly lonely.

Although she had plenty of companionship, thanks to her four children, parents and siblings, Katie longed for the special bonds and closeness she had once shared with her girlfriends (Betty Lou, Tiffany and Susie) from the vocational school. Sadly, the pact they had made to keep in touch after graduating in June of 1969 had fallen prey to life's inevitable modifications, even under the most honorable of intentions.

Last summer, Betty Lou had married a nice young fellow who whisked her away to Huntington Beach, California, where the couple decided to begin their new lives together beneath the endless sunshine of "The Golden State," and where they would be able to escape their nine-to-five office jobs in the city to surf the bountiful waves each weekend in "Surf City."

Shortly after graduation, Tiffany had taken her sec-retarial diploma to the metropolitan city of Cooper's

Dam, Minnesota, where she secured a very demanding position as secretary to a corporate executive in one of the downtown high-rise buildings in the elite business district. Tiffany rarely made it back to Lumberton anymore since starting her new life and cultivating a new harvest of friends. Katie had not heard from Tiffany in months.

The last of their tight-knit group from secretarial school, Susie (who still resided in Lumberton), fell in love with a seemingly charming young beau, who turned out to be anything but charming. He ultimately became very controlling of Susie's activities, dictating where she could go, the people she could associate with, which jobs she could accept, etc.

Katie knew all too well the direction in which her friend's relationship with that young man was headed, and so she made it very clear to Susie that her life was destined for disaster as long as she stayed with him. Unfortunately, Katie's friend didn't heed her discerning warning.

The following weekend, while in the midst of a drunken rampage, Susie's "charming" boyfriend beat her so badly that she was hospitalized for two days, after which Susie unhesitatingly decided to move far away from her abuser and start a new life with her grandparents in the state of Vermont. Katie never heard from Susie again.

Not only did Katie long for the female companionship and camaraderie of women her own age, she had often thought about the loneliness she felt with regard to the special kind of comfort that only a man can provide.

When she realized that it had been eight years since she had been on a first date (that being with her ex-husband, Darren, on New Year's Eve, 1962), Katie knew that she had to do something about her social life, or lack thereof.

At the same time, however, since Katie Munson was the first and only divorcee to reside in the small community of Stone Valley, her acceptance was rather ambiguous. Ever since she had moved to the tiny town three years earlier, many of the townspeople treated the single mother like an interloper, as if by infiltrating their tightly knit Catholic society, she might start some sort of "divorce epidemic" amongst the citizens of Stone Valley.

Consequently, Katie had not attended the Stone Valley Catholic Church for quite some time, given that the priest had informed her one Sunday morning after mass that she was no longer eligible to receive the sacrament of communion. Apparently, according to him, Mrs. Munson was deemed "unworthy" to accept the "Body of Christ," for she had committed the cardinal sin known as "divorce."

Katie found that proclamation appalling, as she had always believed that the church was for the sinners. "If we were all perfect," she argued with the clergyman, "then why would we need to go to church at all?"

Feeling that she had made a valid point, Katie remained true to her convictions. Therefore, following the priest's unforeseen chastisement, she didn't see much point in attending mass at all anymore. The parish's clerical staff, however, proceeded to mail the collection envelopes to Mrs. Munson's home address every week, without fail.

With the dawning of each new morning, Katie resumed her search for adult companionship. Then one day, on a frigid wintry afternoon, while enjoying her brown-bag lunch (consisting of a tuna salad sandwich, a red delicious apple, blueberry yogurt and a half-pint of skim milk), a glimmer of hope presented itself.

Katie peered up from her half-eaten sandwich and happened to notice a newspaper clipping tacked to the cork bulletin board in the employee lounge at the Lumberton Community College. The notice read: "Solo Parents Club--Join now to meet other single parents--Fun social events and family activities--Call the YMCA today!"

"Wow, that's just what I've been looking for!" Katie thought, and so she wasted no time at all. Since she had another ten minutes left of her lunch break, she quickly dialed the number listed in the ad and called the YMCA. Katie Munson was happy to learn that she would soon become a member of a social club.

"Once we receive your membership dues, Mrs. Munson," the pleasant female voice at the other end of the line instructed, "we'll send you an itinerary for upcoming events and a list of members...or you can simply stop by our office in person to pay the dues and pick up your new membership packet."

"Thank you very much," Katie replied. "I'll stop by tomorrow on my lunch break."

"Wonderful," the woman acknowledged. "We're always eager to recruit new members."

Katie gleefully joined the Lumberton chapter of the Solo Parents Club in January, with high hopes that some social interaction and fun for the kids might help them all trudge through the remaining cold winter months ahead.

The next social engagement of the Solo Parents Club was to be held the following Sunday at the local YMCA in Lumberton. The agenda advertised an open gymnasium and swimming pool for the children during the afternoon hours, followed by a potluck supper in the kitchen, with each member's contribution being that of a dish to pass.

"Hey, kids!" Katie hollered to the children in the living room on Saturday morning. Not surprisingly, since all eyes were glued to the television screen for this week's haunting episode of *Scooby Doo, Where Are You?*, their mother's page went unnoticed, as usual.

"Kids, I'm trying to talk to you," Katie reiterated, as she stuck her head inside the doorway of the living room. "Wait 'til the commercial, Mom!" Keith insisted, while he and his little sisters smacked and munched relentlessly on their red licorice whips and penny candy they had purchased earlier that morning at the Stone Valley grocery and candy store.

During the next commercial break, about halfway through their all-important cartoon program, Katie seized the opportunity to vie for her children's attention. "Guess what, kids!" she zestfully announced. "Tomorrow we're going to the YMCA, where you kids can play in the gym, and go swimming in the indoor heated swimming pool, and then we're gonna have a potluck supper there too."

"Really?" Judith Ivy reacted, astonished that they were going to have access to a swimming pool. None of the Munson children had ever swum in a real-live swimming pool, only those plastic wading pools they had in their yard or at Grandma and Grandpa's house.

"Yeah," Katie answered. "And there will be lots of other kids there for you to play with too." Oddly, she received no reply from the other children. "Well, what do you think?" Katie pressed the preoccupied youngsters, hoping that they might show some enthusiasm as well.

"Shhh!" the kids retorted, putting their index fingers to their lips and/or waving their mother away. "Quiet, Mom...'Scooby Doo' is back on," 3-1/2-year-old Samantha sassed.

"Well, excuuuuse me!" Katie mumbled, as she turned away. At that moment, she knew precisely where her place was—anywhere but the living room.

Katie retaliated to the kitchen and searched the cupboards for enough ingredients to throw together a side dish to make for tomorrow's potluck supper at the YMCA.

In the refrigerator she found a pound of fresh ground beef, and in the freezer Katie recovered half a bag of tater tots from underneath the frozen pizzas, along with a package of frozen mixed vegetables. "All right!" Katie uttered, relieved. "I can make a tater tot hot dish."

On Sunday afternoon, Katie met at least a dozen grownups with whom she could relate, as they all shared similar circumstances. The Solo Parents Club was comprised of divorced and/or widowed singles who were raising their children single-handedly, which they unanimously perceived to be the biggest and most difficult challenge of their lives.

Through the help and support of its members, this select group of intelligent and caring single parents had devised a way to offer their underprivileged children a sense of continuity and attachment in an otherwise disassociated existence.

One Sunday afternoon each month, the children of the Solo Parents Club members looked forward to the potluck get-togethers and a variety of playmates in any given age bracket, while the parents enjoyed some very gratifying adult conversation and respite from their monotonous daily routines.

At long last, Katie Munson had found her social

niche. She finally felt accepted by a group of her peers and was enjoying a sense of belonging that she had not experienced in a very long time.

Katie was so exited about joining the Solo Parents Club that she called her parents right away during her Monday morning coffee break, apprising them of the wonderful time the five of them had shared yesterday at the YMCA gathering.

Buster and Sally were extremely pleased that their daughter had found some new friends and that the children were getting some exposure to other kids who also suffered the lonesome misfortune of being raised without a father or a mother in their lives.

"I'm so happy for you, Katie!" her mother exclaimed. "It's been such a long time since I've heard you get excited about anything," Sally declared. "You deserve to be happy, Sweetheart...and so do the children!"

"Thanks, Mom," Katie returned. "This single parents group is just what I was looking for, I mean...I get to engage in conversation with actual adults while the children play with the other kids in the gym," she expounded. "It's so great, Mom, it's...it's like having the perfect babysitter for all of us!"

"That's wonderful, Katie," Sally replied. "Not to change the subject, but are you bringing Keith over to stay this coming weekend?"

"Oh, yeah, that's right," Katie recollected. Ever since Keith's little "expedition" on Christmas Eve (when he had snuck away on his bicycle to be with his Grandpa), Katie and Keith had made a deal that Keith could alternate weekends between his house in Stone Valley and his grandparents' home in Huntington.

"Uh, yeah, Mom. I'll be coming over sometime Friday night after work to drop Keith off for the weekend," Katie confirmed. "I sure hope it warms up by then," she related. "It was twenty below zero this morning, and I had the hardest time getting my car started."

Although Keith had a wonderful time at the Solo Parents function, nothing compared with the satisfaction he derived when he was with his grandfather. The seven-year-old was already looking forward to spring, which meant fishing and gopher trapping with Grandpa Buster.

As the days grew warmer, and winter blended with springtime, Buster Wiederman made the life-altering decision to retire from the truck hauling business. In view of his upcoming sixtieth birthday in July, he started selling his inventory of dump trucks and supplies, having chosen to live his golden years as a man of leisure, spending quality time with his family and helping his wife with the planting, gardening and harvesting of their homegrown produce.

The Wiedermans had long since sold their livestock and farm animals, once all their children had grown and moved out of the house. Managing the hobby farm, in addition to Buster's trucking business and Sally's numerous berry patches and vegetable gardens, without any extra helping hands left at home, had become increasingly burdensome on the aging couple.

Now that his newly retired grandfather had liberated his days from the constraints of working a full-time job, Keith had already begun to daydream about hanging out at the boathouse that summer and/or fishing for walleye and northern pike in the deeper waters of the Mighty Mississippi from Buster's flat-bottom fishing boat, just he and his grandpa.

When Katie picked up Keith the next Sunday evening, after his weekend stay with his grandparents, she had barely started the car when her son made a startling request. "Hey, Mom," he began, after clearing his throat, "now that Grandpa doesn't have to go to work anymore, I was wondering if I could spend the whole summer at their house."

"Oh, no…I don't think that's a very good idea, Keith," his mother declined. "Why not?" the lad whined. "Because I need you to help me around our place this summer," Katie countered. "Who do you think is gonna mow the lawn and take out the garbage…and shoo the bats out of the attic?"

"Oh, Mom," Keith bewailed. "The girls can do all that stuff."

"Oh, really?" Katie questioned. "Keith, your sisters have their own chores, doing the dishes and cleaning the house…and they're much too little to be running the lawnmower," she rebutted. "Besides, that's man's work."

"But, Mom," the seven-year-old pleaded. "No, Keith...I said no!" his mother retorted. "Now, give it a rest and let me drive!" she scolded. Katie then cranked up the volume on the radio, in an effort to drown out Keith's annoying whining.

As the late Janis Joplin belted out her posthumous hit ballad, "Me and Bobby Magee," through the air-waves, Katie rolled the windows halfway down. With her long blonde ponytail blowing in the wind, she drove off into the fresh spring night air in her blue 1958 Chevy Impala, singing and humming along with the peppy song.

While her former relationships with Darren Munson were a far cry from the love affair described in Joplin's ballad of Bobby Magee, Katie Munson still remained hopeful that she would one day find true love and enjoy a stable, nurturing relationship with a kind, gentle and decent man.

When the Stone Valley Elementary School closed its doors in June for the summer break, and Keith had successfully completed the first grade, he was off to spend his first week of summer vacation with his grandparents in Huntington.

As a result of her seven-year-old son's repeated requests to spend the summer in Huntington, Katie had made a compromise with her son, granting him permission to spend every other week in Huntington and every other week in Stone Valley. That way, Keith would still be able to tend to his chores at home while enjoying plenty of quality time with his grandpa over the summer vacation.

Every Sunday thereafter, when Katie and the girls drove to Huntington to either pick up Keith or drop him off, the clan enjoyed a family feast of Grandma Sally's choosing, and then they all gathered around the living room to watch Buster and Sally's new favorite hit television show, *All in the Family*.

Mr. Wiederman couldn't get enough of the Archie Bunker character, with his blatant bigotry and verbal assault upon the English language. Mrs. Wiederman, on the other hand, didn't much care for Archie's outspoken prejudice and condescending remarks, particularly when he referred to his wife as a "dingbat," or when he called his son-in-law "Meathead."

It was Edith Bunker's character who lured Sally to the living room on Sunday evenings, for Edith Bunker and Sally Wiederman shared several personality traits; and while Sally tried to conceal her contempt for Archie Bunker whenever he got on a rant, she knew that Edith would put him in his place when he really had it coming, which pleased Sally immensely.

While the Munson/Wiederman clan were laughing and enjoying the popular television program, their merriment was interrupted by a commercial they had never seen before, and so they paid close attention to the new advertisement.

The ad campaign revealed a middle-aged, Native-American gentleman paddling his canoe down a murky, industrialized river whose banks were littered with trash and Styrofoam cups. Moments later, a car drove past on the highway up above, spewing a bag of fast-food containers and garbage at his feet. The Indian then turned toward the camera, and a heavy tear rolled down his dispirited cheek.

Judith Ivy instantly felt sorry for the Native American. In fact, she was so moved by the image that she started to feel tears welling in her own eyes. "Grandpa, why is that nice Indian man crying?" his six-year-old granddaughter beseeched.

"Well, Snuffy," her Grandpa Buster started to explain, "I think it's because he's sad to see all the garbage polluting our beautiful land and rivers."

"But, why do people throw garbage in the roads and the rivers, when they could just put it in a trash can?" his soft-hearted granddaughter so innocently inquired.

"Unfortunately, Snuffy," he alerted the youngster, "some people simply just don't care." Buster could sense his granddaughter's woe, and so he picked up the six-year-old and placed her on his knee, cradling her in his rocking chair while he puffed away on his tobacco pipe. At that moment, Buster realized that his little "Snuffy" was a very sensitive young lass and that she had a caring nature and a gentle, kind heart.

"If it's something you feel that strongly about,

Judith, honey," Grandma Sally encouraged, "then why don't you do something about it?"

"I think I will, Grandma!" the passionate young lady exclaimed. Her big brown eyes grew even larger with excitement as she gave her grandmother's suggestion further thought. "Starting tomorrow," Judith Ivy reported, "I'm gonna start cleaning up all the garbage around our yard and out in the street…and in the park across the street too." The little girl was bound and determined to help that grieving Indian.

"Well, I think that's a wonderful idea," Katie remarked. "Maybe your brother and sisters can pitch in and help too," their mother hinted, in the hopes that her eldest daughter's zeal might ignite the interest of her siblings as well.

The next morning, while Keith was in Huntington for the week, and the girls would be spending their days at Linda Reed's house across the street for daycare, Judith Ivy Munson asked her daycare mom for a large garbage bag. "What do you need with a garbage bag?" Mrs. Reed curiously inquired.

"I'm gonna help the sad Indian man so he won't cry anymore," the six-year-old answered. "What Indian man?" Linda Reed queried. "The one on TV," Judy clarified. "We saw him last night when we were watching Archie Bunker."

James and Linda Reed had also caught last night's episode of *All in the Family*, as well as the "Keep America Beautiful" ad campaign. Thus, Mrs. Reed was able to interpret the juvenile ramblings of the pre-cocious six-year-old. "Oh...okay," Linda consented. "Just be back in time for lunch at noon."

Keeping true to her word, little Judy ventured outside that Monday morning with her big garbage bag and initiated her quest to clean up her surroundings. She started picking up trash around Jim and Linda's yard and the adjacent street.

After that, she cut across the street to the Stone Valley Park, where she noticed some refuse peeking out from underneath the merry-go-round and some trash hiding behind the slide. Judith Ivy continued to scrounge the entire playground area, plucking dozens of sharp pop tops from the ground along her path, safeguarding the area for her sisters and friends, who also ran barefooted all summer long.

To the little girl's surprise, it didn't take long at all to fill up that big garbage bag with litter, cigarette cartons and butts, as well as soda pop bottles, beer cans and Styrofoam cups. Therefore, Judy was back at the Reeds' place in plenty of time for lunch, with a half-hour to spare.

Having worked up a hearty appetite, Judith Ivy consumed her grilled cheese sandwich and tomato soup lunch in record time. As she slurped the last remnants of soup from her bowl, it suddenly occurred to the do-gooder that there was still a lot more work to be done (more than she could handle on her own), so Judy decided to bring in reinforcements.

The following weekend, as soon as she and her two little sisters had returned home from their Saturday morning trip to the candy store (where they each traded their weekly allowance of 10 cents for a bag of penny candy and bubble gum), Judith Ivy called Laverne Crawford on the telephone.

"Wanna go for a long bike ride with me and pick up trash along the way?" Judy beseeched. "We could pack lunches and everything!"

Laverne immediately agreed to assist her little buddy in her quest. "That sounds like fun," she concurred. "My mom said it's gonna get really hot today, so we should bring a bottle of pop too," Laverne suggested.

"That's a good idea," Judy returned, adding, "I'll bring a bottle of Dr. Pepper and a bottle opener."

"And we have some root beer at our house," Laverne offered, "so I'll bring one of those and then we can share."

"Hey," Judith Ivy proposed, "let's bike out to that place with the big weeping willow tree on the other end of town later, and then we'll eat our lunches under the willow tree and go wading in the creek."

"Yeah, that sounds cool!" Laverne blurted. "I'll meet you outside in five minutes," the eager six-year-old confirmed. "I gotta go to the bathroom before we leave."

It was a warm and sticky morning in July of 1971 when the determined duo set out on their bikes with their brown-bag lunches. Laverne had packed a peanut butter and grape jelly sandwich, while Judith Ivy had prepared a tuna salad sandwich with a slice of American cheese.

When they met outside, Judy securely stuffed their sack lunches into the basket on the handlebars of her blue Huffy bicycle (which her mother had bought at a garage sale two months earlier for her sixth birthday), along with their two bottles of soda pop and three plastic trash bags.

By the time the young girls had thoroughly combed Main Street, Washington, Broadway, and the entire downtown area, they had already filled the garbage bags they had brought with them, which they subsequently deposited in the dumpsters between the Stone Valley Saloon and the butcher shop.

The charitable children felt proud of the work they had already accomplished, yet they couldn't help but feel overwhelmed by the amount of debris that still remained along the roads leading in and out of their small town of 395 residents.

Feeling somewhat defeated in their pursuit, the girls decided to call it a day. They were exhausted, dirty and hungry, so they rode their bikes out to the big weeping willow tree on the outskirts of town, where they took a well-deserved break beneath its shaded boughs and enjoyed their packed lunches while reflecting upon their work.

"I guess Stone Valley is a lot bigger town than we thought it was," Laverne conceded. With a heavy sigh, she plopped herself down and sat cross-legged in the plush green grass.

"Yeah," Judith Ivy agreed, as she crouched down on her knees beside her best friend. "There's no way we can clean up this whole town all by ourselves," she reasoned. As she opened the two soda pop bottles with the metal device she had packed, Judy asserted, "It'll take us forever and a day!"

"We gotta get some more kids to help out," Laverne acknowledged, after taking a big bite out of her peanut butter and jelly sandwich. After masticating on that for a few seconds, she proposed, "Why don't we try this again, like maybe next spring, when it's not so hot…and we'll trick Darcy and Jeannie into helping us."

"Hey, yeah!" Judith Ivy remarked, handing Laverne her lukewarm bottle of root beer. Her big brown eyes then widened with clarity as she blurted, "They don't have anything else to do anyway…and we don't even have to trick 'em," she reminded her buddy. "They're always begging to tag along with us!"

"Oh, yeah, that's right!" Laverne recalled. "But, let's do it in the spring," she reiterated. "I'd rather go swimming or run through the sprinkler on hot days like this, wouldn't you?"

Following that first "garbage day," as it came to be known, as soon as the snow melted and the frigid winter temperatures were a part of the season past, the Munson girls, along with Laverne and Jeannie

Crawford, rallied together each spring on their bicycles and began their annual spring cleanup of Stone Valley, Minnesota.

While some of the townspeople were grateful for the more aesthetic landscaping on their way to church or work that week, they never really knew who to thank for the enriching transition.

Sadly, it was most unfortunate how many of the passersby from the small village, those who were all wrapped up in their daily toils and troubles, rushing to and fro without taking a moment to look around, didn't notice any difference whatsoever. Nevertheless, Mrs. Munson and Mrs. Crawford were extremely proud of their daughters for their good deeds and their hard work.

When the arrival of fall mandated the beginning of another academic school year, Keith Munson was none too happy about starting second grade. His mother anticipated that he would be difficult for a while, especially after spending half of his summer vacation with his grandparents, but Katie wasn't at all prepared for just how unhappy her son would become and how miserable he would make the rest of the Munson household.

During those first few months of school, with Judith Ivy starting first grade and Darcy starting kindergarten, Keith was faced with added responsibility, now that he had to walk his two sisters home from school each day and watch them afterwards until their mother got home from work at 5:30 p.m.

Keith grew increasingly gloomy, moping around the house, whining and complaining about being bored, having to be stuck with his sisters all the time, and expressing how he wished he could just go and live with his grandparents. "I hate it here!" he often spouted.

As a result of his persistent irritability and argumentative temperament, which was causing his sisters to become grumpy as well, while gnawing away at his mother's patience, Katie talked it over with her parents, at which time they decided to let Keith continue alternating weekends between Huntington and Stone Valley.

Katie's daughters, on the other hand, were hardly understanding of this arrangement. As the weeks went by, and Keith told story after story of all the good times he was having during his weekend visits with Grandma Sally and Grandpa Buster, his sisters became jealous, wondering why they couldn't stay with their grandparents as well.

"How come Keith gets to stay at Grandma and Grandpa's every other weekend and we don't?" Judith Ivy barked. "That's not fair, Mom!"

"Yeah!" Darcy interjected, smacking her lips as she ate her macaroni and tomatoes entrée at the dinner table. "Just because Keith's the oldest," the five-year-old ranted, "that doesn't mean he should get whatever he wants!"

"And if they get to stay at Grandma and Grandpa's

on weekends," Samantha chimed in, "then I wanna go too!"

"Oh, for cryin' out loud!" their mother snapped. "You kids are driving me bananas, you know that?" Katie looked around the table at all the grouchy faces and commanded, "Just be quiet and finish your supper…and nobody leaves this table until your plate is clean!"

Later that evening, after having had some time to think about her daughters' concerns, Katie realized that they were right. It wasn't fair to the girls that Keith was granted special privileges. Therefore, she brought up the subject with Keith while he was watching television.

Just as she had presumed, Keith was unreceptive to what his mother was telling him. "No way, Mom!" he refuted. "I don't want my sisters staying at Grandma and Grandpa's while I'm staying there…they'll just ruin everything!"

"Well, I've got to come up with some sort of a compromise," his mother countered. "It's really not fair to your sisters, you know, that they have to stay home every weekend and pick up the slack from your chores."

On that note, the displeased seven-year-old ran upstairs to his bedroom, slamming the door shut. Keith then locked himself inside, where he pouted for the remainder of the night, until he fell fast asleep.

The following Sunday, at the monthly potluck

gathering at the YMCA, Katie learned from one of the Solo Parents Club members that the YMCA had recently initiated a "Big Brothers Program," whereby young adult males (mostly college students) volunteered some time each month to spend with boys who were being reared without a father in their lives.

These compassionate and caring "Big Brothers" offered a variety of activities, such as softball and basketball, fishing and swimming, hiking, biking and horseback riding, or whatever interested the willing participants.

Katie felt certain that the Big Brothers Program could benefit her son, Keith, especially during the weekends he spent at home in Stone Valley. If Keith had a "Big Brother" to take him on special outings on Saturdays, doing the types of masculine activities that he cherished with his grandfather, they might all enjoy a more peaceful existence inside the Munson house.

As a member of the Solo Parents Club, Katie had been introduced to many other singles, and she began to delight in some of the more grownup activities that had eluded her for so many years. It felt a bit unnatural at first, but after four long years of solitude (since her divorce in the fall of 1967), Katie Munson had even begun dating again!

Although she kept her engagements discrete from her children, whether good or bad, Katie was thrilled to be socializing with members of the opposite sex. After all, she was a very attractive 26-year-old woman, and it didn't take long for the single men from the club to take notice of her pretty face, petite build, and vivacious personality.

Katie felt comfortable and at ease with these gentlemen because they already knew about her circumstances—that she was divorced, with four young children—so she had nothing to hide. Therefore, the single mother was free to enjoy herself, without having to worry about those relationship-killing questions surfacing later on, in the midst of an otherwise potentially promising date.

Furthermore, the young divorcee felt strongly that any other man (outside the realm of her singles group) would most assuredly run in the opposite direction upon learning that Katie was not only a 26-year-old divorcee, but that she had four young children under the age of eight!

As the weather turned colder that fall, and the bitter northwest winds began to howl, the atmosphere in the Munson household seemed to be warming up. Keith had a new Big Brother named Joe Bigelow, an eighteen-year-old freshman student at the Lumberton Community College, where Katie Munson was employed as a secretary in the Education Office.

Joe came by the house every other Saturday afternoon, never missing a single visit with his new "little brother." Keith raved about the good times he was having with his pal Joe, to his mother's delight. His little sisters were equally pleased because Keith was in much better spirits all around…and when he (the man of the house) was cranky, everybody was cranky!

Although Joe Bigelow was no match for Grandpa Buster, he was a sound second choice. For the first time in nearly eight years, Keith Munson truly felt like he had a big brother in his life—someone to hang out with, whom he would learn to respect and aspire to emulate.

When Keith's eighth birthday came around in December of 1971, Joe bestowed his "little brother" with a birthday present. "This is for you, little buddy," he affirmed. "Hope you like it."

"Oh, boy!" the excited eight-year-old lad exclaimed. Keith quickly tore open the wrapping paper, to reveal a sturdy rectangular box encasing a chess set.

"What a thoughtful gift," Katie told the young man, as she finished frosting her son's birthday cake. "I didn't know you knew how to play chess, Keith," she remarked.

"I don't…not really," her son replied. "But I've been wanting to learn how," the pleased birthday boy blurted. "I mean, I know the gist of it and all, but I wanna learn the strategies."

"Don't worry, Keith," Joe assured the birthday boy. "I'll teach you how to play," he promised, as he tousled the youth's shaggy blonde hair.

Mr. Bigelow then lowered his head for a moment and shared a very special memory with the Munsons.

"My dad taught me how to play chess when I was about your age, Keith," he divulged. "And I've been playing ever since."

"I bet your dad's a really good chess player," Keith presumed.

"Yeah, he sure was," the tall, lanky brunette returned. "Actually, he was a champion chess player," the big brother added. "He won trophies and everything."

"Cool!" Keith yelped. He couldn't help but wonder why a champion chess player would give up the game and relinquish his crown, so he curiously inquired, "Did he get tired of the game and just quit playing, or what?"

"No, he, uh…he died," Joe sniveled, as he wiped his nose using the sleeve of his navy blue turtleneck sweater. "It's just me and my mama now."

At that moment, Katie set her frosting spatula down on the kitchen table. She and her son suddenly realized that their guest was going through some hardships of his own. The room filled with a chilling silence as the Munsons awaited Joe's next words.

"My dad got killed last Christmas," Mr. Bigelow disclosed. Although Joe did his best to hide his tears from the lad he had been mentoring these past few months, his raging teenaged emotions had gotten the better of him.

"He was walking home from my grandma's house after helping her trim the tree," Joe narrated, "when a car came out of nowhere and crashed into my father...and then just took off!" At that point, he started to cry. "The police said it was probably someone who had been drinking and that's why they didn't stop," he divulged. "All I know is...while everyone else was gathered together on Christmas Eve, singing Christmas carols and opening presents, someone mowed my dad down in the street and just left him there to die, all alone."

The poor young man was obviously distraught. Katie Munson, along with her young son, had uncovered a new appreciation for the kind young man who had entered their lives just months before and who was now weeping in their kitchen, in desperate need of some consolation.

Although Katie didn't know much about consoling others, her instincts led her to walk toward the young man with her arms wide open. Joe Bigelow instinctively accepted Mrs. Munson's open invitation, and then the troubled teen wept openly in her arms.

Shortly thereafter, Keith walked up to his "big brother's" side and placed his hand on Joe's arm, lending his empathy and support as well, which brought comfort and relief to their newfound friend.

"How would you like to stay for supper?" Katie asked their grieving guest, in an effort to change the subject and elevate the overall mood. "We're just having spaghetti and meatballs with garlic toast, but there's plenty if you'd like to join us," she kindly offered.

Their forlorn friend quickly dried his weary eyes, and then he stood up tall and sighed heavily. "I'd...I'd love to stay," Joe stammered. "Thanks for the invitation, Mrs. Munson."

"Please, call me Katie," the hostess insisted, as she spread butter on a warm slice of toast. "You make me sound like an old lady," she added, which brought a welcome chuckle into the room. "Besides, I'm not Mrs. Munson anymore," Katie elucidated, as she sprinkled the buttered toast with garlic salt. "I'm... well, I guess you could say...I'm happily divorced."

During Keith's birthday supper, the Munsons learned that Joe's father had set up a college fund for his only son, before his untimely demise. It was through the Lumberton Community College that Joe had learned about the Big Brothers Program.

He proceeded to share with Katie and Keith how miserable he had been feeling since his father's death, and how he couldn't imagine not having a dad at all, and so that is why Joe decided to become a Big Brother—to help those poor, young, fatherless boys. Fortunately, for Keith Munson, he was to become Joe Bigelow's very first client.

That winter of 1971, on a bitterly cold December morning, a school bus parked outside the Stone Valley Elementary School while school was still in session. The children looked out the window in wonder, each student secretly hoping that school had been called off for the remainder of the day, for reasons unknown.

Instead, the school's principal visited each classroom and called out a handful of names of students from each class. Among those children selected from the first grade, second grade and kindergarten classes were Keith, Judith Ivy and Darcy Munson.

The principal then rallied the group of children together, instructing them to go to the coatroom and get dressed in their outerwear, and then he marched them outside and onto the school bus.

The remaining students in the classrooms were left to wonder about what was going on. Despite their unawareness of the situation, the children on the bus felt uniquely special, while those left behind felt downright cheated.

When all the children were seated on the school bus, they were informed that they were part of a select group who had qualified to benefit from the generosity of the "Goodfellows" charity, which provided children of low-income households with warm clothing during the frosty holiday season.

One day each year, during regularly scheduled classes, these chosen students were escorted onto a bus and taken to the JCPenney department store in Lumberton, where each child was allowed to choose one brand-new clothing or necessity item, which was granted via the munificence of the Goodfellows organization.

The Munson kids were absolutely delighted, as they had never had such an experience. To walk into a department store, pick out something brand new from the rack, try it on and take it home was simply unprecedented.

Darcy's boots had been leaking for so long that she had to wear plastic bread bags inside of her boots to keep her stockings from getting soaked. She, therefore, headed straight for the shoe department, in search of a new pair of warm and sturdy winter boots.

Keith had been in need of a new winter coat for quite some time, as the strings on the hood of his brown parka had been ripped right out, so he was unable to keep his hood on tight. There was also a large tear underneath the left armpit, where the cold drafts were always getting through, so Keith marched over to the boys outerwear department, in search of a brand-new parka of a different color (navy blue).

Judith Ivy decided she wanted a new outfit. She had never had any new apparel before. Ever since she could remember, she had been forced to wear her brother's old hand-me-downs or used clothing and shoes that were donated to Katie's children by other members of the Solo Parents Club, whose kids had outgrown them.

A nice saleslady was more than happy to assist the first-grader with her ensemble choice. The little brown-haired, brown-eyed lass had ultimately selected a pantsuit, which included red slacks and a matching white top with red ruffles on the sleeves, with a decal of a gray elephant on the front that had plastic eyes glued in place.

At long last, Judith Ivy Munson finally had a brand-new outfit of her very own! She was so pleased with her new purchase, in fact, that she insisted on wearing her new pantsuit for the remainder of the school day.

While the Munson children delighted in the day's extracurricular activities, and being treated to new clothing items by the good people at Goodfellows, there were others who weren't nearly as happy about the arrangement.

As a matter of fact, when these "privileged" children returned to school after their field trip to the JCPenney store, they were snickered at and belittled by their fellow classmates. It had become clear to them that, during their absence, the remaining student body had been made aware of the reasons for their eligibility to benefit from Goodfellows.

Consequently, on the playground at recess, these beneficiaries of the charitable organization's compassion and generosity were often teased, taunted and degraded for being "poor," which resulted in the tainting of an otherwise magnificent day.

The Munson kids hated getting harassed every year after their special field trip on (what became known as) "the poor bus," but they learned to deal with their tormentors by retaliating, "You're just jealous!" and walking away with their heads held high. Katie's children were just happy for the new clothing items. They handled them with care and wore them with great pride.

When their mother got home from work that evening, she was reasonably satisfied with the children's choices, with the only exception being that of the elephant pantsuit; but, as long as Judith Ivy was happy with her new outfit, then so was Katie.

Mrs. Munson felt truly grateful and indebted to the Goodfellows organization for those wonderful yearly gifts to her children. She hoped and dreamed that someday she might even be able to give back to this benevolent charity and help clothe another mother's needy children.

"Mommy, how come Keith and Judy and Darcy all got new clothes and I didn't?" little 4-1/2-year-old Samantha questioned. She couldn't help but feel disappointed and left out.

"Well," her mother began, "that's because they all go to school and you don't," she explained. "The nice Goodfellows people came and picked up the kids from school to take them shopping," Katie clarified, as she kissed her daughter's chubby cheek. "And since you're not in school yet, you'll have to wait until next year when you start kindergarten."

"But, Mommy, I really need some new mittens," the toddler moaned. "Mine have big holes in 'em, and my thumbs always freeze to death," Samantha complained.

"I'll tell you what," her mother conceded. "After breakfast on Sunday, we'll drive to Lumberton, and then you can pick out a brand-new pair of mittens from the JCPenney store…how's that sound?"

"Yippee!" Samantha rejoiced. She then skipped off to the living room and started changing the diaper on her dolly, who had been napping peacefully on the sofa.

"But don't throw your old mittens away!" Katie hollered after the teetering toddler. "We'll take them to Grandma Sally on our next trip so she can darn them for you," her mother clarified. "That way, you'll have a backup pair in case you lose your new mittens."

As an added surprise, once they had finished shopping for Samantha's new pink knitted mittens, and a fresh pair of pantyhose for Katie to wear to work at her secretarial job, Mrs. Munson took the children to the Dairy Queen for an ice cream treat.

While digging into her purse for some change, Katie commended her children on their behavior. "Since you kids were so good today and behaved so well at the department store, you get to choose whatever treat you want from the menu."

"Really? Anything?" the children asked. "Yep, whatever you want," their mother reiterated, "but only one treat apiece."

"Oh, boy! I'm gonna get a banana split," Keith declared. "I'm getting a strawberry sundae," Judy asserted, licking her lips. Darcy settled on a hot fudge sundae, while Samantha remained undecided. "I don't know what I want, Mommy," she fretted.

"Well, Honey," Katie coaxed her youngest, "why don't you go on up to the window with your brother and sisters, and then you can look at the menu and make up your mind when you get up to the counter."

Mrs. Munson watched in wonder as her children walked up to the Dairy Queen window by themselves and purchased their own frozen treats. She was amazed at how independent they were for their young ages. Although they were very small in stature, they sometimes seemed so very grown up, and the single mother couldn't have been more pleased...or more proud.

Cherishing the next several minutes that she had all to herself, Katie scanned through the car's radio stations, ultimately stopping when she heard one of her most beloved artists, Olivia Newton-John, singing her lovely ballad, "If Not For You."

As Katie sang along with the beautiful Australian songstress, she noticed how her children had all lined up in single file, with the tallest (Keith) in front, right on down to the smallest child (Samantha) at the rear of the line.

"How precious," their mother murmured, her heart overflowing with love. Tears welled in her eyes, for at that moment, Katie realized that she would truly be lost if not for her children and all the joy, wonder and laughter that they brought into her life each and every day.

When it was finally Samantha's turn to order her frozen delight, the tiny tot reached up as high as she could, standing on her tiptoes. The

4-1/2-year-old then plopped her change down on the countertop and placed her order with confidence. "I'd like a violet ice cream cone with a curl on top," she announced.

The man behind the counter couldn't help but let out a chuckle before he confirmed the youngster's order. "Did you mean a *vanilla* ice cream cone...with a curl on top?" he asked the little girl, whom he could barely see. "Yes, please," Samantha politely answered.

When the children returned to the idling car, Keith told his mother how their baby sister had ordered "a violet ice cream cone with a curl on top." Katie immediately burst into giggles, which infected the rest of the Munson clan and ultimately steamed up the windows.

Katie's blue Chevy Impala was quickly roaring with laughter, at Samantha's expense. The vexed toddler, however, didn't seem to have a care in the world, for she was preoccupied, lost in the immense pleasure of her vanilla soft-serve ice cream cone (with a curl on top).

The Munson family had just shared a remarkably pleasant Sunday afternoon, which got Katie to thinking. "Hey, kids," she addressed the children, as they slurped, sucked, and licked their way to happiness in the back seat of the '58 Chevy. "Why don't we do something fun like this every Sunday?" their mother proposed. "We'll call it 'family day'."

"Hey, yeah!" the kids shrieked, in unison. "Well,

all righty then," Katie declared. "From now on, every Sunday is going to be a family fun day!" That joyous day marked the beginning of a new weekly family tradition and launched the Munsons' first "family day" adventure.

## Chapter 4
# Riders on the Storm

For the remainder of the harsh winter months, Katie Munson and her boisterous brood settled into a comfortable weekly routine, which included Friday night pizzas and Saturday morning cartoons, followed by housecleaning chores and the disbursement of weekly allowances.

Saturday evenings meant bath time right after supper, during *The Lawrence Welk Show*, followed by soda pop and buttery popcorn in front of the television set, where the entire family gathered to watch *The Carol Burnett Show,* which always made them laugh until their bellies ached and/or soda pop spewed forth from one of the kids' noses.

While seated on the sofa for Saturday night television viewing, Katie often set the girls' wet hair in rollers, so that they could attend Sunday morning mass with shiny, bouncing curls, which would last through the rest of their fun-filled "family day" outing, whether it be ice skating, sledding, bowling, or a Sunday matinee.

When Sally Wiederman had learned that Katie was no longer attending regular church services, she harshly reprimanded her daughter, stressing the importance of providing the children with spiritual guidance and religious education.

Therefore, despite Katie's ambivalence toward the Stone Valley Catholic Church and its principles, she made sure that the Munson family attended mass each and every Sunday morning, even though it frustrated Katie that she had to remain seated in her pew while her children and the rest of the assembly were allowed to line up and receive the unleavened wafer during the sacramental communion.

Subsequently, as soon as Keith had turned eight years of age, he was cajoled by the catholic priest into becoming an "altar boy," which his mother endorsed without prejudice. Katie's girls were somewhat envious of their brother's participation in the ceremonial mass, but their mother explained to them that only boys were allowed to be altar boys and that there was no place for girls in the weekly ritual.

In April of 1972, as her sixth birthday approached, Darcy Lynn Munson beamed with excitement, for she had been wishing and hinting for a bicycle of her very own, just as her big sister, Judith Ivy, had received a blue Huffy bike last spring on her sixth birthday.

Traditionally, in the Munson household, it was the decision of the birthday boy or girl as to what to have for supper on that special evening. "I want pork roast with taters and sauerkraut," Darcy declared.

"Mmm, that sounds like a marvelous choice," her mother remarked. "When I get groceries on my way home from work tomorrow night, I'll be sure to add your birthday supper ingredients to my grocery list," Katie asserted.

"Hey, Mom," the almost six-year-old interjected, "since my birthday is on a Friday night this year, would it be okay if I ask Jeannie Crawford to come to my birthday party and stay overnight?"

"Sure," her mother answered. "I don't see why not. I'll just buy a little bit bigger roast, that's all."

"Gee, thanks, Mom!" the excited youngster acknowledged. "I'm gonna go call Jeannie right now," Darcy bellowed, as she bolted for the telephone.

"You know what, Darcy?" Katie proposed, halting Darcy in her tracks. "Why don't you go ahead and invite both Laverne and Jeannie Crawford, since it is a Friday night. That way, Laverne won't feel left out."

"All right!" Judith Ivy piped in, with a clap of her hands. "Now we have enough girls to have a slumber party!"

"Hey, Mom," Darcy beseeched, "can we camp outside in our sleeping bags?"

"Oh, I don't know," her mother returned. "We'll have to see how cold it gets at night. But, if it does get too cold to sleep outside," she suggested, "you could always have your slumber party right here on the living room floor."

"Oh, great," Keith grumbled. "That means I gotta spend another Friday night with five screaming girls in the house, doing all that stupid girlie stuff."

"Now, don't go getting all squirrely on me," his mother scolded. "I have an idea that might interest you, my only boy," Katie added, brushing Keith's long blonde bangs away from his irate baby blues with her fingertips. "You really need a haircut, Keith," she remarked.

"Mom, quit it!" the grumpy 8-1/2-year-old lad hissed, pulling his head away.

"I was thinking," his mother continued, "that since your grandparents will be here for Darcy's birthday party Friday evening, how would you like to go home with them after the party and stay in Huntington for the rest of the weekend?"

"Really? Can I, Mom?" Keith exclaimed, with wide-eyed anticipation.

"Sure," his mother returned. "But you'll have to call your Big Brother, Joe, and let him know…so he can make other plans for Saturday," Katie reminded the lad.

"Oh, yeah," Keith remembered. "I'll call him right now," he asserted, as he darted into the kitchen. "Thanks, Mom!"

When Katie arrived home Thursday evening with a trunk full of groceries, Judith Ivy and Darcy immediately pitched in to help their mom unload the car. Even the Crawford girls rushed over from the park across the street to help their friends' mother with the heavy brown paper sacks.

"So, girls…how's your dad doing since he fell off

that telephone pole?" Katie asked her neighborly help-ers. Mr. Crawford, an established telephone lineman for Northwestern Bell, had been injured the week be-fore after cascading 30-40 feet from a telephone pole while making a repair.

"He's doing okay," Laverne submitted, with a sigh, "but he hurt his back pretty bad, so Mom said he'll be out of work for a while."

"Oh, that's too bad," Mrs. Munson replied. "I hope he'll be up and about soon. Please give him and your mother my utmost sympathy," Katie extended. "And tell your mom to call me if there's anything I can do to help."

"Okay, I will," Laverne replied, as she attempted to heave the heaviest grocery bag of all--the one filled with all the canned goods. Unfortunately, the bottom had ripped open, and all the cans spilled out onto the floor of the trunk, rolling away in opposite directions, like banking billiard balls after a good hard break.

"Whoops! Sorry 'bout that, Mrs. Munson," the sev-en-year-old apologized. The two women then shared a hearty chuckle as Laverne and her best friend's mom fumbled to retrieve the wayward cans of sauerkraut, creamed corn, green beans, peas and carrots, as well as the canned spaghetti rings and stewed tomatoes.

"Ah, don't worry about it," Katie replied, waving her hand away. "This has happened to me on more than one occasion, I'm afraid," she regrettably re-marked. As she redistributed the loose canned goods into the five other grocery bags, Katie turned to her little helper and exclaimed, "When will those bag boys learn that you can't put all the canned goods in one bag!"

Darcy's sixth birthday party was a rip-roaring success. Katie's pork roast dinner in the crock pot with sauerkraut and quartered potatoes was a big hit with all the partygoers, although it was her Devil's food cake with chocolate frosting and vanilla ice cream that the kids anticipated most.

As soon as Darcy had blown out her six white candles, they all sang the traditional "happy birthday" song.

"Happy birthday, Darce," her big sister yelped. Judith Ivy then punched her sister's left upper arm and asserted, "Now you're six too…just like me!"

"But only for another month or so," their mother intervened, "before Judy turns seven…and with Samantha turning five in just a couple more weeks," Katie sighed, "you girls are gonna wear me out!"

While Katie started cutting into her daughter's birthday cake, Buster and Sally showed their granddaughter her bank book (the Wiedermans had opened a separate account for each of their grandchildren at their hometown bank in Huntington).

"See here, Darcy," Grandma Sally pointed out, "we deposited two more dollars in your account this morning for your birthday."

"Gee, two whole dollars!" the birthday girl

boasted. "I only get a dime a week for allowance," Darcy reminded her grandparents, "so that's like… way more than I get in a whole year doing chores!" she screeched. "Thanks, Grandma and Grandpa!"

Grandpa Buster then pulled the grateful little lass up onto his lap and gave Darcy a hearty whisker rub, which caused her giggle and wriggle.

"Quit it, Grandpa!" Darcy shouted, as she struggled to crawl down from his lap, but the scrawny 35-pound weakling was no match for her grandfather's brawny arms.

"So, tell me, 'Gravel Gertie'," her grandfather coerced, "what did you wish for when you blew out your birthday candles?"

"You know I can't tell you that, Grandpa!" Darcy snapped. "If you tell, then your wish won't come true!"

"Oh, yeah, that's right," Grandpa Buster conceded, as he dug into the front pouch of his blue denim overalls, reaching for his black onyx pipe and spicy tobacco.

"Can I light the match for you, Grandpa?" Darcy implored, as she climbed down from her grandfather's lap. "All right, Gravel Gertie," he granted, "but then I think you should open your birthday present, don't you?"

"Well, where is it?" Darcy inquired, looking around the kitchen. She hadn't seen a wrapped birthday gift anywhere in the house, and she had already snooped out the entire downstairs level after school that day, in hopes of finding her birthday present and trying to guess what was inside.

As Buster ignited his tobacco pipe, Darcy's mother snickered and hinted, "Why don't you go outside and look on the front porch?"

The children followed Darcy out onto the porch, where she discovered a red, white and blue Schwinn bicycle with a white woven basket on the handlebars and a big red bow stuck to the seat. (Buster and Sally had brought the bicycle along with them in the Scout, having hidden it away at their place until the little girl's party.)

"Oh, boy!" Darcy hailed. "I got my very own bike! Now I don't have to ask Judy to borrow hers anymore...and she always says no," she informed her guests, the Crawford girls, before sticking her tongue out at her mean big sister.

"Now, I know you wanted a bike with a banana seat, Darce," her mother apologized, "but I couldn't find one. I went to every garage sale in town, but this is the only bicycle I could find...well, that we could afford anyway."

"That's okay, Mom," her daughter replied. "As long as I got a bike, that's all I care about!"

"And I'm sorry your new bike is rusty," her mother lamented, "but with a little TLC and some paint," Katie alluded, "I'm sure you kids can fix it up real nice!"

"Sure, Mom," the birthday girl squealed, before

she wheeled her new bicycle off the front porch and down the steps.

"Me and Jeannie will help you fix it up, Darcy," Laverne Crawford offered.

"So will I, Darce," her big sister asserted. "Hey, you guys," Judy proposed, "now that Darcy has her own bike, maybe we should all go out and do 'garbage day' tomorrow and clean up the roads around town."

"Yeah, yeah, whatever," Darcy retorted, with a wave of her hand. The happy birthday girl was extremely eager to take her new set of wheels out for a test drive on the street. "Come on, Jeannie," Darcy beckoned her best friend. "Hop on Judy's bike and go for a ride with me!"

"Are you sure that's okay, Jude?" Jeannie asked Darcy's big sister. "Yeah, go ahead, Jeannie," Judy reluctantly consented. "But be careful…and make sure you don't wipe out!"

While Darcy and her best friend were taking the bikes for a spin, Keith had already begun working on his grandparents, as he was anxious to hit the road and depart from all the womenfolk. "Can we go pretty soon, Grandpa?" the impatient lad begged.

"Yeah, maybe we'd best be getting on home," Grandpa Buster conceded, with a prolonged yawn and stretch. "I'm starting to get tired, after that delicious pork roast dinner and birthday cake," he remarked, while rubbing his full belly.

"Me too, Buster," Grandma Sally concurred. "It's been a long day."

After Buster had finished smoking his pipe, he dumped the ashes into the ashtray on the kitchen table and announced, "Besides, Oscar and I gotta get up early to go fishing tomorrow, so we'd better hit the sack early tonight."

"All right!" Keith joyfully exclaimed. "I'll run up to my room and get my fishing pole and tackle box...be right back, Grandpa!"

Once the girls had returned from their bike ride through the streets of Stone Valley, and Keith was all packed and ready to go, Mr. and Mrs. Wiederman hugged their daughter and all their grandchildren farewell, and then they loaded up their grandson and his overnight bag, fishing pole and tackle box.

"Bye, Mom," Keith beamed, as he bounded out the door, ecstatic to be spending the weekend with his grandparents in Huntington. "See you Sunday night."

With the overnight low temperature being predicted at 49 degrees, Katie decided that the girls had better camp out in the living room. She locked the front door and retired to her bedroom with a good book, letting the girls have full command of the house for the remainder of the evening.

Once she had gotten her back propped up with two pillows against the headboard of her double bed, and her legs were snuggled comfortably beneath the sheets and bedspread, Katie was content and settled in for the night. She did, however, listen halfheartedly to the ruckus in the living room as she slowly opened her novel.

It didn't take long for the spirited girls to raid Mrs. Munson's record collection. As soon as Katie overheard one of her all-time favorite songs, "Hound Dog," emanating from the other side of her bedroom wall, she felt confident that Elvis Presley would keep her girls and their little friends entertained for hours, much like "The King of Rock and Roll" did for Katie, when she was just a youngster herself.

While enjoying her leisurely reading of *Jonathan Livingston Seagull—a story*, the best-selling novel written in 1970 by Richard Bach, Katie reveled in her seclusion. She presumed that inviting both Laverne and Jeannie Crawford to stay overnight, in addition to sending Keith to Huntington, was a surefire bet that she would be able to indulge in some long-overdue time to herself.

"Gee, I gotta do this more often," Katie declared. The sound of dancing feet was like music to the young mother's ears, and she became further lost in her serenity.

Katie awoke at 9:10 a.m. Saturday morning, with the popular paperback novel still splayed across her abdomen. "Wow!" she proclaimed, after acknowledging the time on her night stand clock. "I haven't slept this late in months!"

The girls' slumber party had, obviously, gone on for hours after Katie's retirement to her bedroom, as there were sleeping bags scattered all over the living room floor…and all five of the sleeping beauties were still tucked inside them, fast asleep.

"Aww, how adorable," Mrs. Munson muttered. She couldn't help but let out a soft giggle when she noticed that seven-year-old Laverne Crawford was snoring.

Katie backtracked across the kitchen floor on her tiptoes, and then she carefully and quietly reached into the top left kitchen drawer to locate the Polaroid camera. She was able to successfully snap off one photograph before the loud click and intense bright flash had awakened the slumbering party girls.

"Oh, Mom, quit it!" the birthday girl growled. "Just leave us alone and let us sleep!" Darcy had always been a bit of a bear in the morning, and her grisly disposition upon wakening seemed to grow more unpleasant with each passing year.

"My, aren't we a Grumpelstiltskin today!" her mother reacted. With that remark, Katie's now six-year-old middle daughter just grunted, hoisting the sleeping bag cover over her tiny blonde head, and then she disappeared into oblivion.

"So, anyone want breakfast?" Katie announced, ignoring her crabby birthday girl.

"I do, I do!" the Crawford girls echoed, as they exploded from their sleeping bags, with Judy and Samantha following close behind. Darcy, however, didn't budge.

Saturday morning breakfast had always been a cereal-and-toast kind of meal in the Munson household. "Do you girls like Cheerios?" Katie asked the Crawford sisters. "Yeah, we love 'em!" Jeannie replied.

"We don't get Cheerios at our house," Laverne clarified, shaking her head. "All we get is generic cereal, like puffy rice and bran flakes and stuff...blech!"

"Well, your mom has a lot of mouths to feed, with nine kids," Katie returned, in Mrs. Crawford's defense. "Besides," she further explained, "we don't waste food, or anything else, for that matter, at our house... and I've learned that if I don't buy my kids the foods they like, then they won't eat it, so I'm better off just spending a little extra to make sure they do."

(The Munson children had no idea that their mother had, indeed, purchased a box of Cheerios cereal at one time. However, once the big yellow box had been emptied, Katie continued to replenish the name-brand cereal box with generic toasted oats... and since her children never seemed to notice the difference, Katie was anxious to share her discovery with Mrs. Crawford.)

Darcy Lynn finally joined the rest of the group around 10:30 a.m., after they had already finished their breakfast and were cleaning up the morning dishes. "Mom, the Cheerios are all gone!" Darcy whined, as she held the cereal box upside down, shaking it continuously, even though nothing poured out.

"Well, that's what you get for sleeping the whole

morning away," her mother retorted. The irate birthday girl then stormed out the front door in her nightgown. "I bet Laverne and Jeannie ate all my Cheerios," she grumbled to herself, as she slammed the screen door. "That's the last time I invite them to my birthday party!" she griped.

The perturbed six-year-old subsequently took out her frustration by hopping up onto the porch railing, balancing atop the narrow ledge, walking back and forth in her anxiety, when she suddenly lost her footing.

"Ahhhhh!" the youngster screamed, as she tumbled down onto the unforgiving porch floor, which the homeowner had replaced with cement two years earlier. Everyone inside the old white Munson house heard the chilling scream. In their panic, they immediately rushed out to the front porch.

"Oh, my God!" Darcy's mother squalled. Katie could visualize bright red blood blotting the dirty gray cement. It seemed to be emanating from the back of her daughter's skull.

Katie panicked, becoming increasingly short of breath as she fell to her knees beside her traumatized little girl. Darcy's sparkling blue eyes were open, but she seemed to be dazed from the fall, and her thin blonde hair became increasingly dampened with oozing red blood.

"Don't worry, Mrs. Munson...she'll be okay," Laverne Crawford stated, as she tried to console her best friend's mother. "All you gotta do is take Darcy to the emergency room," the seven-year-old advised. "Believe me...in my family, with nine kids, we're like regulars there."

"Yeah, our family does go there a lot," her little sister, Jeannie, confirmed, offering Mrs. Munson the only comfort she could muster at that moment.

"Okay, listen up!" Katie bellowed, taking charge of the situation. She asked Samantha to run back into the kitchen and grab a towel. She then ordered Judy to find her purse, after which she hollered, "Now, everybody get in the car...and hurry up!"

Katie applied pressure to the back of Darcy's head with the white cotton towel, and then she carefully laid Darcy in the back seat of her blue Chevy Impala, placing her battered head in her big sister's lap.

"Here, Jude," her mother instructed. "Hold this towel firmly right here, against your sister's head, like this, until we get to the hospital...and don't let up!" That was the longest drive to Lumberton Katie Munson had ever made.

"Your daughter is going to need some stitches, I'm afraid," the emergency room physician assessed. Darcy was terrified and started to cry. "Shhh, don't worry," her mother assured the frightened birthday girl. "I'll be right here with you the entire time, and you're gonna be just fine!"

With the aid of some local anesthetic, the stitching went as well as could be expected with a six-year-old patient. "That should do it," the doctor announced, cutting the suture material after making the final stitch. "Six stitches in all."

After the doctor had finished giving Katie the wound care instructions, the emergency room nurse gave Darcy a great big sucker for being such a good little patient. Darcy enjoyed that strawberry lollipop all the way home, which greatly helped to take her mind off of her throbbing head.

"We'll get you some baby aspirin when we get home, Darcy," her mother stated, while driving back home to Stone Valley. "And then I think you should lie down and try to rest, so you Crawford girls are gonna have to go home."

While Darcy napped, Katie called her parents and told them of their recent ordeal with Darcy's injury. Buster and Sally were overwrought by the news, so they insisted that Katie bring the girls over right after church on Sunday so that they could spend the day together before taking Keith back home for the week.

The next morning, Katie cleansed and dressed her daughter's head wound and stitches. In light of the stimulating day they had all experienced on Saturday, Katie decided that it was all right to skip church that morning and let everyone sleep in, including herself. She treated the girls to their favorite breakfast dish (blueberry pancakes), and then they scrambled to get ready for their trip to Huntington.

It was a beautiful crisp spring morning, with the

sun shining brightly and the birds singing in harmony to welcome the season. As soon as she had walked through the Wiedermans' back door, Darcy was swept up into the loving arms of her grandparents, who showered the dainty lass with love.

"How's my little Gravel Gertie?" Buster asked his granddaughter, while inspecting the back of her head. "Oh, my…that's quite a bump you've got there on the back of your noggin," he commented.

"I got six stitches, Grandpa!" the six-year-old announced, seeming oddly proud of the gash in her head and the large gauze bandage. "Six stitches on my sixth birthday…one stitch for every year," she fervently blurted.

"Gee, that's really something," Grandma Sally interjected. "Do the stitches hurt at all, Sweetheart?" her grandmother inquired, as she gently stroked her granddaughter's soft cheek with her hand.

"No, not anymore," Darcy answered. "But they sure do itch a lot, and I have a bad headache still," the birthday girl reported.

"Well, we can take care of that right now," Grandma Sally assured. She reached into the refrigerator and removed a cold bottle of soda pop. She then retrieved a plastic cup from the cupboard and a couple of ice cubes from the freezer. The former nurse then poured her granddaughter a glass of cola, letting the fizz die down while she retrieved two orange baby aspirin tablets from the bathroom medicine cabinet.

"Here...take these two pills and drink this cola," Grandma Sally insisted. "The caffeine in the soda and the aspirin should have you feeling better in no time at all."

"Thanks, Grandma," the grateful little girl returned. When Darcy got to feeling better, just as her grandmother had predicted, Sally made lunch for the clan. While the family enjoyed their tomato soup and grilled cheese sandwiches, Buster suggested that, since it was such a gorgeous day, it might be nice to take the whole family out for a long Sunday drive in the country.

"Hooray!" the children rejoiced, as they soaked up the last drops of tomato soup from their bowls with their grilled cheese sandwich bread corners. Then, as soon as Katie and Sally had cleared away the condiments and dirty dishes, Buster began to rally the children out the door.

"But, what about the dishes?" Sally objected, as her husband hustled her towards the back door as well. "Don't worry about the dishes, Sweetheart. We can do those later. It's a beautiful day and the road is calling," her willful husband persisted.

The family quickly piled into the Wiedermans' new purple station wagon, with Keith riding up front in the middle, right beside his grandfather. Darcy had requested a window seat. Thus, in light of her birthday and recent boo-boo, she was pretty much permitted anything her little heart desired.

With the windows partially rolled down and the breeze blowing their hair in every direction, the purple station wagon traveled at a steady 55 miles per hour along the peaks and valleys of some of southern Minnesota's most scenic country roads.

"Grandpa, when are you going to teach me to drive?" eight-year-old Keith inquired. "I think you're going to have to wait a little while for that, Oscar," Buster answered his precocious grandson.

"Wow, look at all the cows!" Samantha pointed out, as they drove past a large dairy herd on the driver's side of the vehicle.

Grandpa Buster, who was always goofing around with his grandchildren, slowed the car down, turned his head and started "mooing" at the cows through his open window. "Moo...moo....moo," he chanted.

Interestingly enough, the black-and-white dairy cows lifted their heads from their collective grazing and turned toward the car, to investigate the peculiar sound.

Darcy, who was sitting directly behind her grandfather, then stood up and knelt on the car seat. She stuck her face out her open window and shouted out to the curious herd, "Don't let him fool ya...he ain't really a cow!"

The Wiederman family station wagon howled with laughter as the grape-colored automobile propelled down the highway beneath the abundant April sunshine. Darcy's silly retort was a welcome sign that she was feeling back to normal.

Although she had been injured and had to go to the emergency room that weekend, Darcy knew that she would always remember her sixth birthday fondly, for she had many good things to remember too—the Friday night slumber party, getting her first bicycle, and the fun Sunday afternoon spent with Grandma and Grandpa.

It wasn't long before the cool comfort and mild temperatures of April became lost in memory, as the blazing hot summer of 1972 was soon wreaking widespread havoc all across the Upper Midwest.

Consequently, Katie and one of her girlfriends, Gail Benson (from the Solo Parents Club), decided to take a summer vacation together, along with Gail's two children, Brad (7) and Tara (5), as well as Katie's four kids (8-1/2, 7, 6, 5).

Through their singles club connections, Gail had learned of a semi-affordable resort near Waterloo, Iowa, nestled along the Cedar River, where they might escape the heat for a spell, lying on the beaches of the sandy river's edge, soaking up the sunshine in the fresh summer breezes, and then cooling off in the invigorating, sparkling waters.

Gail had informed Katie that it was a family-oriented resort, sparsely populated, with only six on-site rental cottages. With Katie's approval, Gail had promptly made the reservations for the second week in July and booked two cabins, side by side.

Keith wasn't very excited about the Iowa vacation

initially, as he would be taken away from his grand-parents for an entire week of his summer vacation, but when Katie told him that the cabins were built right on a river bank and that he would be able to do plenty of fishing, Keith began to warm to the idea.

Once Katie had gotten her family through the ag-ony of packing, she, too, became excited about their first on-the-road family vacation. She and her kids had never really had a summer vacation together, so she was excited to create some special and lasting family memories.

Katie filled up the gas tank at the Stone Valley Shell station, had them check the oil and wash the windshield, and then they were on their way. She had previously packed bologna sandwiches and a canister of Pringles potato chips for the long journey south, so as to save money and limit their stops along the way, as she was certain that her children's tiny bladders would disrupt their journey plenty enough already.

The plan was to meet Gail Benson at the Cedar-Loo Resort, since one can never calculate the estimat-ed time of arrival with four youngsters in the car for a nearly three-hour drive. Then, once both families had arrived, checked into their cabins, and unloaded their vehicles, Katie and Gail would make a quick trip into the city of Waterloo to buy groceries and supplies for their week-long stay.

Little did Katie know that her children would choose that particular outing to exhibit their worst behavior. She felt more like a referee than a chauffeur. Katie was constantly chastising the children and putting out fires.

"Mom, Keith won't stop squishing me," Samantha whined. "He keeps pushing me over more and more, and hogging all the room."

"Keith, knock it off!" his mother bellowed. "I'm tired of this constant bickering!"

"Well, I don't want their cooties all over me!" Keith retorted, as he gave his baby sister yet another nudge with his bony elbow.

"Stop it!" five-year-old Samantha demanded, and with that, the feisty little sister shoved her big brother over as hard as she could. That's when the hitting began, as Darcy and Judith Ivy came to their baby sister's rescue, ganging up on their bullying big brother. Within minutes, the children were all at one another's throats.

"That's enough!" Katie hollered, as she pulled the car over to the shoulder of the highway. "Keith, you get in the front seat right now, where I can keep an eye on you!" their mother ordered. "And put all these bags and stuff on the seat in the trunk."

"But, Mom," the 8-1/2-year-old complained, "the trunk's already full."

"Well, you'll just have to make room then, won't you?" she snapped. Katie then turned her attention to the back seat and issued her threat to the girls. "And if I hear any more screaming, fighting, bickering, hitting or slapping, I'm turning this car around, and there won't be any vacation...understood?" Katie's face became flushed with anger.

The children corrected their behavior immediately, for they knew when their mother meant business... and this was one of those times! Even though they weren't at home, where their mother had easy access to the metal yard stick that she used to whack their naked bottoms when they misbehaved, the children feared that they might still "get it" when they arrived at the cabin.

The remainder of the drive across state lines went fairly smoothly, except that the temperature steadily increased and the kids started to complain about being hot and sticky. With all the windows already rolled down in her 1958 Chevy Impala, there was nothing more Katie could do about the suffocating heat. "Just sit still and quit wiggling around," she suggested. "Then you'll stay cooler."

In order to drown out the persistent grumbling, Katie decided to crank up the radio, as she'd had enough of her kids' incessant whining. The Doors' moody melody, "Riders on the Storm," aided greatly in quelling her children's annoying behavior.

Using the dashboard radio as a weapon, Katie's strategy had proven victorious, and for the remainder of their pilgrimage to Iowa, whenever Katie heard even the slightest complaint or argument, she would just crank up the volume to shut them up!

When the Munsons finally arrived at the Cedar-Loo Resort, it was just as Gail had described. There were six small green cottages with white shutters, situated side by side along the Cedar River, about 20 feet apart from one another.

The sun was brightly shining, and it was hot! The mercury on the thermometer outside the resort office read 99 degrees, but the humidity in the air that day made it feel more like 120. The sparkling river water, now just footsteps away, was beckoning.

Their six children wasted no time. One by one, they sprinted toward the river's edge, baptizing themselves in blessed relief. Katie and Gail soon joined their offspring. They kicked off their thong flip-flops and waded in up to their knees, enjoying the respite from the long, unruly, hot and sweaty drive; but since they still had a lot of unpacking yet to do, the grown-ups didn't care to get their shorts wet.

"Hey, Gail, what time is it getting to be?" Katie asked the tall, slim brunette, who always wore a wristband watch with a black leather band. "It's about 5:30," Gail answered, reveling in the respite of the cool river water on her achy and overheated feet.

The moment Gail glanced down at her wristwatch, she and Katie became the targets of their children's shenanigans. "Hey, stop splashing us!" Gail bellowed. "If you get my watch wet, you guys are gonna get it!" she warned the kids. "I mean it!"

Katie, in turn, tried to shield her face and hair

from the large water droplets, as she knew how hard it would be to comb through all of that sticky aerosol hairspray in her ponytail, once her hair became completely saturated.

The adults quickly retaliated by splashing a small wave of water back at their sons, who were most likely the instigators. The mothers were ultimately forced out of the playing field, however, since neither Katie nor Gail felt like getting soaked to the skin.

While the children frolicked in the refreshing waters of the Cedar River, Katie and Gail unpacked their vehicles and hauled their belongings into their respective cottages.

"Wow, these cabins are really nice," Katie acknowledged, when she and her friend met again by their cars. "Yeah, I thought so too," Gail happily concurred. "You never can tell what a place will be like until you get there, so this is pretty cool."

Once the women had finished unloading their automobiles and opening the windows in the cabins to air them out, Katie summoned the children for supper. Gail and Katie pushed the picnic tables together between their two cabins, and then they divided up the remaining sandwiches and potato chips they had pre-packed earlier that morning.

While the two families devoured the last of their available food, the two mothers mandated their orders for the evening. Katie addressed the children first. "Okay, listen up, kids! Gail and I are gonna drive to Waterloo to get some groceries and charcoal and stuff," she explained. "You children are to stay here and unpack your things while we're gone...and stay out of trouble!"

"That's right," Gail agreed. "And while we're gone, we want you kids to be on your best behavior...and absolutely no swimming, under any circumstances!" she dictated, shaking her index finger at the children. "There's no lifeguard on duty here."

"We'll probably be gone for a couple of hours," Katie instructed, "so I'm putting Keith in charge of our cabin, since he's the oldest." Gail then addressed her two children: "And Brad, you'll be in charge of Tara and our cabin, since you're the oldest."

The children seemed to be in agreement, however, their mouths were full of bologna and chips, so they didn't have much at all to say about the arrangement.

As soon as their parents had departed for the city of Waterloo, Iowa (about a half-hour drive), the children began to celebrate their emancipation. Gail's very well-behaved children did as they were told and started unpacking their belongings.

Next door in the Munson cottage, however, Katie's girls had stripped down to their underwear, hanging their soaking-wet clothes anyplace they could find—the sofa, the backs of the kitchen chairs, or slung over the headboard on the single bed in the cabin's only bedroom.

Katie's girls loved to run around naked in the

summertime, which they typically did at their house following their weekly Saturday night baths. On one occasion, Katie had managed to capture her little Samantha as she was trampling through the house, like a wildebeest galloping through the African prairie lands of Tanzania, and asked the wild child (who was three years old at that time), "Why are you running laps around the house?" Samantha just gazed up at her mother, as if her actions were self-explanatory, and candidly stated, "I'm drying my hair!"

In the living room of the Munson cottage, Judith Ivy noticed a radio on top of the table next to the heavy green floor lamp. It took some time for her to tune it in to a clear station, but when she did, she immediately recognized the song and started to twirl and spin around in her underwear. She urged her sisters to join her in the dance. "Come on, you guys, this is a nifty song!" the seven-year-old exclaimed, singing along to Don McClean's smash hit, "American Pie."

Their playful song and dance was rudely interrupted, however, when an emergency broadcast came over the radio station, warning of a severe thunderstorm for several counties until 10 p.m. It was now 6:30 p.m., and it still looked beautiful outside their cabin door. The children had no idea, however, that their current location was included in the severe thunderstorm warning, so they continued to enjoy themselves and savor their brief bout of freedom.

While his three little sisters amused themselves in

ways that only girls can, Keith began to unpack his fishing gear, getting his tackle organized for the morning's highly anticipated fishing expedition.

He painstakingly separated his tackle into two piles—the first being his shallow-water collection, consisting of sunfish, bass and crappie fishing jigs and bobbers, and the second pile comprised of deep-water lures and setups that he used to angle for northern pike, walleye and catfish (and any other unique species that might be lurking in these foreign, uncharted waters of the Cedar River).

Keith had just about finished organizing his fishing gear when, suddenly, a strong wind swept through the screened windows on the front side of the cottage, blowing the curtains with great vigor, and turning his orderly pile of lightweight fishing jigs into a messy clutter.

The frustrated young lad hastily gathered his things together and separated them into their proper compartments inside his prized tackle box, which he had received from his grandparents for Christmas last year. He then stepped outside to investigate the weather situation.

As he glanced across the Cedar River towards the west, Keith noticed that it was getting awfully dark beyond the river's horizon. Just then, it started to sprinkle, and the gray ominous mass from beyond seemed to be skating straight for them, swallowing up everything in its path.

The wind had suddenly picked up as well, and litter was being tossed about freely across the landscape. Keith found himself shielding his eyes from the pounding rain, which was now blowing straight at him with great force. Then, just as he had turned away to go back inside the cabin, a resounding blast of thunder pierced the stillness of the evening, followed by a massive bolt of lightning from the heavens.

Frightened by the unexpected explosion from the tumultuous sky, the 8-1/2-year-old boy sprinted for the cabin door, as yet another blinding flash lit up the skies, chasing the lad into submission. Once inside, Keith latched the screen door and locked the front door of the cabin. Meanwhile, the temperature had dropped rather significantly, so his three little sisters had already begun to dress into some warm, dry clothing.

"I'm scared!" five-year-old Samantha wailed, as she clung to her big sister, Judy. Samantha had always been terrified of storms. Whenever she heard that first rumble of thunder, she empirically ran to her mother and oftentimes slept in her mom's bed when the disturbance occurred at nighttime. Katie Munson feared those summertime thunderstorms as well, as it was more likely than not that she would go without sleep on those dreaded nights.

"Keith, what are we gonna do?" Judith Ivy beseeched her big brother, who was the person in charge, as per their mother's orders. "Mom won't be home for at least another hour or so," the eldest daughter deduced, "and you know how long it takes to get groceries!"

"Don't worry, you guys...everything will be okay," their big brother assured, even though he secretly shuddered in his shorts. "Hey, Jude, help me get all these windows closed!" Keith dictated. "Darcy and Samantha, you two go and listen to the radio and see what they say about the storm!"

"Oh, my God!" Darcy shrieked, as she reported the most current weather update. "They said there's a tornado warning for the whole Waterloo area!"

Just then there was a knock at the door. Darcy unlocked the front door, but the violent windstorm did the rest. She couldn't even step out of the way in time before the door blew back open, hitting hard against the wall. In its path, it smacked Darcy in the face and sent her tumbling to the ground.

The six-year-old managed to pick herself up and unlatch the screen door just in time to get their frantic neighbor kids safely inside, at which time Darcy witnessed a huge tree branch being taken down right behind them! The leaves at the tip of the hefty branch actually brushed the front side of the Munson cottage on its way down to the ground, taking down the white window shutters as well. Panicked, Darcy unleashed a chilling scream, which further frightened the youngsters.

Brad and Tara Benson were completely soaked,

as the rain had since evolved into a steady down-pour, mixed with some intermittent pea-sized hail. As frightened as the Benson children already were by that time, their terror became even more intensified when they observed the chaos that was building inside the Munson cabin.

"Keith, help!" Judith Ivy beckoned her brother. The wind was so strong that the seven-year-old couldn't keep the indoor window shutter closed long enough to get the latch clasped. The gales continued to force the wooden flap back open, until one final gust dismantled the shutter from its hinges and hurled it to the ground, shattering a small table lamp along the way.

Samantha started to cry. "I want my mommy… where's Mommy?" the five-year-old bawled, using the bottom of her old yellow T-shirt to soak up her face full of agonizing tears. Although the toddler needed her mother now more than ever, Samantha was also genuinely concerned about her mom's safety.

"Mom's not here, Sam, so we're just gonna have to get through this by ourselves…and quit acting like a baby!" her eldest sister scolded. That got Judy to thinking about their mother as well. "Poor Mom!" she exclaimed, placing her hand over her mouth. "What if Mom and Gail are stuck outside in this storm somewhere?"

Brad and Tara then began to sob as well, fearing for their mother's welfare. "Oh, nice going, Jude," Keith rebuked, in response to his sister's tactless comment.

"I'm sure they're safe inside the Red Owl by now," Keith reassured the children. "Besides, you know Mom would never drive in this kind of weather."

For that brief moment, Keith's little sisters, as well as Brad and Tara Benson, had all felt a little more safe...until the power suddenly went out! The radio fell eerily silent, the cabin grew dark, and all the kids could hear were the howling winds whipping through the cottage, the door and window shutters banging repeatedly against the walls, in addition to the torrential rain mixed with hail that relentlessly pummeled the rooftop of the tiny shack. The six terrified, unsupervised children screamed out into the darkness, but their cries went unheard.

As the tiny cottage's wall hangings and various décor items began to fly about the shack like feathers in the wind, Keith decided to take charge of the situation and organize their group of horrified juveniles.

"Brad, help me with the table!" he shouted. Frantic, the two young men each grabbed an end of the kitchen table, dragging the heavy furniture to the far corner of the cabin, as far away from the windows and door as they could get.

"You girls get under the table and stay there!" Keith commanded, as his overgrown, long blonde locks irritatingly kept finding their way into his eyes and mouth. (For the first time in his life, the stubborn lad wished that he had taken his mother's advice and gotten that long-overdue haircut.)

Keith suddenly recalled that he had packed a flashlight at the bottom of his tackle box. He quickly retrieved the flashlight and handed it down to the girls, who were hunkered down under the kitchen table. Then he summoned the other man of the house.

"Brad, help me push the front door shut," Keith shouted, over the chaotic storm and raging winds. "Then we'll shove that recliner chair in front of the table to help shield us from flying objects and stuff!"

When the boys had successfully completed their tasks, they joined their little sisters beneath the homemade fortress they had constructed and rode the storm out together.

Keith clutched the flashlight in one hand and his baby sister, Samantha, in the other. He could tell she was shivering, both inside and out, so he rubbed Samantha's skinny little arm repeatedly, back and forth, in an effort to generate some warmth, smooth out her goose bumps, and calm her fears.

Brad, likewise, consoled his little sister, Tara, while Judy and Darcy cradled and comforted each other, not knowing whether they were going to make it through the night or not. *The Wizard of Oz* instantly came to mind, as it was a classic film that all the Munson children had looked forward to watching each and every year at Thanksgiving.

In Judy's vivid imagination, she couldn't help but think of their tiny vacation shack being whisked high up into the sky, getting tossed about in the eye of a cyclone, and then dumped far, far away in some foreign place, like Munchkinland, with a wicked witch seeking revenge upon them for disturbing her perfectly evil euphoria, while they struggled to find their way back home to Stone Valley, Minnesota, with the aid of a bunch of defective misfits.

Although the children were utterly terrified by nature's ongoing fury, and the fact that they were all alone and worried about their moms, the youngsters found solace in one another. As they huddled together underneath the table of terror, their tensions and anxieties heightened, in conjunction with the climax of the raging tempest.

Judith Ivy was the first to penetrate the apprehension by singing a familiar ditty that she knew would evoke a response: "Row, row, row your boat, gently down the stream; merrily, merrily, merrily, merrily, life is but a dream…"

Darcy and Tara readily joined in the chorus, followed by Samantha, and eventually even Keith and Bradley joined in the sing-a-long. As the earsplitting thunder booms resonated throughout the shack, the children answered back by increasing their melodic volume. Each verse became stronger than the previous, until they found themselves literally screaming out the lyrics, with all the power their lungs could emit.

It seemed as though they had spent hours seeking refuge under that table weathering the storm, when, in fact, nature's unleashed fury had already begun its progression out of Iowa, heading east, where it was predicted the storm would terrorize the states of Wisconsin and Illinois, in just a little over an hour.

Before the children even realized that the storm had blown over, Katie and Gail had already made their way back to the resort. They were both surprised and shocked at what they found when they returned. "Oh, my God!" the moms cried out, in unison.

The quaint white shutters had been ripped apart from the cottage windows. Metal trash cans were scattered about the resort, and the clothesline connecting their two cabins was lying flat on the ground. Even more disturbing was that young trees had been completely uprooted, and the limbs of mature trees had been brutally amputated.

As the cold black clouds began to separate and the sky turned clear, Katie and Gail quickly exited the blue Chevy. The frantic mothers first ran to check out Gail's cabin, as it was the closest. The front door was blown wide open, but there was no one in sight. "They must be in our cabin," Katie surmised. "Let's go!"

The frightened women scurried over to the cabin next door. Along the way, much to their disbelief, Katie and Gail thought that they heard humming. As they drew nearer, the humming, or singing voices, grew louder.

Soon, their fear turned to hope, as Katie had instantly recognized the familiar tune. It was a little ditty that her children had often chanted during their Sunday afternoon drives on family day outings. "Oh, thank God!" Katie uttered, feeling faithful and relieved that their children would be found safe and unharmed.

Together, Katie and Gail heaved the enormous tree branch that had fallen in front of the Munson cabin, blocking its entrance. Given their state of hysteria, the distraught mothers hurled the massive limb, with brute strength, off to the side of the shack.

To their surprise, as they entered the small cottage, they found it to be in complete disarray. "Oh, my heavens!" Gail gasped, covering her mouth with her hand as she and Katie visually inspected the room. "Just look at this mess!" she shrieked.

"Kids, where are you?" Katie bellowed to her loved ones. The two boys then peered around the recliner chair, ecstatically relieved to discover that their mothers had made it safely back to them.

"Mom!" Keith and Brad cried out, as they ran into their mothers' arms. The girls then followed suit, one by one, crawling out from the protective fortress their brothers had built during the raging storm's reign of terror.

Alas, the children rejoiced, for their mothers had returned, and they were all back together again. "Praise the Lord!" Katie hailed, as she knelt down and embraced her spared son and daughters.

While the children took turns hugging their

mothers, Katie and Gail took notice of the protective sanctuary the children had made for themselves. "Looks like the storm hit here a lot harder that it did in Waterloo," Gail remarked.

"What an impressive fort you kids made!" Katie commended the children. "But, how on Earth did you kids know what to do?"

"It was all Keith's idea, Mom!" Judith Ivy asserted, making sure to give her big brother the credit that he so rightfully deserved. "He just seemed to know what to do," she proudly stated.

"Good for you, Keith!" his mother congratulated. "Well, Brad helped me a lot too," her son inserted. "We did it together."

"Well, I'm very proud of you...all of you," Katie acknowledged. "And so am I," Gail concurred. "You know what, Katie?" she added. "I don't think either of us could have done any better!"

Katie started to snivel, and tears welled in her pretty blue eyes as she observed the shambles the severe thunderstorm had made of their rented hut. "I'm so sorry that we weren't here for you kids when you needed us," she sobbed. "We had no idea that a storm was coming, let alone a tornado in the area...you poor kids must have been scared out of your minds!"

"We were, Mom!" the children replied. "We thought we were gonna die!" Samantha exclaimed. "But then Keith saved us," she clarified. "He's our hero!"

Katie then smiled affectionately at her only son, who suddenly looked so grown up. "My little man," she uttered, as she tousled his long golden locks.

While the youngsters inundated their moms with their individual accounts of the evening's disaster and all the exciting events they had missed, the two families stepped outside to assess the damage out of doors.

"Boy, were we lucky!" Gail maintained. "Look at all the destruction out here!"

The sky was completely clear now, and the air was unbelievably clean and fresh. As they walked towards the river's edge, Katie inhaled deeply. She then exhaled a cleansing sigh, thanking God for keeping watch over their kids that day.

As they watched the sun set, Katie reflected upon her personal experience with tonight's storm, realizing that whatever she and Gail had endured, it was nothing compared to what their children must have suffered while being left alone in their cabins.

Katie felt a sudden shiver, and then her eyes welled with tears. Her son unexpectedly brushed up alongside her and rubbed the cold, clammy skin on her upper arm with his warm hand, to offer her some comfort. "Don't be sad, Mom," Keith assured his worried mother. "It's all over now, and we're all okay."

"I'm not sad, Honey," Katie replied. "These are happy tears because…well, I know one thing for certain," she proudly told her son. "I sure left the right man in charge, didn't I?"

She brushed Keith's long bangs away from his red-dened, strained blue eyes, reiterating his need for a haircut, to which Keith shockingly replied, "All right, Mom. You can cut my hair tomorrow, if you want… nice and short for the summer." Katie raised her eye-brows in disbelief.

Amazingly, Samantha's debilitating fear of thun-derstorms vanished after that harrowing night. Not only did she feel more courageous for having gone through it, she also knew that she was in good hands, whether her mother was around or not. Samantha was very proud of her big brother, Keith, for she had seen him in action when the going got rough…and he didn't let them down!

The Munsons' first family summer vacation, in July of 1972, was quite memorable, indeed, for in the midst of a threatening tornado, the Munson children had learned a very valuable lesson about camarade-rie, teamwork, and the reliability of family.

Katie, in turn, was pleasantly surprised at how well-behaved her children were for the remainder of their week's vacation. The long drive home was a treat, when compared to the exasperating drive down to Iowa just one week earlier.

Prior to that hysterical, stormy night, the Munson kids had always regarded themselves as just siblings, but after that unforgettable vacation, they became more than just brothers and sisters…more than just family…they became more like "friends."

During the long drive back home to Stone Valley, Minnesota, at the end of that exhausting week, the radio played The Doors' hit record, "Riders on the Storm," once again. Katie immediately cranked it up loudly and hollered, "Hey kids! What does this song remind you of?"

Realizing how fortunate they were to have survived such an ordeal, five-year-old Samantha said it best, when she described their newfound clarity by declaring, "You know what, Mom? If we can make it through that scary storm, then we can make it through anything!"

## Chapter 5
# I Got You Babe

Following that unforgettable summer vacation, life quickly returned to normal for the Munson family. School resumed right after Labor Day, and none of Katie's children was happy about that. Nobody wanted to say goodbye to the long carefree days of summer, particularly Keith.

Katie, on the other hand, was looking forward to one significant change that the new school year would bring. Samantha was starting kindergarten, which meant that her youngest child would be in daycare for only half of the day, saving her money in daycare expenses. "Pretty soon they'll all be in school full time," she secretly rejoiced.

While Katie quietly celebrated the arrival of the new 1972-'73 school year, her youngest daughter, Samantha, exhibited great anxiety towards leaving the familiar surroundings of her daycare mother, Linda Reed.

Mrs. Reed had played an integral role in Samantha's life thus far, and the toddler was most reluctant to leave the comfort of her safety net. It didn't take long, though, before the five-year-old embraced her academic environment and discovered the wonderful world of learning.

One rainy autumn Sunday evening, in October of 1972, Katie Munson and her three daughters rounded out their family fun day at the movies (to see the popular historical drama, *Sounder*) with a trip to Huntington, as they had been invited over for supper before taking Keith home following his weekend stay at his grandparents' house.

Shortly after finishing Grandma Sally's succulent pork chops, mashed potatoes and gravy, Grandpa Buster retired to his rocking chair in the living room, where he ignited his tobacco pipe and eagerly anticipated the televised baseball game. The Oakland A's (Athletics) were playing the Cincinnati Reds in the World Series.

While the men waited in the living room for the ball game to start, the women remained in the kitchen, cleaning up after supper. During that time, the three little girls became restless, so they started searching for something fun to occupy their time.

"Why don't you girls go in the dining room and play grocery store?" their grandmother suggested. Grandma Sally was more concerned with keeping the girls out of Buster's way during the all-important World Series baseball game. "Here's an empty cereal box to add to your inventory," she offered, handing the box to Judith Ivy.

"Thanks, Grandma," the seven-year-old acknowledged. Judy then walked over to the green canvas cot, upon which Buster took his daily afternoon naps, and pulled the large cardboard box filled with empty containers from underneath the cot.

Darcy set up the plastic cash register, organizing the Monopoly play money into the separate compartments, while Samantha retrieved the baby carriage, which would serve as their shopping cart.

Once they had neatly arranged all the empty boxes, milk cartons, glass jars and plastic jugs on top of the dining room table, their fictitious market was officially "open." Judith Ivy appointed herself checkout clerk, while her two younger sisters played the role of shoppers, filling their stroller-cart with weekly essentials, to include cereal, honey, tub margarine, milk, eggs, peanut butter and ketchup.

When her customers had purchased seven dollars' worth of grocery items, Judy handed them each a receipt, at which point she was reminded that it was past the airing time of her favorite television program, *The Sonny and Cher Comedy Hour,* which was already in session.

Realizing that she was missing her favorite show on account of the baseball game, Judith Ivy stormed out into the living room, during the top of the first inning, and announced, "It's past seven o'clock...Sonny and Cher is on!" she panicked. "Can I turn the channel, Grandpa?" Judy begged, with her tiny hand already clutching the round dial on the television set.

"Sorry, Snuffy," her grandfather declined. "We're watching the game tonight, so you won't be able to watch Sonny and Cher this week." The displeased lass walked away with her head bowed down. Judith Ivy simply adored *The Sonny and Cher Comedy Hour* and had never missed an episode…until that night.

Not knowing how to deal with the harsh disappointment, the 7-1/2-year-old became enraged, throwing a fit. "But, I wanna watch Sonny and Cher!" Judy ranted, with a stomp of her foot. She searched the eyes of her mother and grandmother, in the hopes that someone might side with her and insist that the channel be changed.

"Judith Ivy Munson!" her mother intervened. "Your grandpa said no, so we're not watching Sonny and Cher tonight," Katie scolded. "Now, sit down and be quiet!"

As the minutes ticked away, and Judith Ivy was missing her favorite television program, she gave it one last effort, demanding that the channel be changed, or she would stand in front of the television set for the rest of the night. "Then you guys won't be able to watch your stupid baseball game either!" the angry lass threatened.

That was the last shred of patience Buster could muster. With one fluid movement, he skated across the living room towards the television set, grabbed his misbehaving granddaughter by the forearm, turned her around, and gave his little Snuffy a firm spanking on her backside.

Judith Ivy was so shocked, stunned and upset that

she burst into tears and stomped upstairs to her mother's old bedroom, where she plopped face down on the bedspread and sulked in her humiliation.

Minutes later, the distraught youngster heard the sound of delicate footsteps climbing the steep, creaky old stairs. Her grandmother had come to comfort the disheartened child, who was found lying on her stomach on top of the bed, bawling harder than Sally had ever witnessed.

Grandma Sally started rubbing her sobbing granddaughter's back. "Now, now…there's no need to fret so about this, sweetheart," Sally asserted. "I can't believe your grandfather spanked you hard enough to cause such a fuss as this."

Her granddaughter suddenly turned over on her back to face Sally, who quickly snatched a handkerchief from the pocket of her apron, in order to wipe the poor child's nose. Judith Ivy then proceeded to address her enigma.

"No, that's not why I'm crying, Grandma," the 7-1/2-year-old disclosed. "I'm crying because…well, Grandpa never spanked me before," she sniveled, before blowing her nose. "But I'm not mad at him," she admitted. "I'm mad at myself because I love Grandpa SO much…and I feel bad for making him so mad that he had to spank me!"

She continued to cry, harder and harder, progressing to explosive bawling, at which point Judith Ivy had to gasp for air in between sobs. Grandma Sally put her comforting arms around her granddaughter's slender shoulders, and then she placed little Judy's head to rest upon her bosom.

While gently rocking the hysterical young lady in her arms, Sally brushed Judy's golden brown hair away from her big brown eyes, and then she started singing a very familiar song that was certain to console the shameful young lass…and it did.

As her granddaughter raised her head, Sally stretched out her hand and invited the child to sing along to the rest of Sonny and Cher's theme song, "I Got You Babe." Feeling grateful and appreciative of her grandmother's efforts, Judy placed her little hand in Sally's palm and happily joined in the melody that she looked so forward to hearing each and every week at the conclusion of her favorite television program.

Before even reaching the end of their heartwarming duet, sitting side by side and singing with Grandma Sally, Judy's tears had subsided, and her frown was replaced with a smile. "Thanks, Grandma," she asserted, as she wiped the last remnants of tears from her flushed cheeks. "I feel much better now…like I didn't miss the show after all."

"You know what, dear?" Grandma Sally responded, with a hug. "I'm sure this was hard on your grandpa too, so…why don't you come back downstairs with me, and then you and your grandfather can straighten this whole mess out right away."

Now that she was calm and settled, Judith Ivy

yawned and answered, "No, I'm pretty tired. I think I'll just stay up here for a while and take a nap."

"Suit yourself," Grandma Sally replied, thinking that a nap might be the best thing for her ailing granddaughter at that moment.

"Don't worry Grandma," Judith Ivy assured her grandmother, who was heading for the door. "I'll never make you or Grandpa mad at me like that again, so you'll never have to spank me ever again...I promise!"

"I certainly hope not," her grandmother replied. Katie's former bedroom had since grown dark during their little chat, now that the sun had set for the evening. Sally began to slowly close the door behind her. "Get some sleep now, my dear," she advised, "and this will all be behind us when you wake up...you'll see."

"I love you, Grandma!" Judith Ivy exclaimed. "And tell Grandpa I love him too!"

The tuckered lass slumbered for two solid hours, and then, just as her grandmother had foretold, all had been forgiven by the time she had gone back downstairs to join the rest of the family.

From the comfort of her grandfather's lap, as she clung to the straps of his blue denim overalls, little Snuffy quietly watched the last inning of the baseball game. Resting her head peacefully against Grandpa Buster's soft flannel shirt, the 7-1/2-year-old vowed to keep the promise she had made to her grandmother that night.

While the rest of the Munson/Wiederman clan had eventually forgotten all about the 1972 World Series baseball tournament, it remained forever embedded in Judith Ivy's memory--not because the Oakland A's defeated the Cincinnati Reds, but because that was the night she received her first and <u>only</u> spanking from Grandpa Buster!

The following spring, in 1973, a "peace-with-honor" (ceasefire) agreement had been negotiated in Vietnam. The last American troops withdrew from that nation on March 29 of that year. Unfortunately, the fates of many MIAs (Missing In Action) remained unaccounted for.

Although the Munson children didn't personally know of any returning Vietnam soldiers to their home town of Stone Valley, they had prior first-hand knowledge of that horrible war's devastating effects, which were hauntingly revealed through the vacant eyes of their uncle, William, who had been called to action via the 1969 draft lottery.

William Wiederman (Buster and Sally's youngest son) had completed his full tour of duty in Vietnam, but when he returned to Huntington a year later, appearing physically intact, the emotionally disfigured veteran was acutely devoid of the humorous Wiederman personality that had been characteristic of his disposition prior to his departure off to war.

The amusing son, brother and uncle that the Wiedermans had always known and loved was now a lost, sullen and broken man. William never spoke of the unspeakable acts and bloodshed he had witnessed while serving his country in those primitive jungles halfway around the world; and when pressed about anything relating to his military servitude, he simply retreated by vacating the room or ignoring the subject altogether.

As the newspaper headlines celebrated the beginning of the end of the very protracted Vietnam War that spring, the Munson sisters rallied together on their bicycles, with their brown-bag lunches, and organized their annual "garbage day" town cleanup. If there were any veterans returning home to Stone Valley soon, the children wanted their beloved home town to look presentable for their deserving soldiers.

In addition to the voluntary help of the dependable Crawford girls (Laverne and Jeannie), Judith Ivy also recruited the service of the Brenner sisters, whom they had befriended a few months back while playing in the Stone Valley Park, across the street from their house.

The Brenners were a middle-class family of five, plus one large black Labrador Retriever, named "Coot." They lived just a few blocks down the street from the old two-story Munson house in a quaint yellow ranch-style home with a spacious back yard.

Mr. Brenner was an authoritative game warden, employed by the Minnesota Department of Natural Resources (DNR), while Mrs. Brenner worked as a self-employed cleaning lady. The couple had three children--one son and two younger daughters--and though they were a few years older than the Munson kids, the two families soon became intertwined.

The Brenner girls gladly offered their time and energy to help brighten their scenic little town. Kristi Brenner (11) and Barb Brenner (10) were excited to meet the young Munson sisters in the park on Saturday morning at 9 a.m. sharp, as planned, with their bicycles and sack lunches, and join the rest of the community cleanup crew.

At 9:07 a.m., the Brenner sisters sped to the meeting place by the merry-go-round, where the five other girls waited, and then their bikes screeched to a halt. "Sorry we're late, Jude," Kristi apologized, with a huff. "Our mom wouldn't let us leave the house until we got all the breakfast dishes washed and dried and put away."

"Yeah, but we washed 'em as fast as we could so we could get outta there," her sister, Barb, clarified, before blowing a big purple bubble with her chewing gum.

"That's okay," Judith Ivy returned. "Hey, did you remember to bring the radio, Kristi?" the group's almost eight-year-old manager questioned.

"Yep…got it right here in my basket," Kristi Brenner answered. She then held up her silver-faced Sony transistor radio for all the gang to see.

"Oh, good," Laverne Crawford remarked. "We

have so much more fun when we have tunes to listen to along the way."

Laverne then enlightened the group as to the demise of her former radio, which she had brought along on last year's mission. "My stupid brother busted my yellow Panasonic Toot a Loop radio that I got for Christmas on purpose," she submitted. "He smashed it with a baseball bat, just because I lost his new baseball glove."

"What a jerk!" Kristi Brenner blurted. "Tell me about it," Laverne concurred. "You guys are lucky to only have one brother," she contended. "Me and Jeannie got five older brothers…and they can be really mean sometimes!"

"Well, they're always nice to us when they babysit us," Samantha offered, in defense of the Crawford boys. "Yeah, maybe so, but you don't have to live with 'em!" Jeannie Crawford retorted. At that moment, all seven of the young girls nodded their heads in understanding, for they knew that brothers were never as mean to others as they were to their kid sisters!

"Did you tell your mom and dad what your mean brother did?" Darcy inquired, as she was always the first of the Munson kids to run to their mother in this type of scenario.

"Yeah, but with nine kids in the house, they pretty much just tell us to fight our own battles," Laverne explained. "So, now I have to save up all my allowance to buy a new radio," she heavily sighed, throwing her hands in the air. "That'll take months!"

"Man, what a drag!" Kristi Brenner remarked, just before she saw her brother and Judy's brother screeching down the street towards them on their bicycles.

Since Keith had no pressing plans that Saturday, he decided to pitch in for the Stone Valley cleanup, just as long as his best friend, Kevin Brenner (12), could come along too, so that he wouldn't be the only boy in the group.

"It could be fun," Keith surmised, in an attempt to entice his buddy. "Maybe we'll even find some neat stuff along the way," the 9-1/2-year-old scavenger asserted. "I have a really neat agate collection," Keith added, "so let's be on the lookout for those."

With the larger task force of nine that year, these reapers of rubbish were able to collect twice the debris in half the time, thus finishing their job even earlier than expected. At 12:20 p.m., they called the operation, at which time they elected to relax and enjoy their sack lunches on top of Stone Valley's water tower, erected into the side of the bluff just beyond the Brenner house, on the north end of town.

The nine youngsters (seven girls and two boys) ditched their bikes at the curb and started on foot through the slush and slop of the changing Minnesota seasons during the early weeks of April. Up the steep hill they climbed, with Samantha Munson pulling up the rear. "You guys, wait up!" she wailed, after she had fallen and slid back several feet, soaking her pants both at the knees and on her bottom.

"Don't worry, I got her!" Laverne Crawford assured the others. "Here, grab my hand, Samantha," she instructed the little girl, who was about to turn six in just a couple of weeks. The soggy stragglers ventured to the top of the hill together, where they met up with the rest of the group for their well-deserved lunch break.

Kevin Brenner and Keith Munson were already halfway into their bologna and ham-n-cheese sandwiches, sitting clear across the other side of the flat cemented water tank, while the seven girls sat cross-legged in a large circle.

The women were just starting to open their brown bags when Kristi Brenner announced, "Good thing I grabbed this from my basket before we hiked all the way up here." She then exposed her transistor radio, which had been tucked deep inside the pocket of her raincoat.

"All right!" Judith Ivy exclaimed, with a clap of her hands, as she munched on a couple of crunchy corn chips. "Now we got tunes!"

Kristi adjusted the radio dial until she found a clear station. She then traded her egg salad sandwich for Judy's peanut butter and jelly. At the same time, Barb Brenner traded her Hostess Twinkie for Jeannie Crawford's cupcake.

The Munson girls couldn't help but salivate at the

sight of their friends' luscious dessert treats. The only sweets the Munson children had at their house were usually generic cookies (unless their mother had a coupon), aside from the occasional homemade chocolate chip cookies or brownies, and their birthday cakes, but that was about it.

Although they used to beg for those popular, expensive cake treats and name-brand cookies in the pretty packages during their many grocery shopping trips with Mom, the Munson kids learned early on that it was a waste of time and energy, for those items were prohibited...and Mrs. Munson rarely deviated from her strict policies.

Whenever the children got a yearning for a Hostess Twinkie, Ho Ho, or a pink Sno Ball, their mother always issued the same response: "If you kids want those expensive goodies, you'll have to buy them with your own money!" Fifty cents per week, per child, for allowance didn't go very far in 1973, so that's all there was to that.

In addition, Katie Munson purchased just one 8-pack of bottled Dr. Pepper soda at the market each week, which her four children had to share. Therefore, each child was allotted only two 16-ounce bottles of soda pop per week.

Mrs. Munson's stand against sugary sweets and soda proved triumphant, however, in her yearly savings on dental bills. While she had good dental insurance through her employer (the Lumberton

Community College), any additional expenses, outside of the two covered examinations per child, per year, had to be paid out of pocket.

Fortunately, thanks to Katie's diligence, all four of her children had remarkably healthy teeth, in comparison to their peers, as they rarely encountered cavities, and none of them ever required braces or orthodontic treatments.

As Laverne Crawford chomped away on her big green apple, she started getting some unusual looks from the two Brenner girls. "She's eating the apple core," Barb Brenner loudly whispered to her sister, while pointing across the circle at their new acquaintance.

Judith Ivy couldn't help but laugh, because she'd had the very same reaction the first time she saw her best friend eating an entire apple, core and all. "She always does that," Judy remarked, as Laverne ingested the rest of her apple core, including the seeds.

"That's really weird," Kristi Brenner commented. "No, it's not!" Laverne refuted, flicking her apple stem at the Brenner sisters. Laverne then pulled her long sandy-colored hair over her shoulder and barked, "My mom said it's really good for you and has lots of fiber, so...so don't knock it until you try it!"

"No, thank you," eleven-year-old Kristi rebuffed. "I'd rather eat my apples like a normal person," the dark-haired lass sneered.

Laverne took offense to that snide remark and

retaliated. "There ain't no such thing as a normal person!" the 8-1/2-year-old huffed. "Believe me...I have eight brothers and sisters, so I know for a fact that everybody's weird in one way or another!"

With an argument brewing amongst her friends, Judith Ivy, who typically played the role of peacekeeper at home, promptly improvised. "Hey, you guys," she addressed the group, "guess what? Our baby sister, Samantha, bites her toenails...and then she spits them across the room!"

To Samantha's surprise, the nearly six-year-old found herself at the uncomfortable center of attention, with all the other girls pointing and laughing at her. "Oh, yeah?" the agitated youngster sassed. "Well, my big-mouth sister, Judy, is mean...and she puts peanut butter on liver...blech!"

"Oh, now that's really gross!" Barb Brenner reacted, holding her hand over her mouth in repugnance. The ten-year-old brunette then made a gagging noise and vomiting motion to demonstrate her point.

"I know it's gross, but I can't stand liver!" Judith Ivy retorted, with a grimace. "I've tried ketchup, mustard, onions, everything...but that's the only way I can choke it down!" She then proceeded to explain how their mother makes them sit at the dinner table until their plates are cleaned. "One time," the eldest Munson daughter disclosed, "Samantha wouldn't eat her last piece of bacon, so Mom made her sit there until ten o'clock...on a school night!"

While the crowd guffawed at the two Munson sisters' bizarre idiosyncrasies, Judith Ivy shared a secret about their middle sister, Darcy, in an attempt to divert the focus of attention. "Well, if you guys think me and Sam are weird, get this…Darcy sucks on our bedspread while we're sleeping in bed at night."

All eyes suddenly descended upon the timid seven-year-old, who had just celebrated another birthday. "Yeah," Sister Judy exposed, "our bedspread used to be pink, and now it's half pink and half brown… talk about gross!"

Betrayed by her sleeping partner, Darcy attempted to explain her peculiar nighttime habit by shouting, "It tastes like cookies!" That statement got everybody laughing, all except for Darcy, whose face had turned beet red with embarrassment.

Poor Darcy Munson had always been painfully shy. In fact, she couldn't even walk up to the counter at the candy store on Saturday mornings to give the clerk her change to pay for her candy. Even now, at the age of seven, Darcy still had to summon the aid of her siblings to make the transaction for her, while she watched from afar.

"Man, your sisters are really weird!" Kevin Brenner declared to his younger buddy, Keith Munson. "You ain't kidding," Keith shamefully admitted, before spitting an orange pit over the narrow edge of the water tower. "I'll bet you a hundred dollars, though," the 9-1/2-year-old Munson boy propositioned, "that your sisters are just as strange, I mean...aren't all girls?"

"You got that right!" Kevin agreed, with a chuckle. "I can't even begin to tell you all the annoying habits my little sisters have," the twelve-year-old blurted. "Oh, shut up, Kevin!" his sister, Kristi, snapped, before sticking her tongue out at her big brother from across the way.

At that moment, and just in the nick of time, the midday radio news had finally concluded. The music quickly resumed, playing one of Judith Ivy's favorite hits, "Nice to Be with You," by Gallery. Judy immediately started singing along and shouted, "Let's dance!" while leading the young girls out onto the makeshift dance floor.

Within seconds, all seven of the squabbling females had forgotten whatever it was they had been arguing about, for the song's lively, joyful theme and upbeat tempo had overruled any and all contempt they might have felt for one another during their impassioned lunch break.

Contrarily, while their goofy little sisters and friends were frolicking around on top of the town's water receptacle, Keith Munson and Kevin Brenner became disgruntled, determining that they'd had enough of that scene. "Come on, Keith...let's split," Kevin asserted. "Right behind ya!" Keith returned, shouting, "I'll race you down the hill!"

The two boys sprinted back to town, where they

decided to get a softball game together at the ball diamond behind the Stone Valley Park. They first knocked on the door of the Crawford residence, where they managed to round up three of Laverne and Jeannie's older brothers. They subsequently recruited some neighborhood boys lurking around the swings and, thus, had enlisted enough ball players to start a game.

The girls suddenly found themselves with an entirely free Saturday afternoon, with no foreseeable agenda…and none of them wanted their fun-filled day to end. "Well, what should we do now?" Judith Ivy addressed the group, looking to her circle of sisters and friends for suggestions. "Let's just go back to the park and play on the swings and stuff," her sister, Darcy, replied.

"Nah, I think I've had enough of the outdoors," Barb dissented, "with all the slush and mud on the hill," she clarified. "I vote for playing inside the rest of the day."

"Sounds good to me," Judith Ivy concurred, with a proposal. "I have an idea…how 'bout we go back to our house and play Twister."

"Yeah, let's play Twister!" Kristi seconded the motion, and then the rest of the gang followed suit. The girls quickly collected their things and headed down the sloppy hillside to retrieve their bicycles and pedal on back to the Munson house.

The conversation concerning bizarre habits

continued during their bike ride home, when Judy enlightened her friends as to how their brother, Keith, would cover his milk glass with his hand at the dinner table whenever they sat down to eat.

"Yeah…and he holds his hand over his cup the whole time we're eating," Darcy interjected, with a sigh. "What a doorknob!"

"Why in the world does your brother do that?" Barb Brenner giggled.

"Keith said he's afraid that us girls will breathe on his milk and give him cooties or something," Samantha responded. "If you ask me, he's the weirdo, not us!"

While the girls were scoffing at Keith's quirky behavior, Kristi Brenner offered some insight into their one and only brother. "You know what our brother, Kevin, does that's really weird?" she gossiped. "He eats Bing cherries by the bowlful, one by one, and he stores the seeds in his cheeks, like a gopher, until he can't fit any more in there," Kristi howled, adding, "He looks like a blowfish!"

The girls continued to laugh and poke fun at their goofy big brothers for the rest of the trip back to the Munson residence. "Boys sure are strange!" Jeannie Crawford summarized, as the girls dumped their bikes on the lawn. "Me and Laverne oughtta know," she clarified. "We got five brothers at home to prove it!"

Kristi Brenner won the game of Twister, although she had the advantage, being the tallest of the bunch. The women then played an intense game of Monopoly, dominated by Laverne, and then the gang of giddy girls chose do some stair-sledding.

Although the Brenner girls had initially thought the others were crazy for sliding down those steep wooden steps in brown paper grocery sacks, they couldn't resist the temptation, and once they tried it, they were hooked as well.

When Mrs. Munson returned from her weekly Saturday jaunt to the Piggly Wiggly grocery store in Lumberton, she knew her children were being happily entertained, as evidenced by the amount of bicycles strewn across her front lawn, in addition to the high-pitched squeals and childish laughter emanating from inside.

Katie was most grateful for the abundance of helpers to assist her in unloading the trunk of her car that afternoon. "Hey, Mom," Judith Ivy inquired, as she grabbed a bag of groceries, "can Laverne and Jeannie, Kristi and Barb all stay overnight tonight so we can have a slumber party?"

"Sure, if that's okay with their mothers," Mrs. Munson answered. "But, I don't know how your brother is going to feel about it," Katie fretted. "Who cares?" her daughter snickered. "If Keith doesn't like it, he can lump it!"

"That's not very nice, Jude," her mother corrected. "Well, then," Judy suggested, "Maybe Keith can stay over at Kevin's house tonight."

After the children had gotten it all worked out

with their respective mothers, the slumber party was officially on, and the boys were soon to be gone, spending the night at the Brenner house. "Oh, this is gonna be fun!" the Brenner sisters rejoiced, for they had never been to a slumber party before.

As expected, the seven party girls had a wonderful time together at the Munson house that night. Mrs. Munson baked frozen pepperoni pizzas for supper. Later on, the girls popped three batches of popcorn, drizzled with melted butter, and then they took turns putting rollers in each other's hair during *The Carol Burnett Show.*

Katie hung out with the girls in the early evening hours, as she was very fond of Carol Burnett, her favorite television entertainer. During a scene in which Carol portrayed "Scarlet O'Hara," fashioning a dress from the drapery rod and green velvet drapes she had ripped down from the plantation house window dressing, Katie busted out in hysterical laughter, which started a chain reaction that got the rest of the girls giggling so hard that their cheeks hurt, their tummies ached, Laverne Crawford let out a loud snort, and root beer sprayed from Darcy's mouth, saturating Samantha's pajama top.

Mrs. Munson's happy laughter was, unfortunately, short-lived, as she couldn't stop thinking about Samantha's sixth birthday, now just a few short days away, and she didn't have any money left to buy her baby girl a birthday present.

Spring was always a financially difficult time for Katie, with all three of her daughters celebrating birthdays in April and May. Although it may have been easier for her to combine some of their birthday parties, Katie felt that it was important for each child to have her very own special day, with all focus on the birthday girl.

Therefore, in anticipation of the spring birthday blowouts, Katie empirically started putting money away from her paychecks right after Christmas. She always kept her secret cash hidden inside a coffee can, which she stashed way up high in a cupboard above the kitchen cabinets, far beyond the reach of any of her petite children. Even Katie, who measured all of 60 inches tall, had to stand on top of the kitchen counter or use a step-stool to get at her private savings account.

Earlier that morning, before heading out to go shopping for groceries and Samantha's birthday gift, Katie had opened the coffee can. To her shock, the can was completely empty! She panicked, for the last time Katie had counted her hidden cash (after Darcy's birthday party a few weeks earlier), she had twenty-six dollars and some change left in that old coffee can, enough to cover both Samantha and Judy's birthdays.

In her dismay, Katie first interrogated her children. They, in turn, stressed how they had no idea that their mother even had any stashed cash in the house.

Aside from the fact that her children had no

physical means to access her coffee-can bank, Katie completely trusted her children. Though they may have misbehaved from time to time, gotten under her skin with their bickering and childhood pranks, and even drove her completely bonkers on occasion, the Munson children were good kids who didn't lie or steal.

Only one reasonable explanation for the missing loot entered Mrs. Munson's mind—the new babysitter. Last Saturday night, Katie had gone out to dinner with a gentleman from her Solo Parents Club. The date was very last-minute, so she hired an unknown babysitter, named Betty, whose name and number she had solicited from an index card tacked to the bulletin board at the Stone Valley Post Office.

Although Katie's instincts had urged her to stay home that night, she reluctantly proceeded with the date. The 27-year-old mother now cursed herself for going out that night, for she suddenly found herself more than twenty-six dollars in debt, and with no money whatsoever to buy birthday presents for her daughters.

Even if she had wanted to press charges with the authorities, Mrs. Munson presumed, there was no way she could prove that the new babysitter had stolen her money. "What an idiot I am!" Katie berated herself.

Tears quickly filled her sad blue eyes as the scenario played out in her thoughts. What made it even more agonizing was that Katie had paid the babysitter five more dollars for watching her children, after Betty had already stolen her kids' birthday money. "That's the last time I ever hire a babysitter I don't know!" Katie wailed.

The following morning after church, Katie decided it was time to let her daughters down as gently as she could. Keith was already playing outside, setting up an obstacle course, in order to test run his assortment of army men, tanks and trucks.

"Jude and Samantha, come over here and sit with me on the couch for a moment," Mrs. Munson instructed. "I'm sorry to have to tell you this," she cleared her throat, "but, uh...I don't have any money left to buy your birthday presents this year. All the extra money I had left in this world was stolen from us," Katie lamented.

Her daughters hung their heads in discontent. "I know you girls must be heartbroken, and you certainly don't deserve this," their mother explained, stroking their golden locks with her hands. "You're both such good, sweet girls," she praised, with a sigh. "Unfortunately, the rent's due tomorrow, and after I pay the rent, I'm...flat broke," she admitted, sharing in their disappointment. "I'm so sorry!"

"That's okay, Mom," little Samantha replied. "I don't need anything this year anyways." Katie could hardly contain her tears, given the selfless understanding of her youngest daughter, who lovingly cradled and rocked her baby doll, which was filthy and missing half of its blonde mane, as well as one of its blue eyeballs.

"I promise I'll make it up to you girls...somehow," Katie avowed, as she patted their knobby little knees. "Hey, Mom," Judith Ivy hinted, "there is one thing we've been wanting, and I don't think it would cost any money at all."

"Oh, yeah? What's that?" Katie inquired. "A puppy," Judy replied. "Oh, no," Katie refuted. "I don't think we can have a puppy."

"Why not?" her daughters squawked. "Because a dog takes a lot of work, and your brother is gone every other weekend," their mother reminded them. "Do you girls really wanna take care of feeding, walking, and everything else that comes with having a dog for a pet?" Katie queried.

The girls quickly rescinded. "How 'bout a kitten then?" Samantha bartered, informing their mother that their next-door neighbor's cat had just littered eight kittens, for whom they were seeking good homes. "Okay, maybe a kitten," Katie consented.

Mrs. Munson couldn't have been more proud of her daughters and the manner with which they had handled this year's devastating birthday disappointment. "Come on, girls," their mother urged, as she got up from the couch. "Who wants to help me bake some chocolate chip cookies?"

"Me, me, me," her three daughters answered, in unison. While Katie prepared the batter mix, Judith

Ivy turned on the kitchen countertop radio, and the foursome soon made the best of a sorry situation. While the cookies baked in the oven, Tony Orlando and Dawn entertained the ladies through the airwaves, singing their number-one smash hit, "Tie a Yellow Ribbon Round the Ole Oak Tree."

Katie and her girls had a great time dancing around the kitchen, singing loudly to the lyrics of their favorite Tony Orlando and Dawn song (which ultimately became the number-one hit for the year 1973), while savoring the aroma of chocolate chip cookies baking in the oven on a cloudy, damp and dreary spring Sunday morning.

(In light of her daughters' impressive display of maturity and surprising acceptance of their financial hardship, Katie decided to make sure that both Judith Ivy and Samantha were rewarded with an extra special Christmas gift that year.)

When Samantha's birthday arrived the following week, in lieu of a birthday gift, Mrs. Munson allowed her daughter to adopt their very first pet--a small black female kitten with a white spot on her forehead. Samantha quickly named their cuddly little ball of fur "Petunia," after Grandma Sally's favorite summer flower, and with no dispute from the rest of the Munson clan, Petunia was warmly welcomed into the family.

The following month, when Judith Ivy turned eight, she didn't care about not getting a birthday present. All Katie's vivacious eldest daughter wanted was a big Friday-night slumber party, to which she invited Laverne and Jeannie Crawford, the Brenner sisters, as well as three more of her best friends from school (and Darcy and Samantha, of course), yielding a total of ten young, screaming girls under one roof.

While Keith sought refuge that warm May weekend in Huntington with his grandparents, Katie retreated to her bedroom during the slumber party, where she engaged in some rest and relaxation. The next morning, Katie awoke to find a sea of sleeping bags camouflaging her living room floor.

Judith Ivy sprang from her cocoon and greeted her mother in the kitchen with a heartfelt hug. "Thanks, Mom," the eight-year-old praised. "We had such a blast last night...and you know what?" the birthday girl asserted, with wide brown eyes. "I'd rather have a fun time than a dumb-old birthday present any day!"

During the hot summer months of 1973, Katie's 1958 Chevy Impala began to chug and backfire. Her reliable "blue bomber" was clearly dying a slow and agonizing death while also costing her a small fortune in frequent visits to the mechanic.

Mr. Wiederman, in turn, went in search of a suitable replacement car for his daughter during that Independence Day weekend, while Katie and the children delighted in the Lumberton County fireworks display along the banks of the Mississippi River.

Even though it had been terribly hot and humid

all day long, the Munsons were, unfortunately, unable to enjoy the invigorating cool night air that had finally descended upon the scorched city, due to the massive amount of mosquitoes that swarmed around the vehicle. All the windows, therefore, had to remain tightly sealed.

While the girls eventually drifted off to sleep in the spacious back seat, already donned in their summertime pajamas, Katie and Keith sweated profusely in the front seat of the old Chevy as they "oohed" and "aahed" at the bursting blooms, the kaleidoscopic fountains, and the star-like rockets that lit up the clear blackened sky.

"Those dodo birds, "Keith remarked, as he glanced back at his snoozing sisters. "They're missing the best part," he scoffed, as he and his mom anticipated the exciting grand finale at any given moment.

"Yeah, but that's okay…let 'em sleep," his mother replied. "Tomorrow they say it's gonna hit a hundred degrees, so maybe you could take your sisters down to the pond to cool off in the afternoon," she hinted.

"Oh, all right," Keith reluctantly agreed, even though he thoroughly disliked having to be responsible for his three little sisters.

"You're a good big brother," Katie commended her 9-1/2-year-old son, as she brushed his saturated bangs away from his sweaty forehead. "And don't think I don't appreciate all that you do for this family because I do," his mother expounded.

The Munson kids did a pretty good job of taking care of themselves during the summer months, with no school, and their mom working full time in Lumberton as a secretary at the college. Each morning, Katie left her brood a list of individual chores and provided them with lunch ideas (depending on what groceries she had in stock), which the kids had to prepare for themselves.

Katie's children were well aware of their boundaries, and they kept one another in check. Every evening, when Mrs. Munson got off work at 5 p.m., she couldn't wait to get home and start supper, for there was always at least one exciting tall tale from the day's events to be shared and cherished over the supper table.

The Munsons' next-door neighbors, the Conners (from whom they had adopted their new kitty, Petunia), had a large pond in their back yard, which the Munson children often used to refresh themselves during the hot and sticky summer months. This private oasis was nestled at the bottom of a grassy slope, which the Munson kids (and friends) regularly enjoyed tobogganing down in the wintertime.

Mrs. Munson was sincerely grateful to Mr. and Mrs. Conner for allowing her kids to regularly encroach upon their property, and they seemed more than happy to oblige. Since the couple's three children were all grown adults, they repeatedly told Katie, "We're just happy that someone is enjoying our sledding hill and swimming hole."

Although none of the Munson children knew how to swim, the Conners' pond wasn't very deep, so Katie didn't worry too much when her girls went swimming, just as long as their big brother was with them, since Keith had recently discovered how to doggie paddle.

In August, Keith and his best friend, Kevin Brenner, engineered a tire swing to the towering weeping willow tree that shaded the gateway to the algae-covered pond. With each splashdown into the lukewarm waters below, the green algae would separate from the activity area, creating an ideal target for their next launch.

After his third plunge from the tire swing, Keith staggered up from the murky water's edge, wiping his eyes and shaking the excess water from his blonde locks, when something suddenly leapt out from his short-sleeved shirt. "What the heck was that?" Keith screeched, jumping back about two feet in astonishment.

"I think it was a bullfrog," Kevin returned. He pointed at his little buddy and started laughing out loud, claiming, "It jumped right out of your front pocket!" The two young boys chuckled deliriously when they realized the absurdity of the situation.

"Hey, you know what?" Keith suddenly recalled, while rubbing his chin. "My grandpa told me that bullfrog legs are good eatin'."

"Really?" Kevin responded, with a disapproving grimace. "Yeah," Keith asserted. "He says they taste like chicken…and sorta like squirrels too…only without the gamy taste or the shot pellets," he convincingly added. "Maybe we should give 'em a try."

"I'm game if you are," Kevin assented. The boys spent the next hour trying to grab hold of those elusive bullfrogs. "Dang it! They're just too darn slippery," Keith bellowed, as another big frog jumped through his hands and onto the banks of freedom.

That's when his elder friend hatched a plan to catch those slimy amphibians. "I know," twelve-year-old Kevin Brenner deduced. "Let's try to spear 'em!"

Once they had located a couple of long, sturdy twigs, the two audacious young men retrieved their pocket knives from their cut-off shorts pockets and started to whittle the ends of the branches, creating a sharp point. After a few failed attempts, the boys had, at last, outmaneuvered those mucous mud-dwellers.

To their delight, the bullfrog legs tasted great, just as Grandpa Buster had said they would. Keith was delighted to have discovered a very tasty, natural, and satisfying afternoon snack, which he could access anytime, practically in his back yard.

His mother, on the other hand, was disgusted and appalled to return home from work to find her son frying swampy bullfrog legs in the same pan that she used to cook their bacon, eggs, potatoes and hamburgers. "Ugh," Katie murmured, as she vacated the stinky kitchen and entered her bedroom. "I gotta get me a new frying pan."

When Keith's eight-year-old sister asked to try his pan-fried concoction, with just a dash of salt and pepper, she enjoyed the distinct flavor of those meaty bullfrog legs. In fact, not only did Judith Ivy like eating them, she also wanted to learn how to catch those frisky frogs alongside her big brother...and she became a quick study.

All they had to do was make sure that their two younger sisters were entertained, and then Keith and Judy were good to go frog-spearing. They sat their two younger sisters down in front of the television set, served them each a bowl of Cap'n Crunch cereal, and then the girls were occupied for hours, thanks to those wonderfully amusing weekday afternoon programs of the early 1970s, including *I Dream of Jeannie, The Brady Bunch, The Flintstones, The Monkees, The Munsters*, and *Gilligan's Island*.

A few weeks later, on a foggy Friday evening in late summer, Katie was upstairs in the girls' bedroom, getting their clothes and various other items organized for the children's return to school in just a few short weeks.

Judith Ivy had, once again, inherited some of Keith's outgrown (but still wearable) clothing, while Darcy received Judy's hand-me-downs, and Samantha was bequeathed whatever remained of Darcy's previous wardrobe that was too small and had survived two or three former lives.

Mrs. Munson's youngest was excited to be starting

the first grade. More than anything, though, Samantha was looking forward to her first Goodfellows trip to the JCPenney store in December, and the opportunity to select a brand-new clothing item of her very own.

Katie Munson also rejoiced, for she would soon be released from the encumbering financial burdens of daycare expenses, now that her youngest would be attending school full time and then staying home with her siblings after school.

It had been raining on and off that afternoon. The skies were misty and darkened with cloud cover. The bedroom lamp was brightly lit, and Katie and the girls could hear the television set blaring from the living room below, as Keith sat alone on the sofa, anxiously awaited the airing of *The Partridge Family*.

As soon as Darcy heard the harmonic voices of The Partridge Family singing "Come On Get Happy," the excited seven-year-old bounded down the stairs and joined her big brother on the sofa for the entertaining half-hour program.

Just a few minutes into the highly anticipated episode, however, the television screen suddenly turned black, and there was no audio. Coincidentally, the upstairs lamp went dark, the house fell silent, and Katie's load of whites in the washing machine had stopped banging her clothes around in mid cycle.

"Mom," Darcy wailed frantically from downstairs, "the TV went out!"

"Yeah, I know, Honey," her mother shouted back. "Hang on for a minute and I'll be right down!" Katie hurried downstairs to investigate the problem. She checked the kitchen light switches and appliances, but nothing would engage.

"Keith," his mother requested, "will you go down in the basement and check the fuse box?" Katie had always hated going into the basement, which was nothing more than a damp, smelly, web-filled crawl space that gave her the creeps. At times like this, she was grateful to have a son who didn't seem to mind the long-legged spiders and cobwebs, or that old musty stench from under ground.

The 9-1/2-year-old boy obediently grabbed a flashlight and checked all the fuses, but none of them had blown. "The fuses look good, Mom!" Keith hollered up from the cellar. "Okay…thanks for checking," his mother yelled back, puzzled. "Hmm," Katie uttered. "I wonder what's going on with the power tonight."

The Munsons scrambled together, in search of flashlights and all the candles they could find, as well as matchbooks and their battery-operated radio, as it would be pitch dark soon, and there was no telling when the power would be restored. Keith suddenly remembered that he had a lantern stored underneath his bed—the one he took on camping trips with his den of Cub Scouts.

While the family searched the house for emergency supplies, the serenity of Stone Valley was abruptly disrupted by the frightening wail of an ambulance siren, followed by the alarming warning of multiple police cars. Katie and the children darted out the front door to witness the commotion.

None of the Munson kids had ever experienced such excitement in Stone Valley, so they were rightfully tempted to follow the flashing vehicles as they made their way past the Munson house, stopping just a few short blocks up the road.

"No, no, kids...get back in here!" their mother forbade, waving her brood back inside the house. "Don't you know that it's rude to intrude on someone else's misfortune? Furthermore," Katie educated her children, "the paramedics don't need you or me getting in their way, so get your butts back in this house and mind your own business!"

About ten minutes later, there was a disturbing rap on the Munson's front door. Katie quickly answered the door, to find a very distraught neighbor lady standing on her front porch. It was Mrs. Yvonne Brenner from down the street. The woman's face was drenched in tears, her eyes bloodshot red, and her eyeglasses had fogged over.

"I'm sorry to bother you, but, uh...can you please take my girls overnight tonight, Mrs. Munson?" the frenzied neighbor lady pleaded. "I really need your help."

"Of course, Mrs. Brenner," Katie acceded. The poor woman was visibly beside herself. "But, what's the matter?" Katie sheepishly inquired. "It's my son, Kevin," the thirty-something mother replied, through her tears. "He's had a terrible accident!"

Katie Munson gasped, covering her mouth with her hand. She kept quiet while Kevin's mother attempted to find the words to express her predicament. All four of her children soon joined them at the door, for they, too, wanted to find out what had happened to their girlfriends' brother, who was also Keith's best friend.

"He was playing with a stick, I guess," Mrs. Brenner sniveled, "high up in one of our apple trees in the back yard." She tried to compose herself long enough to complete her sentence, and with a gasp, she blurted, "His hand touched an overhead power line, and...and then he fell to the ground."

"Oh, my God!" Katie shrieked. "Is Kevin all right?"

"I'm afraid not," Mrs. Brenner lamented, shaking her head. "His arms are badly burned...and, uh...the amount of electricity his poor little body absorbed was just too much," Yvonne bewailed. "My sweet little boy is unconscious!"

"Dear Lord! I don't...I don't know what to say," Mrs. Munson stuttered. Although Katie barely knew Yvonne Brenner, she placed her hand upon the distressed woman's trembling shoulder. Mrs. Brenner abruptly pulled away, however, nervously touching her hand to her mouth, and then resting it on her shattered heart.

"My husband's riding with Kevin in the ambulance," Mrs. Brenner disclosed, before wiping her nose with a tissue from the pocket of her house smock. "They're on their way to the Lumberton Community Hospital right now," she added. "Anyway, I really need someone to watch my girls tonight, so…can you do it?"

"Of course, Mrs. Brenner," Katie consented. "Kristi and Barb can stay with us as long as you want," Mrs. Munson asserted. "We'll all be praying for Kevin tonight," Katie offered, "and please let me know if there's anything more we can do for you!"

"Thank you," Mrs. Brenner responded. She then waved to her daughters in the back seat of the car, ushering them to join her. Judging by the appearance of their sad little faces, it was clear that the Brenner girls were in shock and suffering as well.

"Come on inside, girls," Katie greeted, extending her hand. As she welcomed her daughters' grief-stricken friends into her quiet, candlelit home, Katie assured their anxious mother. "Don't worry, Mrs. Brenner…we'll be just fine."

Judith Ivy, Darcy and Samantha instantly surrounded their troubled, expressionless friends, taking Kristi and Barb by the hand. As the Brenner girls were escorted into the living room, Katie noticed how their mother seemed rather lost and out of sorts. "Go now, and be with your son, Yvonne," Katie counseled. "We'll all be right here, praying for him…until you get back."

"God bless you, Katie," Mrs. Brenner replied. Her hands trembled as she rummaged through her overly stuffed handbag for a clean handkerchief. "He just has to be okay," Yvonne wailed. "He's my only son… twelve years old…just a baby."

Katie then embraced the heartbroken woman, offering comfort. She let Mrs. Brenner cry on her shoulder for as long as she needed. When she was finished, the shocked mother collected herself, wiped her foggy glasses with her handkerchief, and then she turned away, fearful to face the worst night of her life.

Watching Mrs. Brenner saunter unsteadily back to her beige family sedan, Katie's heart weighed heavy, for she couldn't even imagine how the poor woman must have felt at that moment. As Mrs. Brenner drove away into the chilly, damp, gloomy darkness, Katie realized that this would be one evening none of them would soon forget!

Throughout the course of that long, harrowing Friday night, the Munson family learned that Kristi and Barb Brenner had been playing Tetherball in their back yard while their big brother, Kevin, was playing on the far side of the lot amongst their numerous apple trees. All of a sudden, out of nowhere, the girls heard the most gruesome, deafening scream of their entire lives, followed by a ghastly and resounding thump.

The sisters then sprinted across the lawn as fast as they could, only to find their big brother lying face down, unresponsive, and utterly helpless—a situation that had, until that moment, seemed unfathomable, as Kevin Brenner had always been extremely bright and responsible, so capable and mature beyond his years.

As critical seconds ticked away, Kristi Brenner stayed by her brother's side. During her repeated attempts to bring Kevin around, their youngest sister, Barb, darted into the house and alerted her parents, who had notified the authorities.

The next morning, while the six children were eating breakfast, Katie Munson received a telephone call from the hospital. It was Mrs. Brenner, calling with an update on Kevin's condition. The good news was that Kevin was stable. However, the wounded lad was going to be hospitalized for quite some time. Yvonne then beseeched Katie's assistance in keeping her girls for a spell longer, and Katie was happy to oblige.

The bad news, unfortunately, was that the Brenner boy was currently in the operating room, undergoing surgery. Due to the extent of shock, nerve damage and extensive burns to Kevin's left hand and forearm, the surgeons were in the process of amputating the necrotic limb, just below the elbow, even as the women spoke.

"The doctors said he'll have to wear some sort of prosthesis on his arm," Mrs. Brenner sniveled. "His father and I had to sign a consent form, giving the doctors permission to cut off our son's arm!" she squawked.

"Oh, dear Lord!" Katie bellowed. "How unbelievably awful…I'm so sorry!"

"We're not sure how long Kevin will have to stay in the hospital, but we don't wish to subject our girls to this sort of trauma right now…it's just too soon," Mrs. Brenner sobbed. "And they're both so young."

"I understand…and don't worry, Mrs. Brenner," Katie assured the grieving young woman. "Your daughters are welcome to stay here as long as you like," she added. "My girls and I will take excellent care of them…and I'll send Keith over to your house to take care of your dog, Coot, for you while you're away."

Mrs. Brenner thanked Mrs. Munson and then asked to speak with her daughters. Katie and the children exited the room to grant them privacy. While the Brenner girls conversed with their mother, Katie explained the tragic situation to her own children, asking each of them to remember Kevin in their prayers at bedtime.

Upon receipt of the alarming news, Keith Munson ran upstairs to his bedroom, slamming and locking the door behind him. He then shuffled through his collection of baseball cards in his bottom dresser drawer, until he located the tribute card of Minnesota Twins player, Rod Carew, which his best friend, Kevin Brenner, had traded him earlier that summer.

Then, to honor his best pal, the Munson lad pinned the baseball card to his cork bulletin board, hanging above the bureau in his bedroom, beside his precious moth collection and tiny jars of assorted insects. Keith vowed never to trade Rod Carew, or to clothespin that particular card to the spokes of his bicycle wheels.

Sadly, Kevin Brenner remained hospitalized for three unbearable months. During that time, the young boy underwent a series of operations, in which the surgeons excised skin from his inner thighs to graft to the burned areas of his arms as well as the amputation site, just below his left elbow.

The long road to rehabilitation included wound cares, prosthesis education and occupational therapy, in addition to the innumerable tasks that the twelve-year-old boy would have to relearn and accomplish using only his right hand, until reaching that point when he could fully master the use of his innovative left arm prosthetic.

While their childhood friend recovered in a far-away hospital in Creslo, Wisconsin, the Munson family went on about their daily lives as usual, but they thought of their brave young friend often and eagerly anticipated his imminent return home to Stone Valley.

Katie rewarded her children with extra gifts that Christmas season. In addition to a set of powder-blue footed pajamas, Santa Claus had brought Samantha Jo Munson a new Baby Tender Love doll, with corn silk hair and bold, clear blue eyes, donning a yellow dress with white polka dots. The 6-1/2-year-old beamed with delight at the sight of her new dolly, whom she readily named "Trixie," after the pretty blonde lady from *The Honeymooners* television series.

Kris Kringle also gave Darcy Lynn Munson a new set of pink footed pajamas, along with a Kenner Spirograph set, which would enable her to create colorful, unique designs and shapes. Inspired by the notion to make a special Christmas gift for Grandma Sally, Darcy selected her grandmother's favorite hues and shades of yellow, pink and periwinkle, and then she sat down and crafted her very first Spirograph masterpiece.

Judith Ivy, in turn, opened her festive gift box, unveiling a full-length lavender nightgown. She immediately slipped the appealing garment over her clothes, modeling her enamored gift for the rest of the Munson clan, to high acclaim.

When the applause died down, Mrs. Munson presented her eldest daughter with her second Christmas gift. Judy took her time opening the package, for she wanted to savor that unprecedented moment. The 8-1/2-year-old slowly tore through the red and white paper, astonished to discover a yellow Panasonic Toot a Loop radio.

Katie's first-born daughter was thrilled to have a portable AC/DC radio of her very own. It was the same model that her best friend, Laverne Crawford, had once owned and Judy had always envied. She unhesitatingly turned the radio on...and as Sonny and Cher sang their signature song, "I Got You Babe," Judy's heart overflowed with joy and love. From that day on, Judith Ivy Munson rarely left the house without her most cherished possession.

Shopping for her only son wasn't nearly as easy as buying for her girls, considering that Katie had just given Keith his birthday present in early December. Nevertheless, when Keith was handed the largest box under the tree that Christmas morning, his blue eyes grew wide with excitement, and he tore right into the shiny silver and blue wrapping paper.

The moment he discovered the Hot Wheels race car and track set, Keith Charles Munson became utterly ecstatic. The ten-year-old instinctively darted out into the kitchen and started setting up his own exhilarating racetrack on the flat hardwood surface. That was one of the best Christmases the Munson children ever had!

On new year's eve 1973, Mrs. Munson made a large bowl of buttery popcorn, and then she and her four children settled in for the evening, each of them excited to watch the enormous, shiny, kaleidoscopic sphere plummet on Times Square during *Dick Clark's New Year's Rockin' Eve* television special.

Since her daughters had fallen fast asleep long before the big ball dropped, Katie turned off the television set at 11:35 p.m., as she and Keith had also exhibited signs of lethargy, each of them finding it increasingly difficult to hold back the mounting yawns.

Katie was grateful to find that her daughters had conveniently passed out on top of one another, ultimately landing in a small heap. After covering the petite party poopers with the large quilted blanket from the sofa, she chucked a few more logs into the wood-burning stove. As mother and son stumbled off to bed, Katie proclaimed, "Happy new year, Keith," with a lengthy yawn. "See you next year."

Although she had been fighting slumber for the last hour of the television program, for some reason, Katie suddenly found it difficult to fall asleep. Even after saying her prayers and counting her many blessings, she continued to toss and turn. Katie then tried counting backwards from one hundred, but nothing seemed to work.

She eventually came to realize that her insomnia was probably caused by the anxiety she was feeling about the coming new year and her unforeseeable future. As she lay awake in bed during those wee hours of the morning, on that first day of 1974, Katie wished that she could just look into a crystal ball and see what the future had in store for her and her four young children.

Thankfully, wishes don't always come true. If they did, and a fortune teller were, indeed, able to foretell Katie Munson's future, the young mother of four would end up being sorely disappointed, for her life was about to take a radical turn...and major changes were, without a doubt, heading their way!

## Chapter 6
# Cat's in the Cradle

In the spring of 1974, right after the first good saturating April rainfall, Keith and Judith Ivy Munson headed outside at dusk with their flashlights and ice cream pails, in search of large earthworms and night crawlers, as they were anxious for the upcoming fishing season.

Keith had also decided that it was time to go into business, selling the slimy invertebrates for cash. The ten-year-old boy was planning to buy himself some new fishing lures, while his sister, Judy, had been saving up for a pair of roller skates, in the event that she didn't get some for her ninth birthday in May, even though she had been dropping hints to her mother for the past two weeks.

The Munson's large front yard turned out to be a rich repository for a variety of worms, and once the two siblings were satisfied that they had collected enough fishing bait to hold a sale, the team started constructing their sales booth, with plans to set up shop right outside on the front lawn, close to the curb along Broadway.

On Saturday morning, just as soon as he had finished his chores, Keith biked downtown to check out the Stone Valley Bait Shop. When he learned that the bait shop was selling night crawlers for ten cents a dozen, the adolescent entrepreneur decided to underbid the competition by pricing his worms at seven cents a dozen--a surefire bet that they would easily sell.

The ten-year-old lad speedily erected a cardboard sign that read: "Worms & Nite-crawlers 4 Sale—7 Cents/Doz." It didn't take long before the passersby took notice and began to stop and purchase a carton or two of fresh fish bait; and when word had gotten around Stone Valley that the Munson kids were selling worms so cheaply, they sold out their entire stock.

In order to meet the high demand for their less expensive night crawlers, Keith and Judy had to hunt and/or dig for worms several days after school to prepare for the following weekend sale. During dry spells, the sharp-witted siblings would turn on the hose, using the sprinkler to saturate their prime worm beds to get them to surface.

Keith split the profits with his sister, 60/40. His cut was higher because he had to man the booth and handle the actual selling of the worms. Judith Ivy didn't object to that arrangement, as she had more interesting things do with her Saturdays.

Charles "Buster" Wiederman had since retired from the trucking business last fall, and after having sold off the last of his dump trucks, he looked forward to this year's fishing season more than ever before.

Grandpa Buster couldn't wait to take his grandson out in the boat and teach him how to fish the dams and spillways of the Mighty Mississippi for the larger walleye, perch and northern pike that lurked deep within those muddy waters.

On the last day of school, in those first days of June 1974, Keith packed his knapsack and went to stay with his grandparents for an entire week. Although Keith would have to miss out on Sunday's "family day" event, it didn't bother him in the slightest, since the girls had chosen to go roller skating (Judy had, indeed, received a new pair of white roller skates for her birthday), and their brother had no interest whatsoever in going to the roller rink with a bunch of girls.

Now that Judith Ivy had her very own pair of custom-fitting roller skates, she found them easier to maneuver and perfect her unique style and dance moves. Before long, she became nearly as talented on the roller rink as had been on the ice, having coordinated many a speed race on the frozen pond behind the Conner house in the wintertime (most of which she had won).

The nine-year-old hopeful had her sights set on entering Skate Capital's roller-limbo contest, which was held every Sunday afternoon at Lumberton's adolescent hot spot, with a grand prize awarded to the winner each and every week. With just a few more practice sessions, Judy felt confident that she would be ready to compete.

Therefore, the next Sunday, since Keith would be away in Huntington, Judith Ivy convinced her mother that today was the day for her to enter the roller-limbo competition. Besides, it happened to be a rainy, overcast summer's day, so it was the ideal setting for indoor family activities.

After church, Mrs. Munson served up a hearty pancake and bacon brunch, and then Katie and her three girls were revved up and ready to roll on down to the Skate Capital roller rink. Upon their arrival, it was apparent that everyone else in Lumberton had the same idea, as the parking lot was jam-packed.

The game room and skating arena were unusually crowded, but that didn't stop the eldest Munson girl from entering the limbo contest on roller skates. Judy was thin and short in stature, but she was also quite nimble from practicing gymnastics and tumbling exercises.

At first she felt a little intimidated by the sheer number of girls who had entered this week's limbo contest (15), particularly since most of them were older and more experienced, but Judy believed she had just as good a chance as anybody else, and decided to give it her best shot.

When the limbo contestants were instructed to line up to skate, Judith Ivy Munson and the other 14 contestants rolled out onto the shiny dance floor. The house lights slowly dimmed, and then the enormous disco ball light was illuminated from the ceiling in the center of the arena.

Given the larger than usual audience, and her family looking on, Judy desperately wanted to win that competition. Her palms started to perspire, so she wiped them on her cut-off denim shorts. "I sure hope I'm small enough," she nervously mumbled. As soon as the words left Judy's lips, she let out a bridled giggle, for she suddenly acknowledged the irony of that statement.

After years of punishment, having been taunted and teased for being poor and small for her age, oftentimes labeled a "midget" or "shrimp" by her classmates, Judy realized that this was the first time in all her nine years that her petite, underdeveloped build might actually be an advantage in this particular situation.

The impatient roller girl couldn't help but fidget while waiting her turn beneath the sparkling disco orb, with its spectrum of brightly colored lights dancing about on the floor all around her. Though she may have been uptight at first, Judy soon began to jive to the thunderous music blasting through the speakers, which calmed her nerves.

Abba's new hit record, "Waterloo," her mother's favorite new song, echoed throughout the arena. Judy quickly glanced over at her mom and sisters for encouragement, and with a wave of her hand, as she was about to shove off, they all flashed her a "thumbs up" signal.

To initiate the contest, the deejay played Chubby Checker's "Limbo Rock." The first few rounds were easy, but as the limbo stick was lowered closer to the ground, the tensions rose. Katie, Darcy and Samantha Munson anxiously watched as, one by one, Judy's competitors either barely touched the limbo stick and/or knocked it off the supports, thereby being disqualified.

From an initial group of 15, the number of remaining contestants gradually dwindled. Ultimately, only two girls were left in the roller-limbo contest, one of whom was Judith Ivy Munson. The limbo stick was lowered one more time, down to just 22 inches, less than two feet high.

Grand Funk Railroad's new hit song, "The Loco-Motion," wafted through the speakers, and the colorful orbs darted to and fro on the floor, ceiling and walls. "This one's gonna be tough," Judith Ivy supposed, taking a deep breath.

Focusing solely on that large limbo stick, about half the distance to the other end of the roller rink, Judy sprinted from the starting point, gaining speed. Then, as she approached the low-lying limbo stick, she crouched down to her knees and extended her right leg straight out to the side.

While hugging her left knee, and tucking her head way down low, Judith Ivy rolled right on through to the other side. She did it! Judy had cleared the limbo stick! As the roaring crowd cheered and clapped, the proud lass skated past her family, acknowledging and welcoming their congratulations and support.

Her mother and sisters watched intently as the last remaining contestant skated up to the starting line. She was much larger than Judy, and at least twelve years of age, but she obviously knew what she was doing, to have made it to the final round as well.

Judy held her breath, crossing her fingers on both hands as the mature blonde girl, donning red shorts with white trim and a yellow "American Graffiti" T-shirt, approached the limbo stick. It appeared quite possible that her opponent might clear the rounded beam, but it was hard to tell with all the commotion from the dancing lights.

The arena became utterly silent, as the spectators held their collective breath, and the "Loco-Motion" song had just ended. A moment later, the only audible sound was the reverberating "clunk" of the large wooden limbo stick hitting the ground, after bouncing off of the girl's back, and then it rolled out onto the empty floor. The limbo contest was officially over!

Judith Ivy couldn't have been more ecstatic, for that was the first time she had ever won anything. The audience, in turn, cheered loudly for the young roller-limbo winner. The announcer publicly congratulated the young lass and summoned the victor to the concessions stand to collect her trophy. The kind gentleman then awarded Judy this week's grand prize--a large ceramic panda bear coin bank.

With the announcement that it was time to resume free skating, the deejay cranked another high-energy dance tune called "Hooked on a Feeling" by Blue Swede. As Judy skated toward the sidelines with her panda bank, eager to share her prize with her family, she proudly chanted, "Ooga chaga, ooga chaga."

"Wow, I can't believe you did it, Jude!" her mother exclaimed. "There were so many other girls in the contest that I really didn't think you could possibly beat all of them...but now I see what a great skater you really are," Katie praised. "Looks like all your practicing really paid off!"

"Yeah, Jude...you were out of sight!" her younger sister, Darcy, concurred, with wide blue eyes. "Really?" the new limbo champion beamed. "Gee, thanks, guys!" Judy exclaimed, feeling as if she were on top of the world. Delighting in the accomplishment of a goal she had set for herself all those months ago, Judith Ivy declared, "Now I know, Mom...if you really set your mind to something, you can do it!"

"Can you teach me to skate like that so I can do the limbo contest some day?" her baby sister, Samantha, beseeched. "Sure," Judy returned. She tousled her sister's dishwater-blonde hair and stated, "You'll be really good at limbo, Sam...because you're so little." Katie Munson and her three young daughters shared a hearty laugh, and then she treated her girls to a large order of cheesy nachos and a pitcher of root beer.

Judy couldn't wait to get to Huntington that evening and tell her brother and grandparents all about her roller-skating triumph. "I only wish Keith could've been there to see me win the big limbo contest," the nine-year-old sighed, during the car ride.

Keith and Judith Ivy had grown quite close since Kevin Brenner's unfortunate accident and lengthy hospitalization. Keith and Kevin were still the best of friends, however, Kevin didn't share Keith's love of fishing and night-crawler hunting, both of which Judy did have in common with her big brother.

As soon as they reached Huntington, Judy was the first one inside the Wiederman house. Clutching her panda bank prize, she threw open the back screen door and summoned her brother and grandparents. "Hey, everybody, look what I won! Come and see!" the lass exclaimed, placing her large ceramic panda on the kitchen table.

"What's that?" Keith asked. "It's a piggy bank," his sister answered. "Well, a panda bank," Judy clarified. "I just won it this afternoon in the roller-limbo contest at the skating rink...first place!"

"Well, isn't that nice?" Grandma Sally remarked. "But, how do you play limbo on roller skates?" she inquired, with a confused smirk. Judy explained the nature of the limbo contest to her grandmother, while Keith inspected the prize. "Gee, that's a really big bank," he blurted, with a look of approval on his freshly sun-burned face.

"You shoulda seen her, Keith! She was out of sight!" Darcy exclaimed. "Jude beat out 14 other girls...and most of them were even older than her," she asserted. Yeah," Samantha concurred. "Too bad you missed it, Keith."

"Cool," Keith replied. "Jude's gonna teach me how to skate like her so I can be a roller-limbo star someday too," seven-year-old Samantha gleefully disclosed.

Grandpa Buster was equally thrilled to learn that his little "Snuffy" had experienced such a wonderful, triumphant day. While Judy was still beaming with pride, her grandfather advised, "Now you'll have to work on filling that panda bank with coins, so you can save up for something really special."

"Like what?" his granddaughter wondered. "Well, I don't know, Snuffy. Isn't there something you've always wanted for your very own?" Buster inquired.

"Hmm," Judy pondered, before rambling on about all sorts of things she wanted to buy when her bank was full of spending cash, such as a new bike, a candle-making kit, an Etch A Sketch, and an Easy-Bake Oven.

While Grandma Sally peeled potatoes for supper, Katie joined her at the kitchen sink. Glancing out the kitchen window, Katie took notice of her mother's bountiful strawberry patch. "How's the berry business going so far, Mom?" she inquired.

"Splendidly," her mother bashfully boasted. "They've been selling like candy these last few years. In fact," Sally expounded, "your father and I are planning to expand the strawberry garden next year, so we can sell even more berries and preserves."

"That's wonderful!" her daughter declared, adding, "You always did have the best strawberries and raspberries in the county, Mom."

"Mmm, strawberries," Keith interjected. "I could really go for some of Grandma's world-famous strawberries right now, especially in a bowl with vanilla ice cream," he hinted, licking his chops like a cat that had just devoured a freshly killed field mouse.

"You'll have to wait until after supper," his grandmother rebutted.

"Hey, speaking of strawberries," Grandpa Buster interrupted, while helping his little "Irish" (Samantha) down from his lap. The children watched in wonder as their grandfather arose from his kitchen chair and then slunk off to the dining room, where he stopped at the record player around the corner.

Buster had the children's complete and undivided attention. He removed a #45 vinyl record from its red paper sleeve and carefully placed it beneath the stylus on the turntable. As the needle found its way to the beginning of the recording, Buster extended his hand outward, to his lovely wife, who donned a faded yellow apron and wielded a silver potato peeler.

"May I have this dance, Sweetheart?" he beseeched his beloved bride. "Buster, I'm in my apron," Sally objected, "and I'm all a mess from peeling vegetables."

"Ah, heck…a little dirt never hurt nobody!" her husband retorted, adding, "Just look at my dirty fishing trousers!" Removing the potato peeler from his wife's right hand, Buster took Sally's left hand in his, and then he led her into the dining room.

Although the Wiedermans had rarely spent a night on the town, and never went out dancing, every now and again, Buster and Sally enjoyed each other's company by swaying and gliding to one of their favorite old-time records, and sometimes even to a more contemporary ditty that the couple fancied.

Thus, when Sally heard the introduction to Buster's new favorite record selection, she couldn't refuse her husband's invitation to dance. After all, this particular song was all about her! Buster immediately started singing along to the fun-loving, cheery and upbeat tune, "Who's in the Strawberry Patch with Sally."

The Munson children soon started dancing around them as well, for they, too, recognized Tony Orlando and Dawn's popular hit single. Even Katie dropped her paring knife and decided to get down and boogie with the rest of her family, nabbing Samantha for her dance partner, while Judith Ivy and Darcy danced together.

Keith suddenly found himself in the midst of another impromptu dance party that even his grandparents had gotten caught up in. "This family is so un-cool," he grumbled, shaking his head. The embarrassed young lad skulked off to the living room and plopped down in Buster's rocking chair, crossing his arms, while the rest of the gang kicked up their heels and enjoyed the time of their lives, for the duration of the record.

Later that evening, as the Wiederman family dined on Sally's peppery pan-fried walleye and sunfish, lumpy mashed potatoes, and crisp garden veggies, the realization soon hit ten-year-old Keith that it was almost time to go home for another long week in Stone Valley, away from his grandparents.

Keith's gloom quickly became apparent to the others when he started to fiddle with his food, making zigzag patterns with his fork in his heaping pile of mashed spuds. "What's the matter, Oscar?" Grandpa Buster probed.

"The same thing that's always the matter," the troubled lad groaned. It was obvious that Keith didn't want to go home for another week and miss out on all those great fun-filled days of fishing and gopher trapping with his grandpa. "There's just nothing to do in Stone Valley," Keith whined, over his dinner plate.

"Oh, Keith," his mother intervened. "It's only the end of June, for cryin' out loud! You still have plenty of summer left to spend with your grandfather," Katie reiterated. "Besides," his mother presumed. "I'm sure your buddy, Kevin Brenner, misses you something awful."

"Yeah, maybe so...but he's starting junior high this fall, and I'll never see him in school no more," Keith fretted. "Well, then...that sounds like a good excuse for you to go out and make some new friends, Keith," his mother advised.

"I don't wanna make new friends!" the youngster

protested. When Keith had finally grown tired of complaining, he started to describe all the good times he had been having in Huntington with his grandparents. In fact, he made it sound so wonderful that his little sisters felt like they were missing out.

"Hey, Mom," Samantha inquired, "when do we get to stay at Grandma and Grandpa's house for a whole week?"

"Yeah…us girls should get to stay here too sometimes," Darcy squawked.

"No way, Mom!" Keith refuted. "This is the only time I can get away from my sisters, and I don't want them spoiling everything!"

"Well, it's not fair, Keith!" Judy chimed in. "Why should you get out of doing all your chores at home and get to stay here all week long having fun?"

"Hey, I do plenty of chores around here!" Keith retaliated. "Don't I, Grandma and Grandpa?" The Wiedermans nodded their heads in affirmation.

"Your sisters do have a point, Keith," his mother responded, suddenly finding herself acting as arbitrator in a heated dispute. The girls ultimately decided that they wanted their turns at spending some quality time that summer with their grandparents as well. Keith, however, was utterly disappointed with the new development.

When the summer custody debate escalated out of control, Buster had to intercede, serving as referee between Keith and the girls. "Looks like we've got ourselves a melluvahess," he declared. (Sally had always forbidden Buster from using curse words in their home, so her husband devised his own clever method of spouting profanity.)

After much deliberation, taking into consideration the children's desires, the amount of weekly Munson household duties, and individual weekly allowances, the Wiedermans reached a decision that would, hopefully, benefit the majority.

Katie ultimately arranged the children's rotations such that her parents could take two of her children at a time for a week, and then they would alternate, if they wished, with the second pair. However, the couple left at home in Stone Valley would have to pick up all the chores for the kids who were 20 miles away in Huntington.

Despite Keith's resentment and ongoing rebuttal, the decision became final. Starting the week after the Fourth of July family picnic at the Wiederman residence, Darcy and Samantha would take their turn at spending a week in Huntington, and then Keith and Judith Ivy would spend the next week, and so on.

The biweekly arrangement worked out remarkably well. While Keith and Judy enjoyed spending their warm, sunny days fishing and gopher trapping with Grandpa Buster, their grandmother appreciated the extra assistance she received from Darcy and Samantha when it was their turn to visit for the week.

Following a brief orientation, Grandma Sally

immediately put her two young granddaughters to work in her colossal gardens, tending to her productive strawberry patch, the diverse vegetable garden, as well as half a dozen raspberry bushes.

One cool early morning in late July, Buster awoke at 4:30 a.m., got dressed, drank a cup of coffee, and then filled his red thermos to the rim, leaving just enough Folgers in the percolator for Sally to enjoy a fresh cup when she arose. Buster cleared his throat and then quietly called up the stairs to his grandchildren. "Time to get up, kids, if you want to go fishing with me in the boat."

To Buster's surprise, Keith was already awake, dressed and ready to go. The eager ten-year-old bounded down the stairs before his grandfather had even finished his sentence. "You're sure up bright and early this morning, Oscar," Buster greeted.

"Well, I kept dreaming that we were going fishing, so...I just got up and got ready to go," the excited lad replied, with his sun-bleached, white-blonde hair standing on end. "Let's go catch some big walleyes, Grandpa!" Keith announced.

Buster tried to tame his grandson's wild mane, to no avail, and then he summoned his granddaughter one last time. "What about you, Snuffy?" Buster hollered up the stairs. "Are you going walleye fishing with us or not?"

His granddaughter glanced at the window. It was still dark outside, which made it easy for her to reach a decision. Judith Ivy bellowed back down from her mom's old bedroom. "Grandpa, the fish aren't even up yet!" She then rolled back over and fluffed her pillow, aiming to get some more shuteye.

The two men just shrugged their shoulders and sighed, "Women!" The early birds then giggled, creeping quietly out the back door, so as not to wake up Grandma Sally, whose bed was just a handful of footsteps away.

The die-hard fishermen returned home later that morning with their limit of "bread and butter" walleye, which is what Grandpa Buster called them. He maintained that it was best to let the little ones go, in order to grow bigger, while releasing the really big lunkers for the sportsmen, who liked to mount them for trophy. "Besides, the medium-sized walleyes make for the best eatin'," Buster reiterated.

Judith Ivy was seated at the kitchen table, enjoying some toast with Sally's delicious homemade raspberry preserves. "Mornin', sleepyhead," Buster greeted, giving his granddaughter a surprise whisker rub on the cheek as he brushed past her on the way to his breakfast chair.

"Grandpa," the nine-year-old groaned, with her mouth full of toast. She instinctively rubbed her chafed cheek, which suddenly itched from Buster's two-day-old, sandpapery, black-and-white scruffy beard scraping.

"You missed out on all the action, snoozey woozey," her brother taunted. "Don't you know, Jude?

You gotta get up pretty early in the morning to catch those walleyes." Judy answered Keith by blowing him a "raspberry," like the kind Archie Bunker often bestowed upon his "Meathead" son-in-law, Michael, on *All in the Family*.

When they had all finished their breakfast, Keith asked his grandfather, "Are we gonna check the gopher traps this afternoon that we set yesterday, Grandpa?"

"You betcha," Buster answered. "Just as soon as I fillet our mess of fish so we can have a fish fry tonight for supper," he added. "There's nothing in this whole wide world that beats fresh-caught walleye fried in your grandma's crispy batter coating! Now, that's some mighty good eatin'," Grandpa Buster affirmed, with a nod.

Both of the Munson kids were eager to go gopher trapping that day. Judy always went along on the days when they checked the traps. Setting the traps, however, wasn't nearly as exciting as checking them, as she got to hang off the back bumper of Buster's Scout and scour the farm fields for their previously set orange or red flag markers, and then she would jump off the back and race her brother to the mound, each of them vying to be the first to see if the traps had been sprung.

For years, Buster Wiederman had been trapping gophers for farmers in the Huntington/Ashton area. While he enjoyed the extra spending cash from his gopher-extermination business (which paid 50 cents per pair of hind feet from each gopher), the farmers were glad that he helped control the gopher population and the bumpy mounds of dirt that the pesky little rodents left behind in their hay and alfalfa fields.

Grandpa Buster gladly accepted the extra help from the kids. All Buster really had to do was drive the Scout, set the traps, and amputate the dead gophers' hind feet with his pruning shears. His grandchildren did the rest.

While Keith had become skilled at digging the holes in the mounds, in which the traps were placed, his sister was blessed with eagle-eye vision, giving Judy the ability to spot the bright flags that marked their traps from far across the field.

Although the Munson boy was the faster runner, he would search his sister's eyes during the bumpy ride on the back of their grandfather's Scout, in an effort to determine which direction she would run next; and once Judy jumped off the back bumper and was in full sprint, Keith was in hot pursuit, racing his sister to the bright red flag.

Buster got quite a kick out of watching his grandchildren compete to be the first to report, "We got one, Grandpa!" Keith would remove the fork traps with the dead gophers, and then his sister would check each rodent's cheek pockets. Judy was always curious to see what the little critters might be stashing in those pouches.

On one occasion, she had discovered a whole

peanut (in the shell) inside the pocket of a gopher, and another time Judy found a dime inside a gopher's pouch, which her grandpa graciously let her keep.

When the parched, dusty gopher trappers returned home with an extra $3.50 to contribute to the household budget, they found Sally to be up to her knee socks in laundry. She was busy hanging one load of linens on the clothesline, while another load of darks and denims agitated in the washing machine in the basement.

"There's some ice-cold lemonade in the pitcher in the fridge, if you're thirsty," Sally announced. Buster kissed his wife on the cheek while she struggled with a stubborn clothespin in the hot July afternoon sun. "That's just what the doctor ordered," he responded. The children wasted no time darting into the house for a refreshing drink.

Before following his helpers into the house, Buster removed the cash from the pocket of his faded blue denim overalls, under which he wore nothing but his mid-summer deep bronze tan, an eagle tattoo on the biceps of his right arm, and a red rose with the name "Sally" imprinted on his upper left arm, near his heart.

Using his forearm, he wiped the gritty sweat from his forehead and readily handed the $3.50 over to his beloved wife so that Sally could add the day's earnings to their petty cash fund, which would be used for the week's groceries. The additional gopher income certainly came in handy, with the extra mouths to feed all summer long.

When Grandma Sally joined the gang inside for a cool glass of lemonade, which her thoughtful grand-daughter had already set out for her, the kids happily shared their news of the day's adventure. Sally couldn't help but notice how tired the men appeared after a full day of fishing and gopher trapping in the sweltering July heat.

"I've got the fish fillets soaking in saltwater," Sally noted, "but it looks like I'll need some more flour to make my coating for the fish fry tonight, so Judy and I will have to make a trip to the grocery store while you boys take your afternoon naps."

"Hey, Grandma," Judy volunteered, "since you've got all that laundry to do today, why don't you let me get the groceries for you?"

"Well, that's very sweet of you to offer, dear," her grandmother replied. Sally was more than grateful for the help, yet she was still a little reluctant. "Are you sure you can handle the grocery shopping all by your-self?" she queried.

"I'm nine now, Grandma, remember?" the confident little lass reminded Sally, holding her hand on her hip in a feisty manner.

"Oh, yes," Sally answered. "I'd forgotten what a grown up little lady you are now," she reconsidered. "I would love for you to do the grocery shopping for me today, Judy...and thank you." Grandma Sally drank her last sip of lemonade and added, "I'll have my shopping list ready for you in a jiffy."

While Buster snored away on his canvas cot, and Keith was sprawled out on the living room davenport, Sally sent Judy to the market, located three blocks up the street, with her grocery list and collapsible canvas cart on wheels. "Now, are you sure you can handle the grocery shopping all by yourself?" her grandmother asked one last time. "That's quite a hefty list I gave you."

"No sweat, Grandma!" the convincing young lady affirmed. "I've gone grocery shopping with Mom hundreds of times, so don't worry…I can do it!"

Everything was going just fine at Glover's Grocery until she got to the bottom of her grandmother's lengthy list. Judy had some trouble finding "Mama Vitale's _____ (something)," scribbled in smeared pencil lead and written in Sally's old-fashioned cursive handwriting. Thus, being the resourceful young girl that she was, Judy asked the store clerk for assistance.

"Hmm," Mr. Glover wondered aloud. "I believe this is a brand of hair tonic," he stated, and then he left to retrieve the item from the top shelf for the petite lass. Sally's little helper then proceeded to the checkout counter, where Mr. Glover gladly helped Judy reload the two dozen or so items into the familiar beige canvas tote-along on wheels.

Judith Ivy was so proud of herself for completing this all-important task for her grandmother, who cooked them such wonderful homemade, scrumptious recipes (which the Munson kids greatly favored over their mother's time-crunched meals, which basically consisted of pre-packaged and canned foods, or whatever could be thrown together in a frying or sauce pan, or baked on a cookie sheet).

During her walk back to the house, Judy stepped lively, her tan bare feet making sure to avoid the cracks in the sidewalk, as she didn't want to "break her mother's back," all the while singing Elton John's hit song, "Crocodile Rock," which had been stuck inside her head ever since she heard it on the radio that morning when she awoke.

Grandma Sally greeted Judy at the back door and helped her heave the nearly full tote cart into the house. After the women had unloaded the cart, Sally meticulously checked off each item on the list against its price on the receipt. Since she was familiar with the cost of most items at Glover's Grocery, Mrs. Wiederman would know right away if something were amiss.

"What's this stuff?" Sally asked her granddaughter, holding up the bottle of hair tonic. "That's the 'Mama Vitale's' stuff you wanted, at the bottom of the list," Judy answered, pointing to the smeared pencil scribbling.

At that moment, Grandpa Buster awakened from his nap and took his rightful place at the kitchen table. "Uh, Buster," his wife addressed, "look what Judy brought home from the grocery store." Grandma Sally held up a clear plastic bottle filled with a yellowish thick fluid, for her husband's perusal.

"Hmm, let me see that," Buster responded, searching his shirt pocket for his black-framed bifocal reading glasses. "Vitalis hair tonic," he read aloud. The corners of his mouth quickly turned up, as he tried to hold back a grin, but it was no use…a snicker had, indeed, gotten away from him.

"What? What's the matter?" their granddaughter fretted. "Didn't I get the right stuff?" After a moment of silence, Judith Ivy demanded an explanation.

"Well, I don't think so, dear," her grandmother returned. "What I had written down on the list was Mama Vitale's spaghetti sauce in a can."

"Oh, no! I'm sorry, Grandma," Judy apologized, her face suddenly flushing as red as last week's sunburn. Feeling embarrassed that she had goofed up her very first shopping trip all by herself, the youngster attempted to explain the mix-up: "Well, I couldn't read it very well…it was all smudged…and Mr. Glover helped find it for me, so it's not <u>all</u> my fault," the nine-year-old contended.

As the excuses poured out from Judy's dry, cracked, sun-beaten lips, her grandparents tried to conceal their laughter, but they couldn't hold back any longer. They decided it was time to let their granddaughter off the hook so that she didn't think she was in big trouble for such a benign little blunder.

Buster and Sally shared a heartwarming chuckle, which greatly eased the humiliation Judith Ivy was feeling…until Keith had to add his two cents. "What a dope!" he teased his sister. "Leave it to Judy to get hair tonic instead of spaghetti sauce."

Grandma Sally reprimanded her grandson, while paying her granddaughter a compliment at the same time. "Anybody could have made the same mistake," she reasoned. "Besides, Judy did a wonderful job getting everything else on the list."

While Sally was putting away the rest of the items in the cupboard, she declared, "As a matter of fact, I think I'll have you get the groceries for me from now on, if you want to, Judy. That would really help me out a lot."

Grandpa Buster's eyeglasses fogged over, as he had been laughing quite a bit. He dried his watery eyes with his red handkerchief, and then he cleaned his glasses. "Don't worry, Snuffy," he asserted. "I'm sure I'm gonna love this here hair tonic...right, Honey?" Buster then winked at his wife, searching her pretty, cornflower-blue eyes for assurance, even though he had never used any such hair product in his entire life.

"Oh, absolutely, Buster," his wife affirmed, calling his bluff. "Um, why don't you go and put some of that special tonic on your hair right now?" Sally suggested, in an effort to make Judith Ivy feel better.

"That's a darn good idea," Buster conceded. "I think I'll do just that!" He got up and walked right over to the mirrored medicine cabinet in the bathroom. Knowing that he had two large brown, curious nine-year-old eyes watching his every move, the

63-year-old grandfather applied a thin coat of the Vitalis hair product to his dark, luxurious gray-tinged head of hair. After grooming himself for a few moments, Buster turned toward his granddaughter and shouted, "I love it!"

"So do I," Sally concurred, while admiring her handsome husband of 43 years. At that moment, Judy's frown had turned upside down. Sally then took a seat beside her relieved granddaughter and gave her some of the best advice the young lass would ever receive. "You know what, Judy?" her grandmother counseled. "Sometimes, the greatest things in life happen through mistakes."

While Grandma Sally prepared to make supper, Judy jumped up on Buster's lap and proclaimed, "I think you look very dapper, Grandpa!" She threw her arms around his deeply tanned neck, and then Buster gave his little Snuffy one of his trademark whisker rubs, which was certain to get the duo laughing.

Grandpa Buster then placed his hand under Judy's chin, turning her face toward his. He gazed deeply and seriously into his granddaughter's fawn-like eyes and uttered, "Your eyes are like pools…cesspools."

Sally was already starting to giggle, because she knew what was coming, once Buster had started talking about Judy's eyes. Her husband was always cracking jokes like that with their grandchildren.

"Oh, Grandpa!" Snuffy moaned. "Hey, you know who could really use some of that hair tonic?" she hinted. "Keith, that's who!" Everyone's attention turned to her brother, whose hair was still standing on end since early that morning.

"Did you even comb your hair today?" his sister scoffed. "Gee, you look like Alfalfa on *The Little Rascals*," Judy teased. That comment got them all laughing, including her brother, for it was a well-known fact that Keith Munson was quite lax when it came to personal hygiene, and he never carried a comb in his back pocket.

After helping Sally wash the dishes from their delicious batter-fried walleye supper, Judy excused herself and headed upstairs to play, while her brother and grandfather watched another boring baseball game. Judith Ivy hated sports on television. "Stupid Twins," she quietly cussed, on her way up the steps.

The Wiederman home was a virtual fun house for Katie's kids and for any of the 20-plus grandchildren who came there to visit. After raising five children of their own, Buster and Sally had collected oodles of fun stuff for kids to play with, which they kept upstairs in the hall closet so that the children could entertain themselves upstairs, leaving the adults to visit without interruption downstairs.

Among these large boxes of treasures, one could find all-time favorite board games such as Monopoly, Pollyanna, Parcheesi, Checkers and Chinese Checkers, as well as picture puzzles. There was also an assortment of army men figurines, matchbox cars and trucks, baby dollies, paper dolls, and a handful of musical instruments, including a small tabletop piano, an accordion, a harmonica and a kazoo.

The only time the television set was turned on at the Wiederman residence was for one hour earlier in the day, when Grandma Sally sat down for a break to watch her two favorite game shows (*Match Game '74* and *Password*), and during the evening hours after supper, when Grandpa Buster liked to unwind with his tobacco pipe and a baseball game after the CBS Evening News.

Therefore, the remaining hours of the long summer days in Huntington were spent doing chores, tending to the gardens, picking berries, canning and pickling tomatoes and vegetables, digging and storing potatoes in the root cellar, hanging the clean laundry on the clothesline, edging the sidewalks and mowing the lawn.

On the rainy days during that summer of 1974, when Judy wasn't gone fishing or trapping gophers with the guys, and Grandma Sally was too busy with housekeeping to play a game of cards, she would retreat upstairs, select a musical instrument with its instruction manual, and teach herself how to play. As the months passed, Judy had taught herself how to play the miniature piano, the accordion, as well as the harmonica.

Judith Ivy Munson had always been a fast learner. Ever since kindergarten, Judy loved learning, which seemed to come easy for her, and she quickly became (and remained) an "A" student in school. Her biggest problem fell in the "citizenship" category of her quarterly report cards, as the energetic, hyperactive nine-year-old liked to jabber during class, and so she was often reprimanded for her disruptive behavior.

Once she had taught herself how to play the table-top piano, and had actually mastered an entire song from the learning book, Judith Ivy played "Heart and Soul" for her grandparents. Her recital was so well received that it made her determined to play a song for them on the accordion one day soon.

During her next weekly visit, Judy taught herself a beloved melody of Grandma Sally's. It was a song that her grandmother had often performed for her family on their antique pump organ. When she felt ready for her concert debut on the accordion, Judy carefully meandered down the steep steps, with the oversized instrument strapped across her back, and found her grandparents and brother relaxing with a bowl of vanilla ice cream, topped with either fresh tart strawberries or robust walnuts.

Her heart began to race with anticipation, for Judy couldn't wait to surprise her grandmother with this particular performance.

As soon as she played the first few chords from "Red River Valley," Sally gasped, setting her ice cream bowl down on the metal TV tray in front of her red rocking chair. She placed her hand over her heart, listening intently as her granddaughter serenaded her with the treasured tune. Sally's eyes grew misty with delight. She reached into the pocket of her yellow dress and removed a handkerchief to wipe her nose.

The following Sunday morning, when they arrived home from church, Grandma Sally and Judith Ivy played "Red River Valley" together, with Judy squeezing heartily on the accordion, and Sally pumping and pounding away at the keys on her majestic pump organ, while pouring her heart out vocally at the same time.

By the end of that enjoyable summer of 1974, Judy had taught herself to play all three musical instruments, wrapping up her last concert of the season with a presentation of "Beautiful Dreamer" on the harmonica.

Buster and Sally could not have been more proud of their nine-year-old granddaughter, who had learned to play three instruments without a single lesson. They were so pleased, in fact, that they occasionally persuaded Judith Ivy to entertain relatives and guests during Wiederman family functions and holiday get-togethers.

The end of August came much too soon, but Judy was excited to get back to Stone Valley and see her friends again, as she had missed them all week long. At the same time, however, she felt a bit melancholy, knowing that she would only get to see her grandparents on weekends, holidays and birthdays, until next summer rolled around.

As usual, Keith returned home in a grumpy mood, facing another long, boring school year in less than two short weeks, particularly since his best friend, Kevin Brenner, was about to start the seventh grade and, thus, would have to be bussed all the way to Lumberton Junior High School.

Poor Keith was feeling left behind, as he was just starting the fifth grade, so it would be two long years before he and Kevin would attend the same school together again. The Munson boy's only comfort was that he had one more week to hang out with his childhood pal, and the Labor Day weekend was coming soon, so he would have one last fun-filled weekend to spend in Huntington with his grandparents.

Since the Munson children had spent an equal amount of weeks in Huntington that summer, Katie insisted that all four of the kids stay home for the final week of the summer, to ensure that there would be no arguing about fairness, which seemed to be the major cause of unrest with her kids. Besides, things had gotten terribly behind at home with chores and projects that Katie wanted help with, and the kids needed new clothes and supplies for the new school year.

Now that the Munson children were all back together again under one roof, after three months of separation, Darcy and Samantha had tons of news to share with Keith and Judy, and vice versa. The reunited sisters, in particular, had plenty to discuss concerning their neighborhood friends, as well as boasting about special memories of their biweekly adventures with Grandma and Grandpa.

While her children were upstairs unpacking and catching up on the town gossip, Mrs. Munson was in the kitchen, wrestling with some very unsettling information that was sure to break their hearts. Katie had been apprised of this disturbing development nearly a month before, but now the time had come for her to break her silence. She summoned her inner strength and called her children downstairs.

Once she had gotten her brood settled down, Mrs. Munson lined up the kids on the living room sofa, tallest to smallest. She absolutely dreaded having to inform her children of the shocking letter she had received at the end of last month, but as Jim Croce's posthumous ballad, "Time in a Bottle," wafted softly into the room from the kitchen radio, Katie found the courage to address the issue.

The evening sun shone brightly through the living room window, illuminating the summer highlights in her children's golden, sun-bleached hair. Katie suddenly noticed how tiny her young children looked, in comparison to that great big green couch. As she prepared to crush their spirit, Katie prayed for strength.

"Kids, uh...I'm afraid I have some bad news," their mother began, pacing back and forth, fidgeting and biting her thumb nail. "I received a letter from the landlord," she stumbled, holding back the tears that formed in the corners of her sad blue eyes. "Well,"

Katie sniveled, "you see…this house is really old and run down and, uh…the owner got an offer from the cemetery to buy the property."

The children dreaded their mother's next statement. Katie took a deep breath and cleared her throat before she finished. "They, uh…they wanna tear down our house and sell the land to the cemetery for more grave sites."

"What?" Keith yelped, astonished. The children couldn't believe what they were hearing. "So, where are we supposed to live?" Darcy bewailed.

"You mean, they're gonna bury dead people where our house is…and in our yard where we play with all our friends?" Judith Ivy paraphrased, as she started to cry.

"Well, eventually, I suppose they will," their mother deduced.

"No way, Mom!" seven-year-old Samantha snapped. "We're not leaving!"

"Now listen, kids…I know you're all upset about this," Katie explained, "and so am I…but I'm afraid we have no choice in the matter. This is not our house!"

"Well, why can't they just fix this house up?" Keith suggested. The girls wholeheartedly supported their brother's plausible solution. "We could even help do the work, Mom," the Munson boy volunteered.

"That's very noble of you, Keith, but this house is just too far gone," Katie admitted. "It's over a hundred years old and not worth fixing anymore."

"Well, it is to us!" Judy refuted. Their mother couldn't agree more. "We have to be moved out of here by the end of the month," Katie clarified, "which is less than two weeks from tomorrow."

As the interrogation ensued, Katie answered their questions as best she could. She then informed the kids that she had already found a place for them to live. "The good news is that we don't have to move very far at all, and we're not leaving Stone Valley," Katie announced. Her children breathed a collective sigh of relief.

"We're going to be moving into the basement of the Ferguson house, on the other end of town," she reported. The children had already begun to moan and groan, so Katie tried to placate them by adding, "Don't worry, we won't be living <u>with</u> the Fergusons. We'll be renting their basement apartment, so we'll have our own kitchen, living room and bathroom... and it's got three bedrooms and a private entrance for us too."

No matter what their mother could have said or promised, Katie's kids were understandably heartbroken. For the past seven years, that old white house had been their home--the only home any of the Munson children could remember.

While Katie felt relieved of the heavy burden she had been carrying, her children had only just begun to feel the sting of that horrendous blow. Judith Ivy stormed out of the house. She ran as fast as she could across the street, through the park, to the back door of the Crawford's ranch-style home. Judy needed to see her best friend, Laverne, in hopes that she might understand her frustration.

At the knock, Laverne's mother hollered for their visitor to come inside. Mrs. Crawford was playing solitaire at the dining room table, smoking a cigarette. "Oh, hi, Jude," she greeted, blowing a puff of smoke in her direction. "Laverne and Jeannie are in their bedroom."

"Thanks, Mrs. C.," Judy returned, with a snivel. Mrs. Crawford could tell right away that her daughter's best friend was upset about something. The Munson girls had spent countless hours playing with her kids under her roof, in addition to helping the Crawford women clean their house in preparation for the Crawford clan's enormous holiday family gatherings.

"Are you okay, Jude?" Mrs. Crawford inquired. "Yeah, uh...I just wanna go see Laverne now," Judy hastily replied.

Looking out from her own front door, Darcy Munson curiously watched to see where her big sister was headed, and then she, too, departed for the Crawford residence. Unlike her sisters, eight-year-old Darcy had always been rather shy and introverted, so she was grateful to have an outgoing big sister to follow around and help her make friends; and whenever Judy was unavailable, she had her sassy little sister, Samantha, to cling to, so Darcy rarely had to worry about being alone.

Once Darcy had been invited inside the Crawford home, she and Judy cut through the spacious living room on their way to Laverne and Jeannie's bedroom. The eldest of the teenaged Crawford daughters, Tammy, was painstakingly working on a "Jesus Christ Superstar" jigsaw puzzle at the living room table, listening to her favorite Carly Simon album and singing "You're So Vain" at the top of her lungs.

Judy had always admired Tammy Crawford's groovy style, in addition to her pretty face and long maize-colored locks, complemented by the yellow-orange-brown crocheted poncho she was wearing. The attractive teenager, however, was so engrossed in her activities that she barely noticed the two young neighbor girls as they paraded through the living room.

"Hey, Jude...hey, Darce," the Crawford sisters greeted their guests. Judith Ivy immediately burst into tears and plopped down on Laverne's bed.

"Oh, no...what's the matter?" Laverne beseeched, coming to their friend's aid and offering her a comforting shoulder.

When Darcy took a seat on Jeannie's bed, with her arms crossed and starting to weep, Jeannie yelped, "What the heck is going on, you guys?"

The Crawford girls listened intently as Judith Ivy and Darcy Lynn Munson relayed the information they had just received from their mother. "They're gonna tear our house down!" Judy bewailed. "And now we have to move!" Darcy bawled.

Laverne and Jeannie were shocked and upset as well, for they were going to be losing their closest friends and neighbors. Feeling like a rubber tire that had just been deflated, Laverne sighed heavily and re-marked, "What a total drag!"

"Well, at least you're not going too far," Jeannie acknowledged, after learning that the Munsons were just moving down the road. "We'll still hang out," she promised, "just like we always do." Laverne nodded her head in agreement.

The Munson girls felt a little better, just know-ing that they could count on their best friends to be there for them, both now and then. "Who knows?" Laverne asserted, in an effort to help her friends see the brighter side of this major change in their lives. "Maybe you'll like it there even better."

"Hey, does anybody want a Shasta?" Jeannie of-fered, hoping that some bubbly sodas might rid their room of the doom and gloom. After taking their or-ders, Jeannie trotted off to the kitchen to retrieve three cans of root beer and one lemon-lime soda pop.

While her little sister was on her errand, Laverne fired up her transistor radio. "This ought to cheer us up," she declared, as music had always played a significant role in the shaping of their youthful souls.

"Ooh, I love this song!" Laverne exclaimed, as "Cat's in the Cradle" started wafting through the speaker. "Me too," Judith Ivy concurred. "Crank it up!"

Laverne and Judy started singing along, mostly to the lyrics referencing the nursery rhymes, as they were really the only parts they had memorized. Darcy and Jeannie subsequently joined in the last chorus before the song concluded, and then it was time for some more local news, so Laverne turned the radio off.

While the four eight- and nine-year-old girls sipped on their Shasta sodas, they held a lengthy conversation covering a wide array of topics, such as the upcoming school year, gossip about their new third- and fourth-grade teachers, foxy Keith Partridge and his talented singing family, "The Fonz" from *Happy Days*, the unfortunate end to *The Brady Bunch* sitcom, the enticing and entertaining drama, *The Waltons,* in addition to the hugely popular, gory and heart-pounding *Jaws* movie, which they had all seen.

When those topics had worn thin, the lyrics of Harry Chapin's sensational hit ballad resurfaced. "So, what do you guys think 'Cat's in the Cradle' is really about?" Jeannie Crawford wondered aloud.

"Well, I'm pretty sure that it's a song about a dad and his son," Judith Ivy surmised. "You know...how dads never have time for their kids."

"Yeah," Laverne understood. "Only, at the end of the song, the son gets back at his dad by not having any time for him either. I still don't get all that nursery rhyme stuff, though," she added, looking to her peers for clarification, to no avail.

"Me neither," Darcy admitted, with a shrug of her shoulders. "Is your dad like that?" Darcy asked the Crawford girls. "Like the dad in that song?"

"Not really, but he used to do a lot more stuff with us, especially the boys, before his accident," Laverne shared. "But then, ever since he fell off that telephone pole, he can't do as much, and Mom says he has to slow down and take it easy."

"Hey, what ever happened to your guys' dad?" Jeannie Crawford asked the Munson girls. Catching them by surprise, Darcy looked over at her big sister, leaving it up to Judy to provide an explanation for that shameful situation.

Judith Ivy started to describe for her friends the disturbing events (bits and pieces of which she had heard over the years) that had destroyed their family all those years ago; and then she thought of an example to share that might help them to better understand their estranged father, Darren Munson.

"Have you ever heard that song called 'Daddy Don't You Walk So Fast'?" Judy asked the Crawford sisters, adding, "I think Wayne Newton sings it."

"Yeah, I love that song," Jeannie answered. "Me too," Laverne concurred, nodding her head. "I like the happy ending, when the daddy moves back home."

"Well, you know what?" Judy repugnantly responded. "Every time I hear that song, it gives me goose bumps." Intrigued by Judy's statement, the girls all moved in a little bit closer. Even Darcy was eager to hear what her sister had to say about that heartrending tune, which she happened to like as well.

"I remember one time when I was about five years old," Judith Ivy narrated. "We were all at Aunt Roberta's house for Easter dinner, and then our dad shows up, only he wasn't invited. We hadn't even seen our dad since the day the cops came and took him away after he beat up our mom...that was on Keith's fourth birthday," Judy clarified. "I guess I was only like two and a half, going on three, when that happened."

The girls took a sip from their soda cans and then waited impatiently for Judy to finish her mesmerizing story. "Anyway," she resumed, "I remember it was a sunny afternoon that Easter Sunday, and we were sitting at this really long dining room table with Grandma and Grandpa and all our relatives...and we had ham with pineapple, and scalloped potatoes, and that yucky fruit salad with the marshmallows...blech!" Judy grimaced, sipping her lemon-lime soda, which caused her to sputter and cough.

"Come on, Jude...don't just leave us hanging here!" Laverne blurted, waiting with bated breath for the climax of her friend's spellbinding tale.

"Well, all of a sudden," Judy cleared her throat, "a car pulls up and there's a knock at the door. A little while later, my mom comes into the dining room to get Keith. She whispered something in his ear...I guess

I wasn't supposed to hear it...but I heard her tell Keith that our dad was here to see him, and...well, heck, I wanted to see our dad too," Judy asserted, with a huff.

"That musta been kinda scary, though...huh, Jude?" Laverne presumed. "You know, after what he did to your mom and all."

"Nah, he was already married to some other lady by then," Judy returned. "Besides, it really didn't matter anyway," she expounded, with a heavy sigh, "because I never even got to see him."

"What? Why not? What happened?" the curious little women beseeched.

"Well, I was sitting all the way over on the other side of the dinner table," Judy explained, "so by the time I got up and pushed through all those chairs and people, I was too late," she lamented. "When I flung open the front screen door, all I saw was our dad's big red car driving away, with Keith in the front seat."

"That's strange," her sister, Darcy, commented. "I don't remember any of this."

"You were only like four then, so you probably just don't remember," her big sister supposed, with a sniffle. "I don't really remember much of anything before that day either, and I was five then," Judy affirmed.

Knowing that she was in good hands, surrounded by friends, Judith Ivy Munson decided to let go of all that pent-up anger, heartache and resentment. "My mom tried to stop me, but she couldn't," Judy sniveled. "I ran after that stupid car all the way to the end of the long gravel road…but he never stopped or turned around to pick me up, and I…I know he <u>had</u> to see me, but he just kept on going anyways," she blubbered. "My mom saw the whole thing…and when I got back to the house, she told me that our dad only came there to see Keith."

"Man, that's a really rotten thing to do!" Jeannie bellowed. "Yeah, it sure is," Darcy agreed, now that she knew of her sister's plight.

Judy wept openly on her best friend's light blue "Janis Joplin" T-shirt (which had been handed down by her older sister, Tammy), wiping her drenched, bloodshot eyes, as well as her nose, on Laverne's shirt sleeve. Judy half expected some resistance, but Laverne didn't say a word about her soiling one of her favorite tops. In that moment, Judy realized what a special friend and great listener Laverne had become.

"That's the only memory I have of our dad," Judy sobbed. Darcy crossed the room and sat on the other side of her sister, placing her arm around Judy's shoulder. "I can't believe he did that to you," she affirmed, wondering if perhaps it was a good thing that she had no recollection of their father. "Hey, you know what, Jude?" Darcy announced, nudging her sister. "We're better of without him!"

"The worst part of all," Judy recalled, wiping her nose on the back of her hand, "is that my mom said our dad was only interested in seeing Keith and that he didn't really care about us three girls at all," she bellowed. "Boy, was that obvious or what?"

"Well, look on the bright side," her friend advised. Laverne was seven months older than Judy, about six inches taller, and tended to see the positive side of things. "Hey, at least when you ask your parents if you can sleep over at a friend's house, or go to the roller rink, or go to the movies, or just go for a bike ride," Laverne expressed, "you only have to ask one person."

"Yeah, that's true," Judy conceded. "And our mom usually does let us do whatever we want...as long as we're not in trouble or grounded or something."

"Believe me," her friend contributed, "every single time I ask my mom to do something, she tells me to go ask my dad...and then my dad tells me to go ask my mom...and so on, and so on, and so on," Laverne repeated.

"Hey, that reminds me of that Faberge Organics Shampoo commercial," Judy responded, with a chuckle. Taking her cue, Laverne interlocked her arm with Judy's, and then they chanted, "You'll tell two friends, and they'll tell two friends, and so on, and so on, and so on." The girls suddenly found themselves giggling, and soon the Crawford girls' bedroom was bubbling over with laughter.

After slurping the last sip of root beer from her soda can, Darcy let out an uninhibited, loud and hearty belch. "Good one," her buddy Jeannie praised.

She reached up and turned her sister's radio back on, and then the giddy girls sang merrily along to Terry Jacks' number-one smash hit, "Seasons in the Sun."

Judith Ivy's spirit had been miraculously revived, and the tracks of her tears soon faded, right along with the memory of her father…for as quickly as the image of Darren Munson had re-materialized, out of the clear blue sky, Judy decided to bury him, once and for all. After that day, the subject of their dad was never mentioned again.

Later on that warm night in August of 1974, Mrs. Munson lay wide awake in her bed, listening to the heartbreaking sounds of her children crying themselves to sleep in their beds upstairs, still reeling from the news of losing their beloved home. A gentle breeze suddenly wafted through her open bedroom window, cooling the beads of sweat that had formed along her furrowed brow.

In an attempt to mask the wailing sounds from above, Katie listened to her radio on the night stand. While Gordon Lightfoot's "Sundown" lulled her into a more relaxed state, Katie couldn't help but fret over the fact that they had only a few nights left to spend together under that leaky roof, in the only home her children had ever known.

Undoubtedly, a new era was about to unfold. Although the Munsons were only moving to the edge of town, it may as well have been a hundred miles away, as far as the kids were concerned, for they would no longer be able to just dash out the front door to meet their friends at the park or the graveyard after dark for a chilling game of Starlight, Moonlight… or go tobogganing down the Conners' steep hill and ice skating on their frozen pond…or go froggin' in the springtime whenever Keith and Judy got a hankering for pan-fried frog legs for an after-school snack.

Lying there in bed, listening to the sultry sounds of "Sundown," Katie recollected the echoing laughter that often seeped through the drafty window panes in her kitchen as she baked chocolate chip cookies and whipped up heaping pans of hot cocoa to thaw the children's bones, once they had finally laid their sleds to rest on a cold winter's day.

Aside from the many joyous memories they had harvested from their seven years of living in that old white house, the move across town also meant a longer hike to school each day. While the Munsons were very active kids who didn't mind the added exercise, unfortunately, they would have to walk right past the gaping empty hollow at the outer edge of the cemetery, where their happy childhood home had once stood.

Mrs. Munson shuddered with regret as she held back the tears. One final walk-through to say good-bye, and then cherished memories would be all that was left to show that the Munson family had ever lived in that old white house on Broadway, in the far corner of the Stone Valley Cemetery.

The only positive aspect regarding their eviction, as far as Katie could surmise, was that, at the very least, they didn't have to worry about cleaning the place after the last porcelain dish had been wrapped in newspaper and the final cardboard box had been loaded into the back of her 1964 Ford Galaxy sedan.

The demolition proceeded as scheduled. The Munsons had left for Huntington early on that Saturday morning, to spend the day and night with Katie's folks, as nobody wanted to stick around for the inevitable destruction of their home. It was just too painful for the family to bear.

It was a cold and cloudy, positively gloomy Labor Day weekend. The demolition crew arrived at the cemetery at noon on Saturday with their leveling equipment, to include a big yellow bulldozer, various sledgehammers and crowbars, donning their most soiled denim coveralls, with either masks or bandanas tied around their faces.

Three of the younger teenaged Crawford boys were among the demolition crew members aiding in the annihilation of the old white house. Two of the boys had been frequent babysitters for the Munson kids, so even they felt a bit melancholy as they knocked down walls, extracted nails, and stacked up boards to haul away from the dilapidated dwelling that had endured in Stone Valley for more than a century.

After church on Sunday morning, the Munsons left Huntington with heavy hearts, for they realized that life would never be the same once they returned to Stone Valley. As she drove through town, Katie's children had never been more silent. The sadness and tension inside the car clearly resembled the dismal climate out of doors.

Although it was to be expected, the Munson family found the sight of the abyss at the outer edge of the cemetery to be most shocking, indeed, and the tears began to fall. The old white house across from the town park, which they had loved so dearly, was gone forever.

"We sure had a lot of fun in that house, didn't we, kids?" their mother remarked, in an effort to break the deafening silence, while holding back her own tears at the same time. Nobody uttered a single word for the next six blocks. Katie struggled to keep her composure as they pulled into the driveway at the Ferguson residence, their new home.

She parked the car in her allotted space, and as she turned off the engine, it seemed as though time had stood still. In that moment, Katie heard nothing but complete and utter tranquility. She hesitated for a moment, taking a deep breath before opening the driver's side door.

As the heel of her white vinyl sling-back sandal contacted the asphalt, Katie reflected one last time on the old white house that had sheltered her family through some of their brightest (and darkest) hours. Once again, she pasted a mental picture in her scrapbook of memories, taking a brief sentimental journey through the years.

Looking back, Katie Munson felt truly grateful, for she and her children had been blessed with scores of friends, neighbors and babysitters who had crossed the threshold of their front door...many of whom would never be forgotten, for they had left their footprints forever imprinted upon their hearts.

## Chapter 7
# Love Will Keep Us Together

The Munson children adapted to their new surroundings even better than Katie had hoped. They made many new friends in the neighborhood, most of whom they already knew from elementary school. For the remainder of the fall months, they were very active in neighborhood softball games and the nightly "kick-the-can" matches, which proceeded until their mothers hollered out into the cool night air for their children to come home and get ready for bed.

Since the Ferguson house was situated at the base of a towering bluff, the four Munson children, along with the three Ferguson kids, were able to enjoy sled riding all winter long, right in their own back yard. Soon the Munsons' new home became a meeting place for their old friends and new pals alike, who frequently gathered together for some of the best tobogganing in town.

Whenever Stone Valley was anointed by a layer of white virgin powder, both Katie Munson (downstairs) and Mrs. Ferguson (upstairs) delighted in the sounds of laughter from nearly a dozen children, for whom they routinely provided hot cocoa, sugary snacks, and nursing care for the occasional boo-boo.

In the spring of 1975, as winter's last snowfall began to liquefy into puddles, and the red-breasted robins were busy gathering twigs and straw to build tree houses in which to raise their offspring, Katie Munson started preparing herself for the conclusion of a notable era as well—her twenties.

Feeling the pressure of her thirtieth birthday closing in, Katie studied her complexion in the mirror, probing her face for the vaguest hint of crow's feet and/or frown lines. "When...how did I get so old?" she whined, to her still-youthful reflection.

For the first time in her life, Katie (Wiederman) Munson was beginning to feel old. Her kids were growing up so fast, and with her three girls' birthdays right around the corner as well, Katie realized that her children were no longer "little."

Samantha was turning eight next month, with Darcy going on nine. Judith Ivy would turn ten in May, and Keith was already eleven. "Where did the last decade go?" Katie wondered aloud, as she stood in front of her bedroom mirror, combing her long, shiny blonde hair. "I can't believe I've been single for..."

She set her hairbrush down on the dresser and counted the bygone years on her fingertips. "Oh, my gosh...almost eight years now I've been on my own!" Katie gasped, in disbelief. She shook her head and took a large gulp from her can of Tab diet soda.

As she examined her appearance in the mirror, it presently occurred to Katie that her youth was no longer something to be taken for granted. Perhaps the time had come for her to seriously consider letting a man back into her life...their lives.

In her past experiences, telling prospective dates that she was the mother of four young children had usually sent most gentleman running for the hills, but now that Katie's kids were more mature and self-reliant, perhaps the notion of seeking a long-term relationship wasn't so preposterous after all, she pondered.

Additionally, since her children were growing up so quickly, and she believed that they were mature enough to look after themselves when she went out on Friday or Saturday nights, while saving herself a bundle in babysitting fees, Katie felt much more comfortable with the whole dating scene.

During those early months of 1975, Katie had, indeed, gone out on a handful of dates with men she had met through various connections from the Solo Parents Club and coworkers at the Lumberton Community College. Unfortunately, not all of Katie's dating encounters turned out to be good ones.

On the second Saturday in May, a group of Katie's girlfriends from the college insisted on treating her to a night out on the town, in celebration of her thirtieth birthday. Their first stop was a pub in downtown Lumberton, where there was no shortage of taverns, with at least two bars to each city block. From there, the party of five did plenty of bar-hopping on foot.

Their final destination of the evening was the

area's most popular nightclub, where the women intended to dance all night long to the stimulating, heart-pounding rock and roll bands that played every weekend at the "Mississippi Belle," named after the famous river boat that cruised through Lumberton once a year on its voyage down the Mighty Mississippi to the Louisiana Delta.

She tried to keep pace with her younger dance partners, however, Katie was out of practice. The nightclub scene had never been a regular part of her life, and she soon found herself exhausted from all the dancing, drinking, ear-splitting music and cigarette smoke, not to mention the electrifying light show radiating from the stage.

Although she had been wanting to leave for the past two hours, Katie had no choice but to stay, as her friends were adamant that she make the most of this milestone birthday celebration, and they were also her ride home.

Finally, during the wee hours of the morning, Katie's friends dropped her off around 3 a.m. She unlocked the basement door and entered the living room. Locking the door securely behind her, Katie crept quietly to her bedroom, where she tumbled onto her bed, fashion boots and all.

While Katie Munson had never been in the habit of drinking alcohol, she was clearly inebriated, thanks to her girlfriends and a handful of gentleman who had purchased the cocktails and toasted far too many birthday wishes. Lying immobile, in complete darkness, Katie could still see the kaleidoscopic stage lights from the night club dancing around on the ceiling of her darkened bedroom.

Shortly after plopping down on her bed, Katie felt unbearably dehydrated. She sat up, steadied herself, and carefully unzipped the sides of her black vinyl high-heeled fashion boots, peeling them off, one at a time. Katie then swaggered into the kitchen, where she plucked a cold pink can of diet soda from the refrigerator door.

Before even popping the top of her soda can, however, Katie was startled by a firm, frightening rap at the front door of her basement apartment. She gasped at the racket, nearly dropping her diet soda. Standing completely still and breathless in the darkness, Katie hoped and prayed that the trespasser would just go away.

A second bold knock soon followed, rattling her front door, accompanied by someone yelling in a deep, raspy overtone. Katie recognized his voice right away. It was the same drunken man who had relentlessly hit on her at the Mississippi Belle. Although she had made it very clear to the guy that she wasn't interested, he apparently didn't get the hint, or maybe he just couldn't deal with Katie's candid rejection.

"Katie, open the door!" the irate man bellowed, as he continued to pound harder on the door. "I know you're in there!" he yammered, in a creepy manner, followed by some slurred inane speech, while hiccupping all throughout his gobbledygook.

"He must have followed us home, all the way from Lumberton," Katie concluded. That really frightened her because Stone Valley was about 20 minutes from Lumberton, which is where the strange man told her he resided. He had no reason for being there.

Katie didn't want anything to do with the scary intruder, so she yelled out from the kitchen, making her intentions extremely clear. "Please, just go away and leave me alone!" she ordered. Unfortunately, the interloper would not retreat.

"C'mon, Katie, open the damn door!" the drunkard demanded. When Katie didn't respond, the outraged man began to pound his fists harder and harder against her front door. Fearing that his intense hammering might awaken the children, not to mention the Ferguson family upstairs, Katie became very frightened, and she didn't know what to do.

After recalling some eerily similar instances from her past, Katie shuddered at the thought of what could possibly happen. For a fleeting moment, horrifying memories of former encounters with her ex-husband, Darren Munson, flooded her fuzzy thoughts...and then the telephone rang.

Katie jumped back, in reaction to yet another startling disturbance in the darkness. The alarming tone resonated like a siren in the middle of the cold dark night. The previously consumed alcohol in her system seemed to instantaneously drain from Katie's body, like blood flowing through an intravenous line, as she suddenly found herself feeling sober as daylight.

She answered the phone after the second ring, to find Mr. Ferguson on the other end of the line, calling from upstairs to see if Katie was all right. "No, I'm...I'm not, actually," Katie stammered, her hands still shaking with dreadful anxiety. "I'm really scared," she admitted, while trying to explain the alarming commotion outside. "He's just some drunk guy that I met tonight at a bar...won't take 'no' for an answer."

Mr. Ferguson instructed his terrified tenant to sit tight while he called the local sheriff. When she hung up the phone, Katie immediately ran to check on her girls, as their bedroom was on the same side of the apartment as the front door, and it had a very large window right above one of the girls' beds. If the drunken fool really wanted to get inside their house, Katie fretted, he easily could, one way or another.

Katie quickly gathered up her three young daughters and corralled them in Keith's bedroom, on the opposite corner of the house. The Munson children were now frightened as well, as they had never seen their mother so scared and out of control.

Once assembled on Keith's bed, the Munsons clutched one another tightly as the harrowing intruder kept pounding on the door, spouting obscenities out to Mrs. Munson. Ironically, that wasn't the first time the Munson children had found themselves in such a predicament, clinging to one another in absolute panic.

Sitting there in the dark, huddled together on Keith's bed, Judith Ivy was reminded of that summer in 1972, nearly three years ago, when the children had to lean on one another for support and strength as they weathered that horrific thunderstorm at a resort in Iowa during their very first family vacation.

Finally, after what seemed like hours, the sheriff and his deputy arrived, in two separate vehicles. The sheriff quickly detained the perpetrator, slapped on the handcuffs, and escorted him off the premises in the back seat of his police car.

The deputy, in turn, secured the area, checked on all the residents, and made the necessary arrangements for the intruder's rusty eyesore of a yellow Ford pickup truck to be towed away, at the owner's expense. Alas, the upsetting nightmare was over!

From that night on, Katie vowed never again to converse with strange men in bars or pubs, and especially not to let them buy her drinks, as they clearly expected something in return for that "free" drink.

Mrs. Munson had learned a very harsh but valuable lesson that night, on her thirtieth birthday. Consequently, she adopted a rule to date only those men introduced to her by friends, colleagues, relatives or acquaintances. Nevertheless, Katie Munson intended to stay home and take it easy for a while.

Once all the commotion had died down, Keith

Munson easily went back to sleep. His mother, on the other hand, was still quite shaken. Katie didn't want to be alone, and she was worried about her girls. Therefore, she decided to sleep in the girls' bedroom.

Katie crawled in between Darcy and Judith Ivy in their double bed. Samantha then hopped out of her twin bed and joined them as well. All four of the Munson women slept together that night, side by side, holding onto one another in a "spooning" position, which made them all feel more safe and secure.

It had been an exhausting night at the Munson/Ferguson residence, and so everybody slept late that Sunday morning. By the time the Munson women had awakened, Keith was already stirring in the kitchen, helping himself to a bowl of cereal.

Mrs. Munson closed the girls' bedroom door, as she wanted to have a serious talk with her girls about what had transpired last night. She sat her three dainty daughters down on the big bed for a little heart-to-heart talk.

"Listen, girls," Katie started, as she brushed their messy, snarled hair away from their sleepy eyes with her fingertips. "You're all such pretty little girls," she fumbled. Katie didn't quite know how to explain what she wanted to convey to them, but she did the best she could. "And…well, there are men out there in this world who want to harm pretty girls…or hurt them, for no reason at all."

The Munson sisters yawned and rubbed their puffy

eyes while their mother wrestled with the words to express her meaning. "I know you're only eight, nine, and almost ten years old, but I think you girls should know that you just can't trust everybody…especially men, because sometimes they can be really mean," Katie advised. "Do you understand what I'm trying to tell you?"

Although her daughters didn't fully grasp Katie's warning, after last night's demonstration, they definitely shared their mother's unhealthy fear of men. The girls were aware that their own father had severely hurt their mother when they were little, and the Munson girls themselves had seen or heard about some of their friends' dads getting angry and yelling, even hitting their kids and smacking them around.

Even though their own mother had spanked, grounded, and/or withheld allowances from her children whenever they misbehaved, the Munson brood unanimously felt that Katie's punishments were actually quite benign, in comparison to what some of their schoolmates had to deal with on a regular basis.

"Yeah, I think we get it, Mom," Judy answered, on behalf of all three daughters. She was more interested in getting up to use the bathroom, so the sooner their talk was over, the better. Samantha and Darcy nodded their heads in agreement, for the impatient youngsters had been doing the "potty dance" for the past five minutes.

"Good…I'm glad," Mrs. Munson replied, with a

lengthy sigh of relief. Katie then opened the bedroom door and excused the children, who scattered like cottonwood seeds in the wind as they blew down the hallway towards the bathroom.

(Katie's speech didn't mean all that much to the girls on that particular spring morning in 1975; however, her eldest daughter, Judith Ivy, would forever remember her mother's daunting words, as she would, unfortunately, one day come to fully understand their intended meaning.)

A few weeks later, Katie's older brother, Walter, and his endearing wife, Amelia, gave birth to their third child. With two sons, the couple were ecstatic to finally be blessed with the daughter they had so keenly desired.

Walter Wiederman worked six days a week as an insurance agent, while Amelia Wiederman complemented the household budget by operating a hometown beauty salon in the basement of their home in Miltgen, Minnesota, a small town not far from Huntington or Stone Valley.

While each of the Wiederman sons had arrived within days of their estimated delivery dates, Walter and Amelia were surprised when their baby girl arrived ten days early. After naming their beautiful bouncing baby girl "Terri-Ann," the proud parents invited all the Wiederman clan to come to the hospital and visit mother and baby.

On that Sunday afternoon, Buster and Sally

Wiederman, along with Katie Munson and her four children, made the trip to Lumberton Memorial Hospital. Katie couldn't have been more happy for her sister-in-law. "You finally got your girl," she congratulated Amelia, with a heartfelt hug. "Can we go see her now?"

"Sure, go ahead," Amelia returned. "That'll give me some time to catch up with the folks." While Buster, Sally and Keith conversed with the exhausted mom, Katie and her daughters meandered down the hallway to the nursery, where they cooed and swooned over their new baby niece/cousin. "She's so little," Samantha remarked, adding, "I can't wait to have a baby of my own."

"Oh, yes you can!" Katie retorted. "Real babies aren't like your baby dolls," she reminded the eager eight-year-old. "They're a lot more work and responsibility!"

When Amelia and baby Wiederman returned home from the hospital on Friday morning, in early June of 1975, she and husband Walter determined that they needed all the income they could get their hands on at that time, considering the extensive hospital bills that would soon be pouring in.

Amelia Wiederman intended to return to work as soon as possible. However, given the baby's early arrival, Terri-Ann's local daycare provider wasn't scheduled to start working until the week after next, and had already made plans to take her summer vacation the week after they brought the baby home.

Finding themselves in a bit of a jam, the Wiedermans racked their brains to come up with a way for Amelia to keep her beauty shop up and running next week. With the whole weekend ahead to rest, Amelia felt confident that she would be able to handle her clients by Monday morning, if only she could find someone to care for baby Terri-Ann from 8 a.m. to 5 p.m. while she was downstairs working in her beauty parlor.

That evening, Amelia called her sister-in-law, Katie, for help. Now that Judith Ivy Munson was ten years old, and on summer break from school, Amelia hoped that her niece might be able to babysit their newborn daughter the following week.

Buster and Sally had recommended their grand-daughter, relating that Judy had always been very reliable, responsible and hardworking whenever she stayed with them; and once her sister-in-law had explained their urgent daycare dilemma, Katie was more than happy to oblige.

"Yeah, I'm sure Judy would be happy to help you guys out," Katie volunteered. "Let me ask her."

"We would, of course, pay Judy for her time," Amelia added. "Oh, heavens, no…we wouldn't hear of it!" Katie objected. "Besides, we're family, and helping each other out during times like this is what family is all about," she asserted.

"Hey, Jude, come out here for a minute!" Katie hollered toward the girls' room. Due to the inclement weather on that wet and dreary Friday afternoon, Judy had sought refuge in her bedroom with the door shut, where she and her best friend, Laverne Crawford, were hanging out, listening to tunes and playing with the hula hoop.

Judy was unable to hear her mother's request, as her yellow Panasonic Toot a Loop radio was cranked to the maximum level. She and Laverne were singing along with Jessi Colter, shouting out the lyrics to her smash hit single, "I'm Not Lisa."

Due to a lack of response, Katie had to yell down the hall again, as she could hear the music all the way from the kitchen. Heeding her mother's second summon, Judy sprinted out to the kitchen. "What is it, Mom?" she asked, catching her breath.

"Aunt Amelia wants to know if you would like to babysit your newborn baby cousin next week while Uncle Walter and Aunt Amelia are at work."

"Really? Are you kidding?" Judith Ivy gushed, astonished that both her mom and aunt had so much faith in her abilities. At last, Judy's maturity had finally been acknowledged, and now it was clear to her that she was no longer considered a "child" in the eyes of her elders. "That would be so cool!" the ten-year-old exclaimed.

"But, next week is your turn to stay with your grandparents," Katie reminded the excited lass. "Yeah, I know…but that's all right," Judith Ivy replied. "I'm sure Keith will be on cloud nine if he can stay in Huntington next week all by himself," she asserted. "I'll just skip my turn and go the next time."

When she found out that she wouldn't be paid to care for her newborn cousin next week, Judy didn't mind. The ten-year-old saw it as a good opportunity to learn how to take care of babies, particularly if she wanted to start taking babysitting jobs and maybe have a baby of her own one day. "What better way to learn?" she speculated.

In just one short week, Amelia Wiederman had taught her niece countless care-giving skills that Judith Ivy would carry with her for the rest of her life. Among them, she learned how to change diapers, carefully pinning the thick cloth in such a manner that she would stick her own fingers before poking the delicate skin on her newborn cousin, how to check the temperatures of stove-heated glass milk bottles, using her inner wrist as a guide, in addition to sanitizing the rubber nipples in boiling water.

It was an eye-opening experience, indeed, for Judy had learned how to properly feed, burp and sponge-bathe a newborn baby, in addition to rocking an infant to sleep. These were all skills that had been completely foreign to the lass just one week earlier, as she had never so much as changed even a doll's diaper before, given that Judy had always been more of a tomboy who preferred hanging out with her brother and grandpa.

Shockingly, at some point during her visit, the ten-year-old girl was instructed to be on the lookout for her newborn baby cousin's retained umbilical cord, which was expected to fall off without warning, as Aunt Amelia wanted to save the blackened coal-like protuberance in a keepsake box for her baby girl.

"Oh, how gross!" Judy thought, now that she had actually seen a newborn's residual umbilical cord first hand. "But, I guess that's all part of the job," the dedicated youngster reminded herself, with a grimace.

Aside from the many marketable skills she had mastered during her stay in Miltgen, Judith Ivy also got to know her two male cousins, as well as her aunt and uncle, a little bit better; and the Wiedermans were more than generous when it came to lavishing their hardworking niece with spending cash for candy, soda pop and carnival trinkets.

That week also happened to be the town of Miltgen's annual summer celebration, commemorating their locally famous Minnesota cheese industry, so Judy was invited to enjoy spools of hand-spun pink or blue cotton candy, oversized beef corn dogs on a stick, and the most delectable batter-fried orange or white cheese curds to be found in the entire county. She was also treated to as many carnival rides as she could stomach. All in all, Judy had the most fabulous time that week during Miltgen Cheese Days!

At the same time, Aunt Amelia was thrilled with the wonderful job her niece had exhibited in taking care of their newborn daughter during her very first week of life, and so she wasted no time in sharing her appreciation with her sister-in-law, Katie.

As a result of that ringing endorsement, Mrs. Munson started bragging about her ten-year-old daughter's precocious maturity and outstanding babysitting skills to her Lumberton Community College coworkers, students and friends. After that, it wasn't long before Katie was booking weekend babysitting gigs for her eldest daughter.

While Judy still enjoyed hunting night crawlers with her big brother, the young entrepreneur knew that she was on the path to making some serious dough (up to 50 cents per hour, far more than she and Keith could ever earn selling worms), and so she gladly let her brother keep all of the earnings from their worm sales. Keith, in turn, supplemented his income by branching out to the lawn-mowing business.

One muggy Saturday afternoon in June of 1975, after mowing two big neighborhood lawns, Keith decided to cool off by trekking out into the hills and forests on a scavenger hunt, which is when the youngster discovered a rippling, crystal-clear stream right across the county highway from the bluff that housed the Ferguson home, where the Munsons now resided.

The serene brook flowed parallel to the town of Stone Valley for about three city blocks before making a sharp right turn, at which point it meandered north as far as the eye could see, until becoming one with the horizon. The sweaty lad immediately waded into the refreshing waters, inching his way in deeper, until the water level reached the bottoms of his cut-off corduroy shorts.

Keith Munson felt as if he had found himself a pot of gold, for the brook was crawling with carp, the largest of which he had ever seen, and it couldn't have been more convenient. The Munson lad now had his very own fishing hole right across the road, up and over a grassy knoll, then down and through some dense trees that shaded the rippling stream from the intense beating rays of the midday sun.

For the duration of that summer, whenever it was their week to stay home in Stone Valley (while their sisters were away in Huntington visiting their grandparents), Keith and Judith Ivy spent a great deal of time fishing in that particular stream.

Mrs. Munson felt a great sense of pride and happiness as she watched her eleven-year-old son and ten-year-old daughter through the living room window as they walked across the road together, carrying a worm bucket, a tackle box, a store-bought rod and reel from Grandpa Buster's boathouse, as well as Judy's homemade bamboo cane pole, on their quest to catch more of those gigantic carp.

As Katie watched her two eldest kids walk away, she noticed how Judy's light brown hair was parted down the back, twisted into two long Indian braids, holding the worm pail in one hand and her cane pole in the other. "Oh, my gosh," Katie giggled, as the thought suddenly occurred to her. "She looks just like Laura Ingalls from *Little House on the Prairie*" (the Munson family's favorite television program).

When the dynamic duo had first arrived at the fishing hole, it was obvious that their spot had been extremely popular at one time, as there were remnants of fishing tackle everywhere--lines with bobbers hanging from overhead tree branches, hooks and sinkers sunken into the mud along the creek banks, shiny lures reflecting the sun's rays from underneath the sparkling clear water, and loose fishing line strung around various weeds and shrubbery.

Keith and Judith Ivy salvaged much of the discarded tackle, recycling whatever they could find, while enthusiastically chanting their ritualistic fish call: "Fishy, fishy, in the brook, come and chomp upon my hook."

Their mother was always impressed when her little anglers returned home with a mess of fresh fish for dinner, especially since the kids cleaned the fish themselves, and Keith usually pan-fried the fillets, making Katie's job a breeze at supper time. The tight-knit pair clearly knew what they were doing, as Keith and Judith Ivy Munson rarely came home from the creek empty-handed.

When their fishing expedition was exceptionally bountiful, Keith would save some of his cleaned carp for Grandpa Buster, so that he could smoke the carp in his smokehouse. Buster Wiederman always looked forward to that, as he loved the taste of smoked carp, accompanied by some of Grandma Sally's homemade pickled herring and a block of sharp cheddar cheese, thinly sliced, with saltine crackers.

Something in Sally's pickled herring always caused Buster to sneeze, yet that never stopped him from eating as much of his wife's special treat as he could get; and once his sneezing fit was over, Grandpa Buster would yank his handkerchief from his overalls or pants pocket, wipe his runny nose and say, "I think God musta made me backwards...'cause my nose runs and my feet smell." That remark always caused his grandchildren to giggle.

When school resumed in September, the fifth-graders were approached by the Stone Valley Elementary School's music teacher, Mrs. Tuttle, regarding their interest in taking up an instrument to play in the concert band. Given her passion for music, the notion intrigued ten-year-old Judy Munson.

Regrettably, Judy knew that her mom could never afford to buy her an expensive band instrument. That didn't stop the eager young lady from bringing up the subject at the dinner table, however. "You know we can't afford something that frivolous and impractical," her mother refuted. "I'm sorry, Jude, but the answer is no!"

Just when Judy had given up on the idea of playing a band instrument, she received a startling surprise. One evening, as the family dined on overly cooked Shake n' Bake pork chops, with boxed scalloped potatoes and canned peas and carrots, her mother made the most unexpected announcement: "If it's that important to you to play a band instrument, Jude, then... well, maybe I can swing it, somehow."

"Really?" Judith Ivy exclaimed. "Oh, Mom, that would be so great!" she screeched. "I'll even give you some of my babysitting money and allowance each week to help pay for it," her thrilled daughter offered.

"That's very sweet of you, Honey, but that's all right…you just go ahead and keep your money," her mother returned. "You've earned it."

"So, what made you change your mind?" her curious daughter inquired. "Well, you're a responsible girl, and you get really good grades in school, and you don't ask for much, so…you deserve this, so long as it's not just a phase that you tire of in a month or two," Katie insisted. "This is something you're gonna have to stick with!"

"Don't worry, Mom…I will," Judith Ivy assured her mother.

With just one week left to sign up for the school band, Katie inquired, "So, what instrument would you like to play, Jude?" Her daughter had decided to try her hand at a woodwind instrument—something far different from the accordion, piano and harmonica, which she had taught herself to play at her grandparents' home.

"Well, at first I wanted to play the flute," Judy expounded, "but then Mrs. Tuttle said they have enough flutes and are short on clarinet players, so she asked if I would try the clarinet instead."

Mrs. Munson juggled some bills and asked for an advance on her next paycheck at work, in order to procure the money to buy a clarinet in time for her eldest daughter to become a member of the Stone Valley Elementary School Band.

Katie stopped at Lumberton's most prestigious music store (one of the city's chief employers) after work and purchased a shiny black clarinet, along with a black carrying case and a box of replacement reeds for the mouthpiece.

When she surprised her daughter with the clarinet that night at the supper table, Judith Ivy was ecstatic. She couldn't believe that her mother had spent $165 on a brand-new clarinet just for her, so that she could play an instrument in the band at school.

Although the additional expense of Judy's clarinet had cost all the Munson kids their Sunday "family day" outings for the coming month, Katie urged her children not to blame their sister, explaining that there may come a time when one of them might want to play an instrument, or take up a hobby or sport costing a large sum of money. Katie was astonished at how well her children took the news, as they didn't even put up a fuss.

When Judith Ivy arrived for her first private clarinet lesson, she felt so privileged, confident, and ready to master her new musical instrument. Unfortunately, when she placed her tongue against the thin wooden reed on the mouthpiece, her body was instantaneously overcome by chills!

Judy had experienced a similar goose-bumpy

sensation whenever her tongue made contact with the wooden sticks from a Popsicle or Fudgesicle, which is why she always used her front teeth to remove the remaining fudge or frozen juice from her favorite summertime frosty treats.

Despite her disabling discovery, the extremely grateful fifth-grader had no intention of ever telling her mother. One way or another, Judith Ivy Munson was determined to tough it out and get through it somehow, at least for the next..."How many more years until I graduate?" she pondered, sighing in frustration.

In light of everything that Katie (as well as her siblings) had sacrificed to buy Judy that very expensive clarinet, how could she possibly tell her mother that the wooden reed on the mouthpiece caused her entire body to break out in goose bumps? "Man, I really screwed up this time," Judy sniveled, while practicing her clarinet lesson in her bedroom. "Oh, how I wish I could have taken the flute!"

On December 31, 1975, Judith Ivy Munson was hired to baby-sit for one of her mother's work-study girls at the Lumberton Community College. Katie told her daughter that she had volunteered Judy for the babysitting job because she was planning to host a small New Year's Eve bash in their apartment.

After getting roped into throwing a party by her Solo Parents Club friends, the thirty-year-old mother of four wanted all of her kids out of the house for the evening. Accordingly, Katie had prearranged for

Keith, Darcy and Samantha to spend the night with their grandparents in Huntington.

The New Year's Eve party list consisted of mainly singles, each of whom was invited to bring a friend or guest. Katie was excited for the opportunity to finally meet some new people; in particular, Burt Pomerance. Mr. Pomerance was a very tall, extremely attractive man with thick raven hair, a full moustache, piercing blue eyes, with dimples and a deep cleft accentuating his very pronounced jaw. "My, my…what a handsome fellow," Katie thought, when Burt first walked into her living room.

Once Katie's dear friend, Gail Benson, had introduced the couple, Katie and Burt spent the entire evening together, conversing with each other almost exclusively. At over six feet tall, Burt towered over Katie's five-foot frame. His black cowboy boots further emphasized his large physique as he gazed down into the hostess's pretty blue eyes.

From that first introduction, it was as if Katie and Burt were the only two people in the room. Gail ended up spending the majority of her evening playing hostess at Katie's party, since her friend was too wrapped up in Mr. Pomerance to tend to the needs of the other guests.

Love was most assuredly in the air on that particular New Year's Eve night, as the radio played one love song after another, from Captain and Tennille's "Love Will Keep Us Together," to Bad Company's "Feel Like

Makin' Love," and Linda Ronstadt crying, "When Will I Be Loved."

Katie felt completely comfortable with the pleasant, overly polite gentleman. In addition, Burt looked and smelled fantastic in his blue western-style shirt, accented with a black and silver bola neck tie, and a splash of Old English Leather men's cologne. Aside from their unmistakable physical attraction and chemistry, the couple soon discovered that they also had much in common; most notably, they were both divorcees.

Although her intuition may have seemed a bit premature, Katie was nearly convinced that her handsome Prince Charming was "the one." By the end of the evening, Katie Munson felt certain that she had just found the man she wanted to spend the rest of her life with, and she prayed that Burt felt the same way about her.

As the clock neared the bewitching hour, there was only one place Katie Munson wanted to be…sitting right beside Burt Pomerance. They counted down the last ten seconds of 1975 together, and then, at the stroke of midnight, the pair impulsively turned toward each other and delighted in their first kiss. Katie blushed as a warm, tingling sensation washed over her entire body, dominating her senses.

From that heart-pounding, blood-rushing moment, Katie knew, deep within her heart, that her dating disasters were finally over. Not only was she beginning a new year in 1976, Katie unreservedly believed that she and her family were on the brink of starting a brand-new life together.

Her instincts had served her well, for when Katie informed Burt Pomerance that she had four children, ages 8-12, he didn't run away. In fact, he hardly even flinched. Catching her by surprise, Burt simply asked Katie when he could meet them, offering that he was himself a 32-year-old, recently divorced father of one five-year-old son named Joshua, who resided with his mother.

Following that magical New Year's Eve celebration, Burt Pomerance started spending a lot of time at the Munson residence. Katie invited him over for supper nearly every night, as Burt was a lonely bachelor, living all alone in a one-bedroom apartment in downtown Lumberton.

Mr. Pomerance wasn't about to turn down a home-cooked meal invitation, particularly since he didn't much care for cooking and had grown weary of the same-old boring meals consisting mainly of frozen Banquet TV dinners, cold meat sandwiches, canned Chunky soup and Hormel chili.

The Munson kids really liked Burt too. They enjoyed his off-the-wall sense of humor, and he was very kind to them. Most importantly, though, Burt was good to their mother. He treated Katie like a queen, bringing her flowers, taking her out on a date at least one night per week, opening doors for her, and Burt kept calling their mom "Pretty Lady," which the children thought was very sweet.

Katie's kids also got a kick out of Burt's big green Ford pickup with the "Keep On Truckin" mud flaps and the rear window sticker that read: "Save Water--Shower With A Friend." When the kids also learned that their mother's new boyfriend used to be a semi truck driver in the past and currently made a living as a diesel mechanic at a large trucking company in Lumberton, they had only one thing to say: "Cool."

Keith, especially, liked riding in Burt's Ford pickup truck. He enjoyed playing with the Citizens' Band (CB) radio and talking to fellow truckers while cruising the country's highways and byways; and since Burt used to be a truck driver himself, he had remained in contact with many of his former trucker pals and colleagues.

Burt Pomerance was better known to the above-mentioned crowd by his CB handle, "Rooster," which was given to Burt because he was such an early bird and usually the first man to report for duty at the trucking garage.

Since Katie had spent a great deal of time riding in the spacious truck cab while they were dating, Burt adoringly selected the CB handle of "Pretty Lady" for his girlfriend; and after allowing Katie's son to choose his own CB handle, twelve-year-old Keith Munson became known henceforth as "Oscar."

During the next month, the happy couple accumulated a wide array of eight-track tapes to play while joy-riding in Burt's pickup on long scenic drives. Katie enjoyed a variety of music including rockabilly, pop, rock and roll, as well as some disco and country, while Burt preferred country western and highway cruising tunes.

The dating duo did share one favorite, however, which they played repeatedly, until it eventually wore out. It was Charlie Rich's multiple award-winning album, *Behind Closed Doors*. Every time Burt and Katie heard "The Most Beautiful Girl" song, Burt would sing the lyrics to his pretty golden-haired sweetheart, and then Katie would snuggle up closer beside her handsome man behind the wheel.

It wasn't long before Burt was invited to join the Munson clan on their Sunday family outings, and he also brought his son along, when it was Burt's weekend to have Joshua. (The divorced couple had agreed to share custody of their five-year-old son, with Burt making monthly payments to his ex-wife for child support.)

The extended Munson/Pomerance clan enjoyed going to the movies together, dining out on pizza, and bowling, which was an altogether new activity for the Munson kids. Burt was a talented bowler, having been part of a men's bowling league during the winter months. He, therefore, had plenty of helpful tips for the kids, who where utterly amazed at how Burt's bowling ball shattered the pins with such force that it sounded like a brick being hurled through a stained glass window.

The more time they spent together, the more contented Burt and Katie and all the kids started to feel with one another, almost like a real family. They just seemed to blend together naturally. Although Burt was in no hurry to remarry, having been divorced fewer than two years, he did share the same feelings that Katie felt for him. It was obvious to everyone in sight that Burt was madly in love with Katie.

As the weeks passed, the icy northwest winds tightened the reins on their fury, allowing the thick blanket of Minnesota snow an opportunity to melt, even if only for a day or two before the gray skies would unload another unexpected snowfall.

At last, winter had begun to blend with springtime, as most residents in the Upper Midwest had grown drained and exhausted from the long cold winter. Burt Pomerance and Katie Munson were no exception, and they were finding their bank accounts somewhat depleted as well.

The couple had grown weary of paying rent at two separate dwellings, running back and forth from Stone Valley to Lumberton (particularly since Burt barely spent any time at his downtown apartment anymore), and the Ferguson's three-bedroom, one-bathroom basement apartment suddenly seemed overcrowded and stifling.

Burt and Katie decided to share their previously discussed plans with the children during their next family affair. The first Sunday in March 1976 also coincided with Burt's thirty-third birthday, which he insisted on spending with Katie and the kids, despite Joshua's absence, as that was his scheduled weekend with his mom.

The most anticipated movie of the year had finally arrived in Lumberton that weekend, and so Katie's girls were excited to see *The Other Side of the Mountain*, starring Marilyn Hassett and Beau Bridges.

The Brenner girls had already seen the unforgettable film and had told the Munson sisters that it was a beautiful and moving love story about a beautiful Olympic champion who was paralyzed following a tragic skiing accident.

Since her daughters had chosen the movie that Sunday, Katie let her son pick the restaurant afterwards. Keith decided on the Ground Round. When the family arrived, the children immediately scrambled to the restrooms, allowing Burt and Katie a moment alone before sharing their exciting news with the kids.

The Eagles' popular hit song, "Lyin' Eyes," was playing in the background as Burt and Katie ordered a cocktail from the bar. When the kids returned to the table, their mother took a big sip from her tall Bloody Mary packed with large green olives and celery stalks, and then she addressed her children. "Say, kids…uh, Burt and I have some news," Katie announced, "and we think you're gonna be really happy about it."

The Munson kids were curious, of course, but

they had no inkling as to what was about to transpire, nor did their mother have a clue as to their immediate reactions. Keith's straw had since found the bottom of his Dr. Pepper soda, and so he continued to slurp every last drop. "Keith, please!" his mother snapped. "Stop that!"

When the waitress returned with the young lad's free soda refill, Katie seized the opportunity. After clearing her throat, she stated, "Well, you know Burt has been spending a lot of time at our place, and…we think that maybe it's time for us to move in together." Katie took another large sip from her spicy tomato drink as she nervously awaited a reply.

Keith, Judith Ivy, Darcy and Samantha just looked around the table, searching one another's eyes for the slightest hint of privileged information. "Is Burt gonna sleep in your room, Mommy?" her eight-year-old daughter, Samantha, inquired. "No, Honey," her mother giggled. "Burt's not moving into our place."

Burt took hold of Katie's hand, in an effort to steer the conversation in the right direction before the entrees arrived and all attention would be focused on dinner. "We both know how much you kids love Stone Valley," Burt interjected. "And I like it too…and that's why your mother and I…just bought a house in Stone Valley."

"What?" the kids shrieked, as they glanced up from their doodling and coloring on the provided place mats. "You mean, we're gonna have our own house?" nine-year-old Darcy paraphrased.

"Yes," their elated mother answered. "That's exactly what we mean!"

"Yippee!" Samantha exclaimed. "All right!" Darcy concurred. "So, where is this house?" Keith inquired, as the children bombarded the adults with questions. "It's right downtown, on Johnson Street," Burt informed the blissful bunch.

"Is it close to the candy store?" Samantha queried, voicing her main concern. "Yep, just down the block and around the corner," her mother expounded. "And, we just finished our lease at the Ferguson place, so, if all goes well, we can move in right away next month!"

"Far out!" Judith Ivy shouted. "I can't wait to call all my friends and tell 'em we're finally gonna have a house of our very own that no one can take away!"

Now that everyone was in agreement and pleased with the impending move, Katie decided it was time to celebrate Burt's birthday. As Glen Campbell's number-one smash hit, "Rhinestone Cowboy," resonated in stereo, Katie approached their waitress privately to notify the staff that they had a "birthday boy" at their table.

At the appropriate time, after all the dinner dishes had been removed from their table, the waitress and several other staff members formed a circle around Katie's table, singing the "Happy Birthday" song to Burt, after which they presented him with a free mini birthday cake with a lighted candle on top.

Once Burt had extinguished his birthday candle, everybody clapped. Katie then inquired about her beloved boyfriend's birthday wish. "I didn't make a wish," Burt asserted. "Well, why not?" Katie pressed. "Because," Burt professed, "it already came true!" Katie and Burt shared a tender, loving kiss, and then the captivated couple devoured the complimentary chocolate cake together.

The Munson kids could hardly contain their excitement during the long drive home to Stone Valley. They were already fighting over the telephone, as each of them wanted to be the first to call his/her friends with the exhilarating news.

As soon as Burt killed the engine, Judith Ivy darted out of the back seat of their mom's Ford Galaxy, reaching the front door ahead of the others. Once inside, she headed straight for the telephone, mounted on the far kitchen wall. Being the first to grab hold of the receiver, Judy turned on the countertop radio, and then she dialed her best friend.

"Guess what, Laverne?" Judy shouted, with exuberance. "We're moving uptown next month, into our very own house!"

"Really, Jude? I'm so happy for you!" Laverne returned. "You guys deserve to have a house of your own," the supportive eleven-year-old remarked, "especially since your old house got torn down."

"Oh, I can't wait!" Judy shrieked. With the long telephone cord stretched clear across the kitchen, she started jiving and dancing to Captain and Tennille's new hit single as it blasted from the radio. The excited young lady couldn't help but sing along to the catchy tune, "Love Will Keep Us Together."

After a protracted pause in conversation, while listening to Judy's singing, Laverne interrupted her caller by shouting, "Hey, Jude...I'm still on the line, remember?" Nevertheless, she was thrilled that her best buddy sounded so happy and upbeat.

"Sorry, Laverne," Judy apologized. "Hang on a second," she added, while turning down the volume on the radio. "I haven't even told you the best part yet," the ten-year-old screeched, pausing for dramatic effect. "I'm finally gonna have my own room!"

# Chapter 8
# Can't Help Falling in Love

In April of 1976, the Munson family moved into a home of their very own, thanks to the love, kindness and generosity of their mother's boyfriend, Burt Pomerance. For the first time in their lives, Katie and her children had found both security and stability, as well as autonomy and independence, for no one would ever have the authority to tear down this house right out from under their feet, and no more would they have to rent space in the homes of others, adhering to their rules and preferences. In conjunction with the reawakening of nature that spring, the family had a renewed outlook on life.

The two-story yellow house was just the right size for a family of six, with three bedrooms upstairs for the kids, a master bedroom on the main level, a large living room with shiny hardwood floors, a full-sized bathroom with a tub and shower, an average-sized kitchen with yellow-brown linoleum flooring, matching brown cabinets and yellow countertops, and an extra room just inside the front door with thick green shag carpeting and a long bar, including four tall barstools and a second refrigerator behind the bar.

The new family dwelling came complete with

amenities, including a washer and dryer set, three-season front porch, yellow aluminum siding (which highly appealed to Burt, as he would never have to paint the house), and a spacious back yard where the kids could play with their friends, shaded by several mature oak trees, and a clothesline on which Katie could hang the family's clean laundry in the fresh spring air, just like her mother always did at her childhood home in Huntington. All that was missing was a garage in which to house their car and pickup truck, but there was a short gravel driveway alongside the house and plenty of curbside parking available out front.

Upon their final trip back from the Ferguson residence, Judith Ivy Munson couldn't wait to finish unloading their belongings. As soon as Katie's champagne Ford Galaxy sedan and Burt's green Ford pickup truck had been completely emptied, and all the boxes were safely inside the house or stacked neatly on the front porch, the overly anxious lass raced upstairs to her bedroom with her first box of personal items. Keith, Darcy and Samantha followed suit, as they were equally excited to check out their new pads and begin to envision the unlimited arranging and decorating possibilities.

The largest of the three upstairs bedrooms had been assigned to Darcy and Samantha, since they were going to be sharing a room. Keith, of course, insisted on reserving the far bedroom, which faced their new back yard, as that room had its own private door that opened out onto a wide ledge running the length of the bedroom, sharing space with the mightiest of the estate's oak trees, whose outstretched limbs extended out towards the aluminum screen door and whose branches gently brushed their leaves against the balcony on that breezy afternoon, almost as if summoning the happy twelve-year-old boy to come outside and play.

The third bedroom on the upper level was the smallest of the three, but Judy didn't mind one bit, as she finally had her very own space, no longer having to share a room with her sisters, and no more putting up with Darcy's constant sucking on their bedspread all night long because she claimed it "tastes like cookies."

As she recalled and scoffed at the many weird idiosyncrasies of her family, at the same, Judy couldn't help but reminisce about all the good times she and her sisters had shared living together in one bedroom all their lives. She realized that she was bound to miss the sisterly girl talks, the tickle challenges, and the heavy pillow fights, which usually left one sibling injured, as the trio often treated their beds like trampolines.

Most of all, Judy would miss the scary bedtime stories that she and sister Darcy concocted while lying in bed late at night, in an effort to scare their tenacious little sister, Samantha. Lost in her thoughts, Judy sighed and looked out her bedroom window, facing the street. "I wonder what it's gonna be like living on this side of town."

The cheerful live-in family worked diligently every evening over the next several days, and they devoted the following weekend to getting things settled and organized. By late Saturday afternoon, Katie and Burt had finally finished unpacking their last cardboard box labeled "bedroom stuff." Exhausted, the couple plopped down on Burt's queen-sized bed, sprawling out to relieve their stiff and aching back muscles.

As The Bellamy Brothers' new hit song, "Let Your Love Flow," wafted softly through the speakers of Katie's night-stand radio, she and Burt grasped a moment for reflection. "Whew! What a busy year 1976 has started out to be so far," Katie declared, wiping away the perspiration on her forehead with the back of her hand.

"You ain't kidding!" Burt concurred, with a chuckle. "Just think…only a little over three months ago, we didn't even know each other," he asserted, turning his head toward Katie.

"Yeah," Katie sighed. "And look at us now! Here we are, moving in together…and into our very own house!" she exclaimed, kicking her feet against the bed with uncontrolled excitement. "I've never seen the kids so happy either."

Lying there on the bed, next to her boyfriend/co-homeowner, Katie looked deep into Burt's tired blue eyes and proclaimed, "This is like a dream come true for us, Burt…and that's all because of you!"

Being a somewhat bashful fellow, Katie's blatant and unanticipated flattery had caused Burt's cheeks to quickly blush. "Well, I…I've never been this happy either," he warmly admitted.

"Thank God my Solo Parents friends forced me into throwing that New Year's Eve party," Katie professed, with a heavy sigh of relief. "Heck, I would've been content to stay home that night with my kids, making kettles of buttery popcorn and watching the big ball drop on Dick Clark's show," she volunteered.

"And I was just happy to have somewhere to go that night," Burt openly divulged. "I couldn't handle spending another New Year's Eve all alone in that drafty, cold apartment with the noisy radiator and that ugly green wallpaper."

"Well, you won't have to be alone anymore," Katie assured her charming boyfriend. "Now you have me…and all of us," she happily reminded her partner, placing her petite, soft youthful hand into Burt's hefty, callused and chafed palm.

Katie subsequently noticed that his eyes were starting to moisten. Although he was a very tall and large fellow, Burt Pomerance was more sensitive, kind and gentle than any man Katie had ever known. She tenderly stroked his prickly, unshaven cheek, and then she planted a moist kiss upon his trembling lips.

Shortly after that romantic interlude, Katie sat

upright on their firm queen-sized mattress. While still holding Burt's hand, she pulled him up and ushered, "Come on, Handsome," in an effort to whisk him through that emotional moment. "Let's go upstairs and see how all the kids are getting along."

"Hey, you really have a good start on your new bedroom, Jude," her mother remarked, as Katie and Burt made their rounds. Glancing around the room, they noticed how Judy already had her Donny Osmond and "Fonzie" posters taped on the brown paneled walls, and her stuffed animals were aligned neatly atop the headboard of her new double bed (Katie's old one), mixed in with her multicolored assortment of candles in the shapes of mushrooms, owls and frogs, which Judy had molded using her Ronco candle-making kit.

While in the midst of organizing her clothes into her dresser drawers and closet, Judy had her yellow Panasonic Toot-a-Loop radio set at the maximum volume level, so that all the kids could enjoy some good tunes while they unpacked, arranged and organized their bedrooms.

As The Marshall Tucker Band's new hit single, "Heard It in a Love Song," blared through the small radio speaker, Judy continued to dance and sing along while dividing her clothes into orderly piles. At the end of the entertaining tune, featuring a beautiful flute solo, Judy wished more than ever that she had been permitted to play the flute instead of the clarinet in her fifth-grade concert band.

Groovin' to the music, Katie Munson strutted her way next into her younger daughters' bedroom, finding their room pretty much divided in half, right down the middle. Darcy and Samantha had arranged their single beds at opposite ends of the room, with their dressers against the wall at the foot of their beds, and their bric-a-brac and memorabilia kept to their own side of the room.

On Darcy's side, just above the head of her bed, hung her Bay City Rollers poster, and across the room, above her dresser, was a picture of David Cassidy, which Darcy had carefully ripped from her *Tiger Beat* magazine. She had purchased the periodical with her Saturday allowance after falling in love with the teen idol when she saw him perform "I Think I Love You" on *The Partridge Family* television show a few years back.

Samantha's half of the bedroom was coming together nicely, decorated with a combination of lacy doilies and Barbie dolls, with the focal point of her dresser being a large palomino horse figurine with a long blonde mane and tail, for which she had traded a new younger acquaintance (Maggie Schultz from down the street) one of her old dolls that she no longer treasured.

Burt and Katie rounded out their tour of the upstairs level with a visit to Keith's room. They weren't at all surprised to find his bedroom in complete disarray. There was no order whatsoever in the young lad's quarters, except that his cherished moth collection had been nailed to the beige paneling, his dart board fastened above his dresser, and a bone-chilling poster from Steven Spielberg's *Jaws* movie taped above his double bed.

Keith's clothes were still strewn all over the floor and bed, and his gopher traps and fishing gear were scattered about as well. "You'd better get to work cleaning up this mess, Keith," his mother warned. "It looks like a disaster area in here!"

"Yeah, yeah," Keith replied. He then kicked some of the clutter out of the way, creating a pathway to the screen door on the far side of his room. "Check it out," the excited youngster raved, as he opened the door. "This is so cool!"

"We already saw it when we looked at the house," his mother commented. "Just make sure you be careful and don't go flying off the edge," Katie cautioned, looking down from the ledge to the ground. "It's a long way down."

"I know...don't worry," Keith assured his mother. "Hey, did you guys know there's a squirrel living in this tree?" he screeched, gesturing with his index finger for them to follow him about halfway down the length of the ledge. "Look!" he pointed out. "I put a small pile of corn out here this morning, and it's almost all gone already."

"Huh," Burt reacted. "I wonder how he got onto this ledge from that tree."

"I've been watching him," Keith answered, before mapping out the bushy-tailed tree rodent's route. "He follows that big branch right there, and then he jumps over to that little branch and makes another flying jump from there onto the ledge."

"That's one gutsy squirrel," Burt remarked. "I'll say," Katie agreed.

"I already gave him a name," Keith asserted. "I call him 'Dummy'...like on *Sanford and Son*." (Fred Sanford often referred to his son, Lemont, as "Dummy" on the hugely popular television sitcom.)

As the days passed, Keith spent a lot of time feeding and befriending that spirited squirrel, and he and Dummy eventually became buddies. Keith would leave trails of corn kernels, acorns and walnuts leading from the ledge, right up and into his bedroom, and then he would prop the screen door open so that Dummy could come and go as he pleased, in and out of Keith's bedroom.

Once Keith had gained the squirrel's trust, and vice versa, it didn't take long before Dummy would crawl up Keith's pant legs, while sitting on his bed, and then creep up his arms and around his shoulders and neck.

"It feels kinda weird," he told his sisters, who often witnessed Keith amusing himself with his naturally undomesticated, furry new pet. "His claws dig in pretty hard, but they don't really hurt," he maintained.

"Leave it to my brother," Judith Ivy mumbled, shaking her head, as she brushed past his doorway. "He shoots squirrels out in the woods for food, and then he keeps one as a pet in his bedroom...what a dork!"

With the most difficult portion of the relocation behind them, Katie needed to redirect her focus to her daughters' upcoming birthday celebrations. Since Darcy's birthday party had to be put on the back burner, due to the added stress of the move, Katie promised Darcy that she and Samantha could celebrate their April birthdays together, at the end of the month.

In addition to their traditional family birthday gathering, which included having Grandma Sally and Grandpa Buster over for supper, cake and ice cream, Darcy and Samantha decided that they wanted to also invite a couple of their girlfriends and have them over for a slumber party, so they could show off their new house and bedroom.

"I think that sounds fair," their mother approved, "considering all the hard work you girls had to do this past month, with all the packing, cleaning and moving...and then unpacking and making up your bedroom."

"All right!" the birthday girls exclaimed, smacking each other's palms high up in the air. "I'm gonna go call Jeannie and invite her," ten-year-old Darcy decided, as she started getting up from the kitchen table.

"Not until after you finish your supper," her mother

interfered, having labored over their cube steak dinner with mashed potatoes and gravy. Katie took another bite of the flavorful pan-fried steak, washing it down with a sip of cold skim milk. Then she turned to her youngest daughter and asked, "So, who are you going to invite, Sam?"

The third-grader pondered the question for a moment, while separating the peas on her plate (which she intended to discretely dispose of later) from the carrots, before making up her mind. "I think I wanna invite…Raquel Kleinschmidt," Samantha asserted.

"Raquel Kleinschmidt!" her sisters shrieked, in disbelief. Judith Ivy quickly enlightened the family as to their surprise, negative reaction. "She's the girl with all those mean brothers who won't let us walk in front of their house, or even on their side of the street, without getting beat up!"

"Plus, her big bully brothers and their jerky friends stole all our candy from us on Halloween!" Darcy alleged. The fourth-grader then shivered, for she was suddenly forced to revisit some of her most haunting memories from Halloweens past.

"Yeah, I know," Samantha understood, while also defending her newfound friend. "Raquel is really nice, though…not like her mean big brothers at all," she insisted. "You'll see!" (In the same breath, the sly little sneak had managed to stuff her entire helping of cooked peas into the pocket of her bright pink windbreaker jacket slung on the back of her dining chair.)

"Her dad nicknamed her 'Mony'," Samantha clarified, "so that's what everybody calls her."

The Kleinschmidts were another large family residing in Stone Valley, about half the distance from the park to the downtown area. Similar to the Crawfords, their clan consisted of nine children as well, but with seven boys and just two girls. Raquel was the baby of her family and two years younger than Samantha Munson. However, despite her younger age, the first-grader already stood taller than the older, petite Munson sisters.

"Well," their mother addressed the group, "that all sounds fine and dandy, but what about Laverne Crawford?" Mrs. Munson inquired. "Don't you think she would feel hurt and left out if you invited Jeannie and not her?"

"Mom's right," Judith Ivy chimed in. "We can't leave Laverne out."

"But…Laverne is Judy's friend," Samantha disputed. "And since it's my birthday party, then I should get to invite my friend, and I wanna invite Mony!"

Burt and Katie glanced at each other, and throughout the course of their family discussion, decided to let all three of the girls invite one friend over for the slumber party. However, for Judy's eleventh birthday in May, the eldest daughter would have to be content with just the family birthday gathering, including her grandparents, but no school chums.

"That's fine with me!" Judith Ivy consented. "But,

wait…what about Kristi and Barb Brenner?" she screeched, having second thoughts. "We want them to come and see our new house too!"

"Yeah," Darcy affirmed, siding with her big sister. "Can we invite them too, Mom…pretty please?"

"Oh, why not?" Katie granted. "What's the harm in inviting two more girls to your first slumber party in our new house?"

"Yippee!" Her daughters rejoiced, with excitement. "We'll make it a combination birthday/housewarming party," their mother declared, and the girls immediately started setting their party plans in motion.

"Well, I'm not sticking around for another stupid slumber party full of screaming girls dancing to records all night long and talking about dumb girlie stuff," the Munson lad refuted. "Oh, don't worry, Keith," his mother returned. "You can stay with your grandparents in Huntington that weekend."

The Munson sisters' birthday/slumber party was just the kickoff the family had envisioned to christen their new home in the spring of 1976. The girls had a marvelous time with their dearest childhood friends. They played LIFE and Twister, after which they pigged out on Tombstone pepperoni pizzas and then decided to dance to records on the spacious hardwood living room floor.

The taller girls carefully slid the couch back and out of the way, while the little lasses picked up the throw rugs and tossed them aside. Judith Ivy, in turn, fired up Burt's enormous home stereo system, having procured his permission earlier that day.

With the addition of Burt's state-of-the-art stereo system in the house, complete with turntable, AM/FM radio, eight-track tape player, and enormous speakers standing almost as tall as her girls, Katie gladly donated her old RCA record player to Judy, so that her eldest daughter could play her own records in the privacy of her bedroom.

Shuffling through Katie and Burt's extensive joint collection of single 45s and LP albums, Judith Ivy elicited requests from her guests, who declined, asserting, "You have good taste, Jude, so just put on whatever you want!"

The appointed party hostess selected a handful of 45s, including many household favorites, starting with her mother's most beloved record, "Harper Valley PTA." She followed that sassy song with Sweet's "Little Willy," "Bad, Bad Leroy Brown," "American Pie," "Billy Don't Be A Hero," Cher's "Dark Lady," "My Maria," "Beach Baby," "Joy to the World," "Brandy (You're A Fine Girl)," "Knock Three Times," "Bad Blood," and Darcy's favorite, "Saturday Night," by the Bay City Rollers.

Once the music festival had gotten under way, the dance party continued straight through until 10 p.m., at which time the Munson girls planned to make some popcorn using their new air-popper popcorn machine and then retire in front of the television set to watch *NBC's Saturday Night Live*.

"I heard the musician for tonight is Rod Stewart," Kristi Brenner informed the group. "Yeah, and I heard he's gonna be singing a new song," Laverne Crawford interjected. "Well, that's what our big sister, Renee, said anyway. She was all fired up about it this afternoon."

"Far out!" Barb Brenner excitedly replied. "Ooh, I hope he sings 'Maggie May' too, 'cause that's my favorite song!" she shrieked. "Hey, we've got that record!" Judith Ivy exclaimed, adding, "I'll play that one next!"

Although Burt and Katie had effectively disappeared several hours earlier (in hopes of savoring some quality time for themselves at the movies), they intended to be home before 10:30 p.m., for they, too, enjoyed the hilarious comedy sketches, Hollywood hosts, and musical guests featured each week on the hit variety show.

When Burt and Katie arrived back home, they were welcomed by the tantalizing aroma of fresh popcorn and the sounds of Hues Corporation's "Rock the Boat" wafting through the air. Judy and Darcy were showing their friends a new dance routine they had choreographed, after learning some trendy disco moves on *American Bandstand*.

By 10:30 p.m., the furniture had been put back in its original layout, the last kettle of popcorn drenched in butter and salt, and the highly anticipated television program was about to begin. Burt and Katie nestled in on the sofa, while the girls enjoyed the show from the comfort of their sleeping bags on the floor.

Chevy Chase, Dan Aykroyd and John Belushi launched the evening's laugh-a-thon by doing a parody of a popular deodorant advertisement, to high acclaim. Katie and the girls, however, were eagerly awaiting the side-splitting satires executed by the show's female actresses, starring Jane Curtin, Laraine Newman and Gilda Radner.

Once Rod Stewart had finished performing his new song, "Tonight's the Night," it dawned on Burt and Katie that the "party" portion of the evening was just about over and, thankfully, the "slumber" segment of the sleepover was about to commence, as the girls were beginning to nod off.

When "The Star Spangled Banner" emanated from the large console television set at midnight, Katie whispered, "At last, we can finally go to bed." Holding her boyfriend's hand, she and Burt tiptoed their way through the sleeping bags and dozing bodies that peppered their living room floor.

Katie couldn't help but giggle at Laverne's donkey-like sounds. "She snores almost as loud as you do," Katie teased her boyfriend. "Oh, I highly doubt that," Burt yawned, as he closed their bedroom door. "Let's hit the sack, Pretty Lady."

A couple weeks later, Judith Ivy celebrated her eleventh birthday, in the company of her family and grandparents. They enjoyed two large pepperoni pizzas, which Burt had picked up from Pizza Hut Saturday morning on his way home from working at the garage, and a marble cake with chocolate frosting.

Once all eleven of the multihued candles had been extinguished, however, the birthday girl appeared puzzled, for Judy hadn't seen a wrapped birthday gift on the countertop, or the kitchen table, or anywhere in sight.

Sensing her daughter's disappointment, Katie intervened. "Jude, honey...would you please go outside and get Grandma's sweater from the front seat of their station wagon?" Playing the pawn in her daughter's ruse, Grandma Sally feigned a chill and started rubbing her bare, fair-skinned arms.

"Sure," the eleven-year-old agreed; but when she opened the screen door on the front porch, Judith Ivy immediately halted, gasping in surprise. Her family quickly joined her on the front porch.

Judy couldn't believe her eyes. On the sidewalk in front of their house, she found a brand-new, full-sized, metallic-blue, girl's Schwinn bicycle with whitewall tires and a big white basket (with pink and blue strands weaved throughout), and a large pink bow taped to the handlebars.

"Oh, my God!" Judith Ivy yelped, flabbergasted. "This is the best birthday present ever!" She exclaimed, as she hopped right up onto the white bicycle seat and pedaled off down the street. From that very first introduction, Judy and her new bike became inseparable friends. "Look, Mom...no hands!" she joyfully shouted.

The Munson children had never felt such happiness before Burt Pomerance had wandered into their lives on that magical night, just five months earlier. In addition to getting a new house with a big back yard, the children had never received such extravagant birthday presents in their entire lives.

Just last month, Samantha Jo got the pink skateboard she had wanted for her birthday, Darcy Lynn was given a brand-new pair of roller skates decorated with colorful disco insignia, and now Judith Ivy had been presented with the bicycle of her dreams.

"Oh, now I have a special treat for all you guys," the birthday girl informed her guests, after returning from her short bike ride. Judy reached into the refrigerator and removed a large metal cookie sheet, plopping it down on the kitchen counter.

"I made some anise candy this morning," she announced. "You gotta try some!" Using her mother's meat-tenderizing mallet, Judy started smashing the sheet of hardened candy into bite-sized pieces.

Although the noise was momentarily unbearable, Judy's family was rather impressed by the smooth, licorice flavor of her homemade anise candy, for which they lavished her with compliments, conceding that it tasted just as good as store-bought.

"Gee, thanks," Judy returned. "It's really not that hard to make. All you need is a double boiler, some

Karo syrup, anise extract, and a lot of patience," she affirmed, adding, "I also make my own pink bubble gum and homemade vanilla ice cream, in the wintertime."

"No foolin'?" Grandpa Buster remarked. He was quite impressed with his young granddaughter's enterprising skills. "How do you make your own bubble gum, Snuffy?" he eagerly inquired.

"It's pretty easy, Grandpa," Judy answered. "You just need some Chickle and a big cookie sheet," she instructed. "I actually learned how to make the candy and gum from Kristi and Barb Brenner, over at their house...but the ice cream recipe I made up myself, using snow. It's super easy and really good!"

Although it was springtime in southeastern Minnesota, all eyes waited with bated breath, as they were curious to learn how Judy made her homemade ice cream, and she was equally excited to share her culinary secrets.

"All you do is fill up a two-quart pitcher with fresh clean snow...really pack it down in there," Judy explained. "Then you add some vanilla flavoring, pour in some milk, add a little bit of sugar, and then mix it with a wooden spoon. Whenever I make a batch," she boasted, with a chuckle, "Darcy, Keith and Samantha always come running."

(Note: Due to the extent of air pollution nowadays, it would be ill-advised to try this homemade ice cream recipe today. However, to test the purity of the snow in your area, simply pack some freshly fallen snow in a white container, let it melt, and judge for yourself.)

"Gee, that does sound awful good, Snuffy," her grandfather asserted, while snatching a second piece of delicious anise candy from the baking sheet. "Seems like you're always doing or making something," Grandma Sally remarked.

"Like I always say," Katie elaborated, "no grass grows under Judy's feet! She has two speeds... full speed ahead and off." Burt nodded his head in agreement.

"Well, I like to keep busy," the birthday girl insisted. "I guess I get bored easily."

Buster and Sally smiled, for they knew exactly what their daughter and granddaughter meant, as Judith Ivy had always managed to keep herself occupied at their house as well, whether it be playing their musical instruments, going fishing and gopher trapping with Buster and Keith, helping them scrape coon and fox hides, playing games with Grandma Sally, or working in the berry patches and vegetable gardens.

"Grandma's been teaching me how to crochet now too," Judy alerted the family. "I saw in a magazine how to make beer can hats by cutting out the sides of beer cans, punching holes around the edges, then crocheting them all together, and adding a brim around the bottom, to make a cute little hat."

She quickly retrieved the photograph of the

finished product to show her guests. "I'm gonna make a bunch of these hats and sell them for a buck apiece at the Bicentennial Bash on the Fourth of July this summer," Judy announced, "which leaves me only two months to get them made, so I've got a lot of work ahead of me."

"My, what a splendid idea," her grandmother endorsed. "I'd like to purchase one of those crocheted hats from you," she added, reaching into her bag for her coin purse. "But, could you make my hat with soda cans instead?" Grandma Sally humbly implored, since she generally didn't condone drinking.

"You got it, Grandma!" Judy promised, with a hug. "And since you paid me first, you'll get the first hat!"

"Hey, I'll buy one of those beer can hats from you too," Burt petitioned, "just so long as you use Schlitz beer cans for my hat, since that's my brand."

"Oh, yeah, that reminds me...I'll need your help collecting the beer cans, Burt," the young entrepreneur advised. Having polished off his first can of Schlitz, Burt smiled and replied, "I don't think that'll be a problem." He shook his empty can and then quoted the popular Schlitz Beer television commercial, hinting, "When you're out of Schlitz, you're out of beer."

"I'll get you one, Burt," Judy responded, before darting off to the refrigerator in the bar room to fetch her mother's boyfriend another cold beer.

Grandpa Buster ignited his tobacco pipe, and as the

flavorful aroma masked the lingering food odors from their birthday luncheon, Judy invited her grandmother upstairs, as she was eager to show Grandma Sally all the candles she had made with her candle-making kit. Darcy and Samantha followed closely behind.

"You can have one, if you want," Judy offered. After Grandma Sally had chosen a pink hoot owl from Judy's collection of homemade candles, the four little women ventured into Darcy and Samantha's bedroom, where their grandmother was bombarded with requests to look at all their prized possessions and décor.

Sally Wiederman seized that opportunity to learn a little bit more about the man who had stolen her youngest daughter's heart. Sally had never heard Katie speak of another man quite so seriously since her ex-husband, Darren. Thus, her intuition led her to believe that Mr. Pomerance was going to be around for a while.

"Say, what do you girls think of Burt?" their grandmother tactfully inquired, while studying the various trinkets and knick-knacks lining their dresser tops and headboards. The consensus was most favorable, indeed. "We really like Burt...a lot!" Judith Ivy volunteered.

"Yeah, Burt's really nice," Darcy maintained. "And he treats Mom like a queen, bringing her flowers and calling her 'Pretty Lady'," she snickered. "Corny, but cute."

"And what do you think, Sam?" Grandma Sally asked the nine-year-old, who was busy taming the mane of the most majestic horse statue on her dresser, using her Barbie doll's hairbrush.

"I like Burt," Samantha proclaimed, as she continued to stroke the black stallion's shiny raven tresses with adoration. "And you know what, Grandma?" she gleefully disclosed. "When we moved in here, and I told Burt how much I loved horses, he just up and gave me all of this nifty horse stuff!"

That statement meant more to Sally Wiederman than anything her daughter had ever shared with regard to Mr. Pomerance's character, for Sally knew how special those equestrian trophies and figurines were to Burt.

"Do you girls know where Burt got all these horse trophies and statues?" Grandma Sally quizzed, as she gingerly handled the precious merchandise.

"I don't know," Samantha answered, with a shrug of her shoulders. "I just woke up one morning and found all this neat stuff on my dresser," she noted. "Mom said it all came from Burt."

"Well, your mother told me that, back in the olden days, Burt and his brother, Daniel, used to compete on the rodeo circuit together," their grandmother informed the girls. "Really? No foolin'?" Samantha reacted, her excited baby blues as large as dinner plates. Her sisters couldn't believe what they were hearing either.

"Yes, it's true," Grandma Sally replied. "Your mother even showed me some pictures of Burt and his brother from their rodeo days. There's this one," Sally started to giggle, "where they're both wearing these fancy white studded suits...you know, like Elvis Presley wears...with great big colorful sombreros on their heads...like the kind they wear down in Mexico."

"Far out!" Judith Ivy exclaimed. "As soon as we get back downstairs," she blurted, "we gotta get Burt to show us those pictures!"

After much pestering, the kids had finally persuaded Burt to share that exciting piece of his past with them. Katie retrieved the large box from under their bed. Inside the highly anticipated time capsule was Burt's collection of priceless photographs, victory ribbons, bandanas, as well as ticket stubs and other miscellaneous memorabilia from his glorious rodeo days.

"Wow! Look at all this cool stuff!" Keith proclaimed, while rifling through Burt's most private possessions. "I can't believe you never told us about this, Mom!" Keith scolded his mother.

"Well, Burt asked me not to," Katie answered. "I made him a promise, and I kept it," she affirmed, looking to her boyfriend for approval, who returned with a wink. Katie then took a seat on Burt's lap. Stroking his soft dark hair tenderly with her fingertips, she disclosed, "He said it was too embarrassing to tell people about his rodeo days."

"What? Are you crazy?" Keith argued. "This is like

the coolest thing in the world!" the impressed twelve-year-old exclaimed. Obviously, Burt's former pastime had just opened up an entirely new world to Keith Munson.

"Yeah, Burt...why didn't you tell us that you used to be a rhinestone cowboy in the rodeo?" Judith Ivy challenged. "And how come you never showed us all these neat pictures before?"

"Yeah, Burt, how come?" Darcy Lynn added to the heckling. "Gosh, I can't wait to tell all my friends!" Samantha Jo chimed in.

Backed into a corner, Burt felt his cheeks turning pink with embarrassment. He had no idea that his past hobbies and activities would spark such interest among his girlfriend's children, who eagerly awaited his reply. Realizing that there was no excuse for hiding his past from them, Burt simply picked up his cold Schlitz beer can, and in his unique, humorous way of apologizing, he uttered, "Gee, sorry I blew up!"

Samantha then selected a handful of her favorite pictures from Burt's keepsake box and hopped up onto Grandpa Buster's lap. "Look at all these pretty horses," she screeched, sharing each individual photo with her grandfather. "Look! This one has lots of different colors on it."

"Sort of like that ugly T-shirt you're wearing," Keith teased his baby sister. "Where'd you get that thing anyway? It looks like someone barfed up all different colors of paint on it."

"Shut up, Keith!" Samantha hissed. "I like this shirt! I got it from my friend, Maggie," she explained, looking down at the top she was wearing, admiring the variety of bright colors that were represented in its unique tie-dyed pattern.

"We don't say 'shut up' Sam," her grandmother reminded the youngster. Buster then intervened. "Well, I think it's a nice-looking shirt, Irish," he complimented, with a snicker. "Too bad it's hanging on such a homely-looking kid, though" he teased, while tickling the young lass.

"Oh, Grandpa," Samantha giggled, as the tickling relentlessly continued. "Stop...help...somebody, please help me!" she hollered, squirming and laughing hysterically. Nobody came to the little girl's rescue, and she ultimately fell victim to one of Grandpa Buster's prickly, late-evening whisker rubs.

Another month had passed, and as June was coming to an end, the Stone Valley townspeople vigorously prepared for the special bicentennial celebration on July 4, 1976. In commemoration of the nation's two-hundredth birthday, the Stone Valley Jaycees had organized oodles of fine festivities.

In addition to the annual parade, the greased pole and sawdust pile littered with coins, the log-rolling competition, firefighters hose and barrel contests, softball tournaments, chicken barbecue with ticket drawings for valuable prizes, and the popular street dance on Saturday night, this year's extravaganza boasted a kiddie parade (for children up to 16 years of age) and skateboarding contest, as well as a dunk tank, in which various prominent citizens of Stone Valley dared to risk being soaked to the skin by a youngster with a good pitching arm.

Judith Ivy Munson, along with the rest of the marching band, met at the park every morning at 8 a.m. for practice, in preparation for the grand parade. Each band member, comprised of Stone Valley band students from fifth grade through twelfth, had been issued a matching blue and white T-shirt with his/her name etched on the front and the band's name, "The Stone Valley Sparklers," embossed on the back in bold white letters, which they were instructed to wear with dark blue shorts.

On the morning of America's bicentennial, as soon as Judith Ivy had finished her obligatory stint in the parade's marching band, she ran home and ditched her clarinet on her bed, while shedding her tennis shoes and socks, kicking them underneath.

She quickly changed out of her stifling band uniform and into a multicolored, striped tank top and blue denim shorts, tying her long, light-brown hair up high into a ponytail. Judy then sprinted back down the street, as she wanted to make sure she didn't miss her little sister's float in the kiddie parade, which followed the main procession.

Samantha Munson and her new friend, Maggie Schultz, worked hard for weeks getting their "Be Kind

To Animals" platform ready for the kiddie parade. The dynamic duo had fastened colorful homemade posters to the sides of two red wagons, with their "Be Kind To Animals" slogan written in bold magic marker, enhanced by their colorful and imaginative artwork to accentuate their important message.

With a little help from their friends, the compassionate nine-year-olds borrowed as many animals as they could fit into their wagons, including puppies, kittens, guinea pigs, bunnies, turtles, parakeets, hamsters, gerbils, goldfish, and Kristi Brenner's pet white rat, Jasper. The girls even bathed their spotlighted animals, cleaning and shining the cages and wagons so that everything would be just perfect for their debut.

While Katie and the kids, Buster and Sally Wiederman, Burt Pomerance and his son, Joshua, were all enjoying the kiddie parade, Grandpa Buster snapped a few Polaroid photos of Samantha and Maggie's adorable parade entry. In turn, Burt recorded the memorable occasion using his home movie camera.

A palpable "Aww" could be heard resonating from the audience when their animal-themed float passed by, which was most pleasing to the two animated young girls, who beamed with pride as they nestled a fluffy, clean, adorable critter in one hand while pulling a wagon load full of crowd-pleasing charmers with the other.

The skateboarding contest was coming up next,

right after the kiddie parade. Thus, Samantha had to dash on home to get her pink skateboard, as she was competing in the timed downhill obstacle course run, which the Jaycees had laid out for the competitors using orange street cones. Maggie agreed to tend to the animals while her partner got ready for the big race.

First prize was ten whole dollars, with a blue, red or white ribbon awarded to the first-, second- and third-place winners, respectively. Despite the nine-year-old's ability and steadfast determination, victory seemed like a long shot, as Samantha Munson was the only girl to compete from her age bracket (8-12), against eight other boys.

When it was her turn to fly, Samantha's family stood proudly by as their youngest member whizzed around each traffic cone, riding barefooted on her bright pink skateboard, wearing nothing but a rainbow tank top and red shorts. They were all very impressed with the great speed, balance and agility she had exhibited.

At the end of the skateboarding contest, the winners were chosen. Samantha's cheerleaders were thrilled when their little daredevil had finished in second place, although Samantha didn't act like much of a winner at all.

"No fair," she grumbled, hanging her head in disappointment, while holding a red second-place ribbon in her hand. "I woulda won, if it wasn't for that stupid boy from Lumberton," Samantha lamented.

"He doesn't even live in Stone Valley, so he shoulda been disqualified!"

"Yeah, well…you'll win it next year," Maggie consoled her burdened buddy. When that didn't work, she put her arm around Samantha's shoulder and declared, "We had the best float in the kiddie parade this year…everyone said so…cheer up!"

"Hey, guess what?" big sister Judy interrupted, in an attempt to brighten the murky mood. "I'm gonna try climbing the greased pole," she asserted, before running back up the road. Judy was anxious to get in line for her chance to ascend the slippery, towering 25-foot telephone pole. "Come on, you guys!" she shouted.

Judy couldn't stop thinking about the twenty-dollar bill anchored to the top of that post, ever since early morning. During the parade, the "Sparklers" band had marched past a yard sale on Broadway, where she noticed a foosball table on sale for ten dollars, and she intended to buy it. Judy loved playing foosball at the arcade, and if she had a table of her own in her bedroom, she could play all the time and get even better.

As she watched the short line of full-grown men who tried and failed at reaching the top of that tall, smooth wooden pole saturated with thick brownish-black grease, she was relieved each time, for that meant Judy was one step closer to getting her shot at nabbing the twenty bucks, even if she was the only female (or kid) to give it a whirl.

"I just know I can do it," Judy chanted, while awaiting her turn. "They're all wearing boots and shoes," she observed. Having had lots of experience scaling neighborhood apple trees, Judy intended to climb that slimy pole barefooted.

On many a lazy summer afternoon, Judith Ivy Munson and Laverne Crawford would pick a paper sack full of crisp, tart green apples and then scramble up behind the scoreboard at the baseball diamond, or sit inside the dugouts, and munch on Mother Nature's sour, juicy fruit snacks until they'd had their fill and their bellies ached.

Since she could also fan out her toes like a monkey, climbing trees seemed to come naturally to Judy, who never wore shoes during the warm spring, summer and fall months. Thus, the soles of her feet were so callused and thick-skinned that she could run across gravel and rocks, or parched dead grass and straw, hot sands and scorching pavement, even broken glass on occasion, without pain or injury.

As the young man ahead of her neared the summit, Judith Ivy winced. Relief was quickly restored, however, as the daredevil had lost his grip and slid all the way back down to the ground, spewing expletives in the company of the young lass and her onlookers, in reaction to his wounded pride and bruised backside.

At last, it was young Judy's turn. Standing at the base of that telephone pole, it suddenly appeared much taller. "Now I know how Jack felt when he climbed the beanstalk," she mumbled, as she started to guide herself up with her bare feet, clenching her tan thighs tightly around the smooth and slippery wooden beam.

Before long, as the young girl inched her way higher and higher, a crowd had gathered below, which made her even more nervous, but Judy kept focusing on that twenty-dollar bill, which drew nearer with each forceful nudge. She was getting tired, and the sun was glaring directly into her eyes, but all Judy could think about was how much she wanted that foosball table at the yard sale. "You can do this!" she ranted.

Just a few feet from the top now, she stretched her left arm as high as it would reach. Then, using the very tips of her long fingernails, Judy managed to pluck the twenty-dollar bill from under the rock that kept it from blowing away in the wind.

The excited young girl exhaled a victorious sigh, and then she slid back down the greasy beam, landing on her feet. "I did it!" Judy rejoiced, jumping up and down in her filthy clothes, waving her money for the whole town to see.

Judy's family and friends, in addition to the curious, growing crowd, happily cheered for the eleven-year-old girl, as Judith Ivy Munson had been the only successful greased-pole climber of the day thus far.

The climbing champion immediately handed her

winnings over to her mother's boyfriend. "Burt, would you please take your truck over to the Miller house on Broadway and buy that ten-dollar foosball table for me?" Judy requested. Burt happily agreed to do her that favor, after which he left the remaining ten dollars on her bedroom dresser.

"Ugh, I am SO hot," Judy complained, as she wiped beads of sweat from her forehead using her fore-arm, which was one of the few places on her body that hadn't been covered in dark grease. "You guys wanna hit the creek?" she proposed. "I could really use a bath right about now." All the young girls consented.

"Race ya!" Samantha challenged, as she mounted her pink skateboard in her tan bare feet and headed down the hill toward the creek behind the lumbar yard, where the Munson girls often cooled themselves on the hottest of summer days.

"Hey, wait up for me!" Darcy hollered, chasing after her sisters and Maggie. When the gang arrived at the swimming hole, Laverne and Jeannie Crawford were already there. "So, that's where you guys ran off to," Judy bellowed, catching her breath.

"Hey, Jude, how come you're all covered in mud?" Laverne asked her friend, from the cool, dark rushing waters below. "It's not mud," Judy clarified. "It's grease from the greased pole....guess who just won twenty bucks!" she cheerfully bragged.

"No way! Really?" Laverne reacted. "Darn, I wish I coulda seen that!"

"Did you guys get to see Maggie and Sam's float in the kiddie parade?" Judy hollered back down to the Crawford girls.

"Yeah, that was really cute. You guys did a great job!" Laverne complimented the youngsters. "Too bad about the skateboard contest, though, Sam," she added. "You really shoulda won."

One by one, the foursome jumped off the ledge and into the deepest pooled area of the creek, trying hard not to touch the bottom, as the creek's floor was made up of a thick layer of quicksand-like, black squishy mud, in which the girls had lost several tennis shoes and thong sandals. The only reason they wore shoes in that particular creek in the first place was because its muddy bottom also happened to be the preferred habitat of big black leeches, which often attached themselves to the soles of their feet.

Judith Ivy had no problem with leeches, since she hunted night crawlers with her brother and always baited her own hooks when she went fishing with Keith and Grandpa Buster. Laverne and Jeannie weren't afraid of them anymore either, as they had yanked several leeches off of each other in the past.

Once they had all gotten cooled off, they decided to head home, as the girls wanted to get showered and cleaned up, grab some supper, and then get ready for the highly anticipated Stone Valley street dance.

As they stood on the creek bank, wringing out

their wet hair and drenched tank tops and shorts, one of the girls shrieked in horror, yelling, "Get it off me! Get it off me!" That eerie shrill came from Darcy Lynn, who was sitting down in the grass, flailing about, because she had a huge black bloodsucker stuck to the bottom of her bare left foot.

"Stop squirming!" Judith Ivy commanded, while attempting to wrangle the enormous bottom-dweller from her panicked little sister's foot.

"Don't be afraid, Darce. He won't suck that much blood out of you," Laverne Crawford teased. "But, if your leg starts turning blue, then you're in big trouble."

"Get it off, Jude...hurry up!" Darcy whimpered, in tears.

"Man, that's gotta be the biggest leech I ever saw!" Jeannie Crawford reported.

Once she had steadied her sister's floundering foot, Judy was able to release the gigantic sucker from its deadly grip, although it did take some of Darcy's skin along with it. "There, ya big sissy...it's off now," Judy reassured her sister, before hurling the black monster back into the murky depths from where it came.

"You okay, Darce?" her best friend, Jeannie, beseeched. "Yeah, I think so," Darcy replied, while Jeannie helped her to her feet. "Here, put your arm around me," she urged her bewildered buddy, as she helped Darcy limp away.

"Oh, she'll live," Judith Ivy avowed, with a wave of her hand. "Come on, you guys," she addressed the gang. "Let's go back uptown and I'll buy us all a snow cone with my greased-pole winnings!"

Later that evening, the tiny town of Stone Valley, Minnesota (population 395), rounded out its special bicentennial celebration with the annual street dance, which typically yielded high attendance from the surrounding communities as well, but never such a crowd as the gathering on that particular night.

The Munson sisters and all their friends had a wonderful time frolicking to the popular live music provided by The Lamplighters band. Their favorite dance tune each summer was "Wipe Out," by the Surfaris, which the girls, of course, requested multiple times. That bicentennial summer of 1976 was truly one to be remembered.

When school started again in the fall, the Munson sisters had plenty of fond summer memories to share with their fellow classmates. Keith Munson, however, was starting the seventh grade, which meant that he would have to ride the school bus all the way to Lumberton Junior High School.

Keith was nervous about starting a different, much larger school and making new friends outside of his Stone Valley classmates, but he was happy about one thing—no more sisters! For the first time in his life, the young boy had found independence from his three little sisters, as well as an opportunity to carve out an identity all his own.

In December, on his thirteenth birthday, Keith's

special wish was to see the new *Rocky* movie playing at the Cineplex, followed by dinner at Shakey's Pizza. His sisters had argued to go to *Carrie* on that Sunday afternoon, but since it was Keith's birthday, he was placed in charge of their family fun day.

Despite the horror film's "R" rating, Katie promised the girls that she would take them to see *Carrie* the following weekend, since Keith had just received a Pocket Fisherman for his birthday and had made plans to go ice fishing next weekend with Grandpa Buster at his boathouse on the Mississippi River.

It was the Munsons' first Christmas in their new house, and everybody pitched in to help decorate the home for the holidays. Burt and Katie had purchased an artificial tree, along with some store-bought decorations and lights, while the children worked together to craft some special homemade ornaments, which their mother favored over anything sold in a novelty store.

While the children enjoyed their favorite Christmastime shows, featuring Frosty, Santa Claus, Charlie Brown, Rudolf and The Grinch, Burt and Katie celebrated the holidays by sipping eggnog on the sofa in front of their beautifully decorated Christmas tree. As soon as the children retired to bed for the evening, Katie would put on one of their favorite record albums, which she and Burt could enjoy alone together.

On the evening before Christmas Eve, as the couple relaxed on the couch, listening to Katie's favorite

Elvis Presley album, something seemed to be bothering Burt. Katie could tell that he just wasn't himself. Fearing the worst, she turned to her boyfriend and implored, "What's the matter, Burt? Aren't you happy?"

Katie received no reply. Then, as Elvis's beautiful ballad, "Can't Help Falling in Love," began to waft through the stereo speakers, Burt became overwhelmed with emotion. "That's just it," he responded, through misty blue eyes. "I'm very happy. In fact, I've never been so happy in my entire life."

"Well, then...what's the problem?" Katie eagerly inquired. She had never seen her boyfriend so anxious and fidgety. "The problem is...that I...I just can't wait another twenty-four hours until Christmas!" Burt finally blurted.

Mystified, Katie watched in awe as Burt turned and reached behind the throw pillow next to him on the couch. Katie didn't have a clue as to what was causing Burt's peculiar behavior...until he pulled out a tiny black velveteen box.

At that moment, Burt dropped down onto his knee and professed, "I love you, Katie Munson...and I think your kids are great too. So, Pretty Lady, will you please do me the honor of becoming my wife?"

Following his marriage proposal, Burt opened the small black box to reveal a diamond engagement ring. "I know it's not much of a ring," he openly admitted, "but I can buy you a bigger diamond when I can get some money saved up."

"Oh, yes, Burt," Katie gladly accepted. As her pretty blue eyes pooled with tears of joy, she avowed, "Nothing would make me happier than to be your wife!"

Burt joyfully placed his diamond ring upon Katie's dainty left ring finger, and then she returned his sincere sentiment with a tender kiss. In that poignant moment, Burt took his fiancé by the hand, and then the happy couple swayed to the music as the beloved Elvis Presley ballad finished its lovely and timely message.

With Burt singing, "For I can't help falling in love with you," in her ear, suddenly Katie was the one feeling overcome by love and emotion. She could feel her heart pounding fiercely against Burt's masculine chest as their intertwined bodies glided in harmony to the beautiful romantic music.

As she looked up at the tall, dark-haired, handsome man who had caused her heart to dance with joy, heavy teardrops rolled down her blushing cheeks, for Katie was about to declare those three little words that she thought she might never utter again. "I love you too, Burt Pomerance...and I always will," she proclaimed. "This has been the best year of my life!"

The newly engaged couple rejoiced in secret for the remainder of the evening, though Katie was anxious to share their wonderful news with the children. Burt, on the other hand, had intended for their engagement to be a Christmas surprise for the kids.

"Well, it's past midnight," Katie hinted, after

glancing at the living room wall clock, reading 12:05 a.m. "Technically, it's Christmas Eve now, so...can we tell them?" she excitedly begged her new fiancé. Burt instantly nodded his head in approval.

Presuming that her kids were still awake upstairs, rustling about in their bedrooms, telling tall tales, or working on private Christmas surprises of their own, Katie took Burt by the hand and led him to the base of the stairs. "Hey, kids...guess what?" she hollered up to the children. "What?" Keith bellowed back down to his mother.

Katie then shouted out with glee, "Burt and I are getting married!" A resounding "Hooray!" was all Burt and Katie heard before all four kids came bounding down the stairs, stumbling over one another to be the first to rush into their open arms for a congratulatory embrace. In that moment, on Christmas Eve 1976, all five of the Munsons realized that their lives would never be the same, and so did Burt Pomerance.

As the bitter winter winds relented, and the springtime crocuses, tulips and daffodils had all but exhausted their perennial bloom cycles, the azaleas, irises and peonies soon took their places as they burst into subsequent blooms of white, yellow, pink, melon, scarlet, magenta and plum. Budding bushes sweetly ushered in the summer season, followed by an explosion of fragrant, multicolored roses and lilies to herald the news of the upcoming Pomerance-Munson nuptials.

The marriage ceremony was scheduled for the first Saturday in June, to be held at a very popular, quaint wedding chapel known as "The Little Brown Church in the Vale," located in Nashua, Iowa. The wedding was to be a small affair, consisting primarily of family members.

Only one song seemed fitting for the bride and groom's processional hymn—the love ballad that had been playing on the stereo the very moment Burt had proposed. As the bride and groom walked down the aisle together towards the altar, to Elvis Presley's impassioned tune, "Can't Help Falling in Love," their eyes grew misty with the affection they felt for each other as it overflowed from their blissful hearts.

In June of 1977, Burton Leroy Pomerance (34) and Katie Ann Munson (32) exchanged wedding vows in the company of Burt's mother (father deceased), Katie's parents, and their combined five children, along with a handful of the couple's siblings who had made the special trip to Iowa on that gorgeous Saturday afternoon in those early, pleasant weeks of summer.

From that day forward, Katie (Wiederman) Munson became forever known as Mrs. Burt Pomerance. As the newlyweds exited the tiny brown church, their five children surrounded them with beaming smiles, throwing rice and congratulations into the warm, fresh June air. That was the happiest day of their lives!

At long last, Katie Munson and Burt Pomerance had found their soul mates, with whom they would spend the rest of their lives. Katie's children, in turn, had been blessed with a loving, kind father who replaced the emptiness, resentment and longing they had felt (for as far back as they could remember) with acceptance, appreciation and devotion.

In addition, the Munson children finally had a home of their very own, as well as a six-year-old stepbrother named Joshua, whom they merrily welcomed into the family through this holy marital union. It was truly a dream come true, for in spite of the many obstacles and detours that stood in their paths, none of them had ever been happier!

### THE END

*In loving memory of our dear friends,*
*Ray and Pat Swanson*

# Epilogue

At long last, Katie Munson and her family had found peace, joy and happiness, against all odds…but how long will the family's euphoria last? Sadly, all good things must come to an end. As the children grew older, they were all being bussed to school in Lumberton, Minnesota, where their parents also worked. Thus, a move to the city was imminent, despite the kids' defiant and outward objections.

Having vacated their home town of Stone Valley, which was as much a part of them as their clothes, the small-town Munson kids faced many new challenges and people in this foreign land known as "the big city." Soon after moving to central Lumberton, some strange things started happening, which triggered a chain of events that most would find impossible to believe.

Then, in the summer of 1983, a terrible tragedy strikes one of the Munson children, turning all of their lives completely upside down. The Munson/Pomerance clan was forced to start over yet again, but in ways they never could have imagined. Life as they knew it would never be the same.

Katie took solace in her wonderfully supportive husband, Burt, who remained steadfast and true throughout the entire ordeal. Unlike her first husband, Katie now had someone to lean on and hold her up when her world was crumbling down. For better or worse, their marriage will be sorely tested, and the family ties strained to the limit. Will this horrible tragedy bring the family closer together, or will it tear them apart?

In Part 3 of *Detours to the Good Stuff*, take a journey back in time through the 1980s (the decade of AIDS, MTV and "yuppies") along with the Munson/Pomerance family as they face one obstacle after another in their relentless determination to rebuild their lives and restore their happiness.

CPSIA information can be obtained
at www.ICGtesting.com
Printed in the USA
BVHW072054310122
627588BV00001B/17